SMITHSONIAN CONTRIBUTIONS TO HISTORY AND TECHNOLOGY • NUMBER 55

The Winton M. Blount Postal History Symposia

Select Papers, 2006–2009

Thomas Lera

Editor

Smithsonian Institution
Scholarly Press

WASHINGTON D.C.
2010

Cover images are objects from the Smithsonian National Postal Museum Collection. From left to right: envelope with ten-cent black Washington stamp (Scott 2) mailed from Doakesville, Ark, 1850 (NPM 2003.2019.7); Leather satchel for letter carriers, ca. 1920–1950 (NPM 1992.2002.70) Parcel Airlift Issue (Scott 1341) used for parcels being mailed to servicemen in Vietnam 1968 (NPM 1980.2493.571).

Published by SMITHSONIAN INSTITUTION SCHOLARLY PRESS
P.O. Box 37012
MRC 957
Washington, D.C. 20013-7012
www.scholarlypress.si.edu

Library of Congress Cataloging-in-Publication Data
Winton M. Blount Postal History Symposia.
  The Winton M. Blount Postal History Symposia : select papers, 2006-2009 / Thomas Lera, editor.
      p. cm. — (Smithsonian contributions to history and technology ; no. 55)
  Includes bibliographical references.
  1. Postal service—History—Congresses. 2. Postage stamps—History—Congresses. I. Lera, Thomas M. II. Title.
  HE6041.W56 2010
  383'.49--dc22
                                                                                                    2010016338

ISSN (print): 1948-5999
ISSN (online): 1948-6006

∞ The paper used in this publication meets the minimum requirements of the American National Standard for Permanence of Paper for Printed Library Materials Z39.48–1992.

Contents

Letter from the Director

July 1, 2010

It is my great pleasure to introduce the Selected Proceedings of the Postal History Symposia. The first of these symposia was named after Winton M. Blount, the first Postmaster General of the United States Postal Service. Through his generous endowment to the Smithsonian National Postal Museum (NPM), the Center for Postal Studies and the Chair-in-Research was created in his name in 2006.

The success of the Postal History Symposia was due in large part to the support and assistance of our partners: the American Philatelic Society (APS), American Philatelic Research Library (APRL), NPM Council of Philatelists and the NPM Museum Advisory Council.

I would like to thank all of the philatelists, scholars, and industry leaders who presented at the first four symposia. Their research and presentations created an environment in which everyone enjoyed participating in each panel.

Special thanks are due to the symposium co-chairs Thomas Lera (NPM), David Straight (APS), and Virginia Horn (APRL). Without their efforts, the symposia would not have been the great success they were.

If you enjoy these papers, as much as I hope you will, please consider participating in, or at least attending, the future postal history symposia. Check our website for the dates and location of future symposia.

Allan Kane
Director, Smithsonian National Postal Museum

Acknowledgments

The symposium would not be a success without the help and encouragement from many people. At the top of the list is Allen Kane, Director of the National Postal Museum (NPM), who provided support and persuaded industry leaders to be plenary keynote speakers. Next I would like to thank the NPM Council of Philatelists and the NPM Museum Advisory Council for their assistance, and all of the staff at NPM who helped at the symposium over the past years.

The symposia could not have happened without the help and co-sponsorship of Ken Martin, executive director, David Straight, vice-president, and the staff of the American Philatelic Society and Gini Horn and the staff at the American Philatelic Research Library.

I would also like to thank the scholars who completed peer reviews. Their knowledge of philately and postal operations along with their suggestions and comments greatly improved the papers.

Finally, I thank Ginger Strader, scholarly publications manager, and Deborah Stultz, publications specialist, both of the Smithsonian Institution Scholarly Press, whose guidance, support, and review is much appreciated.

Introduction

In November 2005, in the quiet corner of the hotel bar at CHICAGOPEX, the annual World Series of Philately stamp show in Chicago, David L. Straight, then an American Philatelic Society (APS) director, and Cheryl R. Ganz, curator at the Smithsonian National Postal Museum (NPM), discussed the state of postal scholarship in America. They agreed that academic scholars rarely connected with philatelic scholars. On a paper napkin, they outlined the idea for a postal history symposium that would bring together researchers from all disciplines.

Postal history is the study of postal systems, how they operate and/or the collecting of covers and associated material illustrating historical episodes of postal systems. The term is attributed to Robson Lowe who made the first organized study of the subject in the 1930s and described philatelists as "students of science", but postal historians as "students of humanity".

Postal history includes the study of postal rates, postal policy, postal administration, political effects on postal systems, postal surveillance and the consequences of politics, business, and culture on postal systems; basically anything to do with the function of the collection, transportation, and delivery of mail.

The first symposium *"What is Postal History?"* took place in November 2006. In the opening plenary panel, Michael Laurence representing the philatelic perspective said, "In the philatelic vocabulary, postal history describes envelopes or folded letter sheets that have passed through the mails."

Richard R. John, a professor at the University of Illinois in Chicago, followed with, "For historians, postal history is the empirically grounded investigation in space and time of a vital, yet often neglected, communications medium. Topics inviting exploration include postal policy, postal administration, postal surveillance, political movements in which postal systems become entangled, and the consequences of postal systems for politics, business, and culture."

John Willis, historian at the Canadian Postal Museum, gave the museum perspective and stated, "Museum curators take a broad territory of research and interpret it for the benefit of the public via exhibitions. Objects in a postal collection become supporting documents of the postal past. Letters, envelopes, stamps, and writing implements are devices that help establish a rapport between a particular theme of history and the public."

Maynard H. Benjamin, president and CEO, Envelope Manufacturers Association, the last speaker of the panel, ended with the business perspective, stating,

FIGURE 1. Winton M. Blount, United States Postmaster General from 1969–1972. Courtesy of the National Postal Museum Library, Smithsonian Institution Libraries.

"Businesses see their postal history as a celebration of past achievements and a springboard for future innovations. Postal history includes the evolution of technologies and manufacturing processes for sorting and moving the mail."

These four perspectives sparked conversations to find common ground, share resources, and inspire new research.

This first symposium was named in honor of Winton M. Blount who, in 1969, became postmaster general in President Richard M. Nixon's cabinet and put an end to the patronage appointment of postmaster vacancies (Figure 1). In 1971, he presided over the shift of the U.S. Post Office from a cabinet department to the United States Postal Service, a nonprofit, government-owned corporation, and became its first chairman. Later, he endowed the Smithsonian National Postal Museum with The Winton M. Blount Center for Postal Studies and the Winton M. Blount Research Chair.

For the past four years, the location of the symposium has alternated between the NPM in Washington, D. C., and the American Philatelic Center in Bellefonte, Pennsylvania. The four symposiums were:

- *"What is Postal History?"* in Washington D. C. on November 3–4, 2006
- *"Further, Farther, Faster: Transportation Technology and the Mail"* in Bellefonte, Pennsylvania on October 21–22, 2007
- *"When the Mail Goes to War"* in Washington, D. C. on September 27–28, 2008
- *"Post Office Reform"* in Bellefonte, Pennsylvania on October 30–November 1, 2009

There have been more than sixty papers presented, many of which have gone on to be published in various academic and philatelic journals. The papers presented here have not been previously published. The theme of the symposium follows a collaborative, interdisciplinary approach which is discussed by various panels. Details on the symposiums and panels can be found on the NPM web site under Research / Symposiums http://www.postalmuseum.si.edu/symposiums/index.html.

Thomas Lera, NPM Winton M. Blount Research Chair
David L. Straight, APS Vice-President
Virginia L. Horn, American Philatelic Research Library
Director of Library Services

The Political Economy of Postal Reform in the Victorian Age

Richard R. John

The mid-nineteenth century postal reform movements in Great Britain and the United States were superficially similar, yet substantively different. The similarities were obvious. In both countries, postal reformers called for a radical reduction in postal rates, an innovation that they termed "cheap postage." In both countries, cheap postage was dependent on the enactment of legislation, since, at this time, both postal systems were owned and operated by the central government. In both countries cheap postage became law: in Great Britain, postal rates were restructured in 1840; in the United States, in 1845 and 1851. And in both countries, cheap postage led to a huge increase in the number of letters sent through the mail at a time when letter-writing was the primary medium for the circulation of long-distance information by the general population.

The differences between the campaigns for cheap postage in Great Britain and the United States were subtler, yet considerable. In Great Britain, the rationale for cheap postage was market-based, in keeping with the tenets of an emerging tradition in political economy that political economists called liberal, and that would later be dubbed laissez-faire. By limiting the taxes that the central government imposed on letter postage, reformers contended, lawmakers hoped to more closely match the cost of mailing a letter with the price that the government charged for its delivery. In the United States, in contrast, the rationale for cheap postage was civic, or what the founders of the American republic might have called republican. By expanding the mandate of the central government to embrace the low-cost circulation not only of newspapers and magazines, but also of letters, lawmakers empowered individuals to circulate at low cost information on personal matters as well as public affairs and market trends. This mandate was in no sense market-based since it entailed the legal suppression of rival non-governmental mail carriers, and the extension to a new class of postal items—that is, letters—based on the presumption that, if necessary, the cost of their circulation would be paid for out of the treasury. This presumption was codified with the enactment of the Post Office Act of 1851, which obliged the Post Office Department to maintain the existing level of service even if this obligation forced it to draw on the treasury for support.[1]

The origins, character, and legacy of the campaigns for cheap postage in Great Britain and the United States raise a number of questions that are worthy of careful historical scrutiny. Who supported these campaigns? What was their rationale? What were their consequences for public and private life? These are large questions, and ones that this essay cannot possibly answer in a definitive way. Yet they are worth posing, since their answers provide a context for understanding later innovations in communications that ranged from the rise of commercial broadcasting to the commercialization of the internet.

The most tireless promoter of cheap postage in Great Britain was the educational reformer Rowland Hill (Figure 1). Beginning in the mid-1830s, Hill lobbied energetically to convince his countrymen of the benefits of a radical decrease in the basic letter rate. The British government at this time regarded its postal system as a branch of the treasury and postage as a tax. The British post office was expected to generate a large annual surplus—which, invariably, it did—which the treasury used to cover the costs of running the government. In fact, the British post office would not run its first annual deficit until 1955.[2] By linking the actual cost of mail delivery to the price a postal patron paid to send a letter, Hill reasoned, the treasury could simultaneously lower postal rates and increase the total revenue it obtained.

Cheap postage had the further benefit of curtailing the special privileges that the British government lavished on the well-to-do. High letter postage was not only inept fiscal policy, but also a regressive tax that fell most heavily on the middle class and the poor. Rich aristocrats had little trouble obtaining free passes, known as "franks," that permitted them to mail letters at no cost to themselves. Franks were harder to obtain by the middle class and unknown to the poor. Cheap postage would, as it were, level the playing field by providing the many with facilities that had formerly been a perquisite of the few.

The principal features of Hill's reform—mandatory prepayment, the rollout of the now-ubiquitous postage stamp, and the reduction in the basic letter rate to a penny—might seem prosaic enough. Yet in the years following their introduction in 1840, many well-informed contemporaries hailed them as a triumph of civilization, an assessment that would be seconded by influential historians for over one hundred years.

The campaign for cheap letter postage in Great Britain coincided with a parallel campaign to reduce the taxes that the government charged on newspapers. Taxed newspapers paid fees that permitted them to be circulated in the mail; the rest of the newspaper press, in contrast, had to rely on other, non-postal means of conveyance. These fees often took the form of non-adhesive labels called "stamps"—a confusing term, in retrospect, since these labels were very different from the adhesive stamps that Hill advocated, and that the British post office began to issue in 1840. The proprietors of the unstamped newspapers resented their exclusion from the mail and lobbied Parliament to change the law. The "war of the unstamped," as the resulting political contest has come to be known, is typically studied in isolation from the campaign for cheap postage. As a consequence, many questions remain. Did the war of the unstamped antedate the campaign for cheap postage and, thus, serve as a precedent for reformers like Hill? Or was it the other way around? Or were the two movements fundamentally distinct? Whatever the answers to these questions turn out to be, it remains suggestive that the two reform movements shared a common grievance—that is, that the cost of circulating information was too high—as well as a common remedy—that the price of mailing a posted item should bear a discernible relationship to the cost of its circulation.

FIGURE 1. Postal reformer Rowland Hill.

Further questions are raised if the war of the unstamped is located in a transatlantic context. The campaign for cheap postage is typically understood as having originated in Great Britain and only later spread to the United States. In the war of the unstamped, however, British reformers looked to the United States, and with good reason. The U.S. Post Office Department admitted newspapers into the mail on a non-preferential basis beginning in 1792. Henceforth, postal administrators were proscribed from discriminating between one newspaper and another. The British post office, in contrast, would not begin to put its newspaper press on an analogous footing until 1836.[3]

Hill's priorities shaped the ways in which the campaign for cheap postage would come to be remembered. For many decades after 1840, historians echoed Hill's contention that the consequences of cheap postage were far-reaching. The "social and economic results" of this innovation, exulted the British cultural historian Llewellyn Woodward in 1938, were "beyond calculation."[4] The hostility of British aristocrats toward cheap postage, Woodward elaborated, owed much to the studied indifference toward material considerations of a haughty elite. Aristocrats, Woodward recounted, arrogantly regarded it as "beneath their dignity to understand anything about a penny."[5]

Woodward was by no means alone in his admiration for cheap postage. French historian Marc Bloch regarded as highly consequential the comparable innovations that had occurred at roughly the same time in France. "When I ask for timbres [that is, adhesive postage stamps] at my post-office window," Bloch observed in 1940, "I am able to use that term only because of recent technical changes, such as the organization of the postal service itself, and the substitution of a little gummed piece for the stamping of a postmark. These have revolutionized human communications."[6] The British political historian David Thompson found particularly notable the consequences of cheap postage for political reform. Cheap postage, Thompson observed in a history of nineteenth-century England that he published in 1950, had given the Anti-Corn-Law League a "new means" of "disseminating its propaganda," an innovation that hastened a dramatic reduction in 1846 in the import duty on wheat, or what the English called corn.[7]

Woodward, Bloch, and Thompson reflected the consensus of the generation of historians who came of age in the years preceding the Second World War. More recent historians have been more circumspect. To be sure, in his justly celebrated *Age of Revolution, 1789–1848* (1962) E. J. Hobsbawm did hail Hill's "brilliant invention" of a "standardized charge for postal matter."[8] Yet Hobsbawm attributed no particular consequences to Hill's innovation, an omission that, in more recent years, has become the norm. Monographs on specialized topics in British postal history abound.[9] Even so, the campaign for cheap postage has failed to take its place alongside free trade and Catholic emancipation in the annals of Victorian reform. More broadly, the postal system itself no longer commends itself to historians as an agent of change. The institution, for example, goes unmentioned in several well-regarded recent overviews of nineteenth-century British history. From the standpoint of the generalist, the British post office is, at best, a bit player on the historical stage.[10]

Postal reformers in the United States shared Hill's conviction that cheap postage mattered. In fact, if anything, they were even more inclined to wax rhapsodic in pondering its consequences for public and private life. The moral effects of cheap postage were a preoccupation of Joshua Leavitt, an evangelical Protestant minister-turned-newspaper editor who combined a faith in postal reform with a hatred of slavery (Figure 2). The British Parliament had lowered postal rates and freed the slaves: why could not the U.S. Congress follow its lead?

The relationship between cheap postage and abolition was for Leavitt far from incidental. Of what consequence was it to "nine tenths of our population," Leavitt editorialized in 1844, "that time and space are half killed, while the absurd United States mail nuisance continues? Time is annihilated, you say? Why a common man cannot carry on a moderate correspondence with his friends, scattered as they usually are, without consuming his whole time to earn the money to pay for it." Cheap postage, Leavitt elaborated, had ironically become a rallying cry for certain publications, such as the New York City-based *Journal of Commerce*, for whom abolitionism remained anathema. Yet by championing cheap postage, the *Journal* was endorsing a political reform that, by empowering ordinary people to circulate information over long distances, was "dealing blows unwittingly at slavery": "Give us the British system of postage and slavery is dead."[11]

The candor with which Leavitt linked cheap postage and abolition was unusual. Yet his faith in the emancipatory potential of cheap postage was not. The campaign united thousands of Americans in a common cause. Newspapers in New York City, Boston, Philadelphia, and many other commercial centers ran frequent editorials on the topic, and postal patrons flooded Congress with petitions demanding a host of postal reforms—including, above all, a reduction in the basic letter rate.[12] This well-organized protest preceded, and almost certainly hastened, the

FIGURE 2. Joshua Leavitt. Photograph by unidentified photographer. From *Portraits of American Abolitionists*. Courtesy of the Massachusetts Historical Society, Photo 81.404.

enactment of two laws—the Post Office Act of 1845 and the Post Office Act of 1851—which instituted a host of reforms that include, in addition to a steep reduction in the basic letter rate, the rollout of the first postage stamps.

Under other circumstances, the campaign for cheap postage in the United States might have taken its place in the historical imagination alongside the better-known reform movements of the period: temperance, abolition, women's rights. Yet it did not. The only general history of the United States to treat the campaign for cheap postage in detail is John Bach McMaster's *History of the People of the United States*, and it was published over a century ago in 1910. McMaster heaped praise on the movement, yet he failed to link it to any larger theme—such as, for example, evangelical reform or abolition—that might have

increased the likelihood that it would become incorporated into general accounts of the American past.[13]

McMaster's treatment of postal reform was the exception that proved the rule. None of his contemporaries treated the campaign for cheap postage in any detail. Henry Adams, for example, ignored it entirely in his *Education*, which Adams had completed by 1907, even though it can be credibly argued to have been no less important an innovation than the three events of the mid-1840s that Adams credited with throwing into an "ash heap" the political universe of his youth: namely, the commercialization of the telegraph, the spanning of the Appalachian mountains by the railroad, and the first regularly scheduled transAtlantic steamship.[14]

Adams's priorities became the conventional wisdom. For historians of the United States, not only the campaign for cheap postage—but also the history of the mail—were long topics that they felt safe to ignore. Had Cornell history professor J. B. Bretz published his long-promised history of the U.S. Post Office Department in the early republic, a project that originated in Bretz's 1906 Ph. D. history dissertation at the University of Chicago, it is conceivable that the situation might have been different. Yet Bretz sat on his manuscript for his entire academic career. Bretz's dissertation has disappeared, making it impossible to know how he might have treated the campaign for cheap postage, or even if he would have taken his story up to the 1840s. In all likelihood, he would not: the two essays that he cobbled out of his dissertation focused on the period before the adoption of the federal Constitution in 1788 and the War of 1812.[15] Yet this much is known: Bretz never published his magnum opus, and the opportunity passed. Not until the 1990s would any topics in the history of the American postal system begin to attract sustained attention, and it would not be until the very recent past that the institution would figure in a more than incidental way in synthetic overviews of the American past.[16]

Modern historical writing on the American postal system began with the publication in 1972 of Wayne E. Fuller's *American Mail*—a thoughtful topical survey of American postal history from the colonial era onward. Fuller's overview included a cursory discussion of the campaign for cheap postage, which he analyzed through a neo-progressive lens as a victory of the "people" over the "interests." While Fuller's account has much to commend it, he was, in the end, less concerned with the campaign for cheap postage than with its implications for postal finance.[17] More recently, Fuller's *Morality and the Mail* expanded our understanding of several related nineteenth-century reform movements, including Sabbatarianism and anti-pornography, without putting either the campaign for cheap postage or its consequences on center stage.[18] Most recent of all, David M. Henkin traced the consequences of postal reform, though not the cheap postage campaign itself, in his engaging *Postal Age*.[19] Even so, much remains to be done. Specialists in nineteenth-century U.S. history have long been aware of the prodigious paper trail that the campaign for cheap postage generated, yet, as the well-known nineteenth-century historian Eric Foner recently observed, no one has yet fit it into a broader historical context.[20] The significance of cheap postage is underplayed even by Joshua Leavitt's biographer, Hugh Davis. From Davis's point of view, Leavitt's campaign for cheap postage was overshadowed by, and largely unrelated to, his crusade against slavery.[21] Even Fuller and Henkin are ultimately less interested in tracing the origins, character, and legacy of the campaign for cheap postage than in mining the documents that the movement generated to generalize about postal policy and cultural trends.

Here lies a conundrum. In both Great Britain and the United States, contemporaries hailed the campaign for cheap postage as an epochal reform. Yet almost never have historians explored the origins, character, or legacies of these campaigns in any detail. As a consequence, they have been largely ignored. The early modern historian Elizabeth L. Eisenstein tackled a related challenge in her justly acclaimed *Printing Press as an Agent of Change*. Frustrated by the hype that had enveloped the invention of printing, Eisenstein traced the influence of this communications medium on three pivotal events in western civilization: the Renaissance, the Protestant Reformation, and the Scientific Revolution. No historian has undertaken an analogous investigation of the campaign for cheap postage in Great Britain and the United States. Might it not be time for someone to write a history of cheap postage as an "agent of change"?

Of the many dimensions of the campaign for cheap postage that would seem to be worthy of exploration, three would seem to hold special promise. These are its rationale; the process by which it was enacted; and its consequences for public and private life. Of these three themes, the consequences of cheap postage is the most ambitious and the hardest to pin down. Historians since the 1990s have become cognizant of the political, economic, and cultural consequences of the Post Office Act of 1792, while, in 2000, historian of technology Daniel E. Headrick posited that two postal "revolutions" transformed the West, one in the 1790s and one in the 1840s.[22] The first of these postal revolutions is no longer obscure; the second, however, remains—at least in the United States—largely unknown.[23] In both Great Britain and the United States,

cheap postage hastened a huge increase in letter writing. How might this increase have shaped the identity of letter writers? What implications might it have had for other dimensions of public and private life?

It would be anachronistic to compare cheap postage with the communications innovations of the recent past, an age in which letter-writing is enjoying an unexpected revival, due first to email, and, more recently, to social network applications such as Facebook and Twitter. Yet there should be no hesitation about comparing the mid-nineteenth century "communications revolution" with what came before—and, in particular, in asking how cheap postage shaped an informational environment in which letter-writing previously had been expensive, and, in Great Britain, the circulation of newspapers limited by onerous taxes designed, at least in part, to prevent ordinary people from gaining access to information on public affairs.[24]

While the consequences of cheap postage are hard to isolate, the process by which it was enacted is better suited to historical inquiry. Here it might make sense to begin with the reformers themselves. Hill and Leavitt were but two members of a small but determined cadre of postal reformers. In Great Britain, their counterparts included the reformist MP Robert Wallace and the career civil servant Henry Cole; in the United States, the anarchist Lysander Spooner and the anti-monopolist Barnabas Bates.

While much remains to be learned about these reformers, a few tentative generalizations can be ventured. Cheap postage enthusiasts in Great Britain often had close ties to the government; their counterparts in the United States, in contrast, did not. In large part for this reason, British postal reformers had less trouble enlisting lawmakers to generate the data necessary for an informed debate on the merits of the proposed reform. Postal administrators in the United States generated mountains of postal data, yet few lawmakers used this data to make the case for cheap postage, and no legislative hearings probed its implications. The most incisive public debate over cheap postage in Great Britain took place in Parliament; the best-informed public debate in the United States took place in the press—and, in particular, in the publications of postal reformers like Leavitt, Spooner, and Bates. This contrast helps to account for some of the differences not only in the evolution of the cheap postage campaigns in the two countries, but also in the ways they have come to be remembered.

In his celebrated 1837 brief for cheap postage, *Post Office Reform: Its Importance and Practicality*, Hill drew on data generated by Parliament. Leavitt, Spooner, and Bates, in contrast, had no comparable body of data to conjure with. Postal data was abundant. Yet contemporaries used it mostly to speculate about the likely implications of cheap postage for public finance. The potential benefits of letter-rate reductions for postal users were downplayed not only by legislators, but also by almost every postal administrator who considered the issue. The principal exception was John M. Niles, a one-time Hartford, Connecticut, postmaster who served briefly as postmaster general in 1840 and 1841. Niles championed cheap postage in his 1840 annual report, to which he appended a prescient report on American postal finance by post office special agent George Plitt. The Plitt report had been originally commissioned by Niles's predecessor, Amos Kendall—a capable administrator who had briefly flirted with postal reform in the 1830s. Yet Kendall eventually changed his mind, and the Plitt report played, at best, a marginal role in the congressional debate over cheap postage in the years to come.[25]

Hill was, of course, an outsider when he published *Post Office Reform* in 1837. Soon thereafter, however, he obtained an appointment in the treasury and following a brief hiatus, he obtained a high-level position in the British post office that he retained for almost twenty years. No American postal reformer ever obtained a comparable government position. In fact, high-ranking American postal administrators were, almost without exception, hostile to postal reform. The campaign for cheap postage was ridiculed in the 1840s by John Tyler's postmaster general Charles Wickliffe, James K. Polk's postmaster general, Cave Johnson, and the veteran postal administrators Selah Hobbie and John Stuart Skinner.[26] Even Amos Kendall challenged the rationale for cheap postage, reversing a position that he had taken as postmaster general in 1836.[27] The hostility of U.S. postal administrators toward postal reform was epitomized by the publication, in 1844, of an anonymous pamphlet ridiculing cheap postage.[28] This pamphlet had the imprimatur of the Tyler administration: it was reprinted, for example, in its official administration newspaper, the *Madisonian*.[29] Although no one in the Post Office Department claimed credit for this document, Bates was probably right to assume that it had been written by a postal administrator.[30] The hostility of American postal administrators toward postal reform goes far toward explaining why cheap postage remained obscure. Had Bates lived longer—he died suddenly in 1853 at the age of sixty-eight—or had Leavitt and Spooner enjoyed closer ties to the levers of power, it is conceivable that a triumphalist narrative would have emerged—with, conceivably, a hero like Hill. Yet they did not, and it did not.

It is beyond the scope of this essay to provide a detailed analysis of the process by which postal reform was enacted in Great Britain and the United States. Yet this much seems plain. In both countries, the railroad and the steamboat created a new communications channel that made some kind of legislation inevitable. In both countries the campaign for cheap postage had considerable popular support; and in both it culminated in the enactment of legislation that mandated a major reduction in the basic letter rate.

Even so, the similarities between postal reform in Great Britain and the United States are easily exaggerated. Postal reform in Great Britain and the United States emerged in different political economies that shaped their legacies in ways both large and small. The campaign for cheap postage in Great Britain drew at least part of its inspiration from the campaign to expand popular access to newspapers, a reform that, in the United States, had been accomplished almost fifty years earlier with the enactment of the Post Office Act of 1792.

Equally notable was the contrasting relationship in the two countries between postal reform and postal finance. In Great Britain, postal reformers campaigned for cheap postage secure in the knowledge that even a radical reduction in the basic letter rate was not likely to throw the post office on the support of the treasury. The British post office generated a substantial surplus, it is worth underscoring, not only before Rowland Hill's reforms, but also for over a century after they were enacted. True, as the historian of British taxation Martin J. Daunton has astutely observed, Hill was overly optimistic in his estimation of the revenue increase that cheap postage would bring.[31] Yet a surplus remained. In the United States, in contrast, the Post Office Acts of 1845 and 1851 preceded a long period in which the Post Office Department generated a large annual deficit that obliged legislators to borrow from the treasury to cover the shortfall, a pattern that would remain the norm until the establishment of the U. S. Postal Service in 1970. Explanations differed as to the cause of this deficit. Some blamed the reduction of letter-postage; others the continuation of a perquisite for lawmakers known as the "franking" privilege. Either way, one conclusion was incontestable: Congress paid far more to facilitate the circulation of information in the United States than Parliament did in Great Britain.

The precarious financial position of the U.S. Post Office Department highlights yet another contrast between the campaign for cheap postage in Great Britain and the United States, and that was its spatial logic. In Great Britain, postal reformers presumed that cheap postage would benefit regions on the periphery of the country's political and commercial center of London. Not surprisingly, a number of prominent reformers—including Hill and Wallace—hailed from the hinterland. Hill was from

Birmingham; Wallace from Scotland. In the United States, in contrast, postal reformers presumed that cheap postage would disproportionately benefit the country's principal commercial centers—including, in particular, New York City, Philadelphia, and Boston. Not surprisingly, the campaign for cheap postage in the United States had far more support in the thickly settled North and East than in the thinly settled South and West. In fact, legislators from the South and West feared, entirely plausibly, that if revenue failed to match costs, they might find themselves obliged to curtail the massive newspaper and stagecoach subsidies that their constituents currently enjoyed.

Just as the process of postal reform in Great Britain and the United States differed, so too did its rationale. Postal reform in Great Britain had much in common with the abolition of the Corn Laws and the ancillary economic innovations that ushered in a political economy that contemporaries termed liberal. Hill himself was very much as part of this tradition. Like a small yet influential cohort of self-proclaimed radicals whose ranks included the utilitarian political theorist Jeremy Bentham, Hill endorsed the then-novel moral philosophy that posited that the purpose of government was to promote the greatest good of the greatest number. Hill traveled in some of the same reformist circles as Bentham, and, like Bentham, was determined to simplify government and make it more economical. Hill did not regard cheap postage as a subsidy for the poor, for a region, or even for a specific kind of mail.[32] Rather, he favored it as economically sound. Like popular education, competitive capitalism, and representative democracy, it would limit the power of the few to take unfair advantage of the many. In fact, Hill went so far as to endorse the abolition of the postal monopoly, a position that was hard to reconcile with the endorsement of internal cross-subsidies of any kind.[33]

In the United States, in contrast, the rationale for postal reform was more expansive. Here cheap postage was championed not as an economic innovation that would match cost to price, but, rather, as a public good—or what a later generation would call an entitlement. Congress had facilitated the low-cost circulation of information on public affairs in 1792 when it admitted newspapers into the mail at low cost, and it had permitted Postmaster General John McLean to surreptitiously expand this mandate in 1825 to embrace information on market trends.[34] Now, or so the champions of cheap postage contended, Congress had an obligation to extend this mandate to information on personal matters such as the health of a distant relative. Postal reform in the United States, in short, was intended to promote the well-being of the citizenry, rather than to limit the role of government in personal affairs. In Great Britain, cheap postage was backed by legislators who endorsed the abolition of the Corn Laws; in the United States, by legislators who approved of large expenditures for public works and favored the reestablishment of a national bank.

The contrasting rationales for postal reform in Great Britain and the United States help explain why the Nobel-Prize winning economist R. W. Coase has hailed cheap postage in Great Britain as a forerunner of what is today called "market liberalism." Coase's parents had both been post office telegraphers in Great Britain, a circumstance that spurred Coase's interest in communications history and that, eventually, led him to characterize cheap postage as a prototype for communications deregulations, including the auctioning off of the electromagnetic spectrum to the highest bidder.[35] No social scientist in the United States has reached a comparable conclusion. This was not because cheap postage lacked a rationale, but, rather, because its rationale was emphatically civic—and, as such, harder to characterize as a prelude to deregulation. Joshua Leavitt supported the postal monopoly; Rowland Hill did not. In one sense this made Leavitt more old-fashioned as an heir to the civic ideals of the founders of the republic and the evangelical aspirations of the Protestant Reformation. In another sense, it underscored the degree to which, in the United States, though not in Great Britain, lawmakers regarded cheap postage as an innovation that fully justified whatever augmentation in the organizational capabilities of the federal government it might require or whatever cost it might incur.

From such a perspective, cheap postage had more in common with certain political projects to facilitate intercommunication, such as the construction of the Erie Canal, than it did with the market-oriented reforms such as the refusal of the Jackson administration to recharter the Second Bank of the United States. Then, as now, American postal policy drew its inspiration not only, or even primarily, from the supposedly inexorable logic of economic incentives, but also from the moral power of civic ideals. The campaign for cheap postage in the United States was but one of several reform movements that reformers hailed as a welcome augmentation in the role of the central government in public and private life. In this regard, it resembled Reconstruction and Prohibition more than free trade or the constitutional guarantee of a free press. Its success has obscured not only its legacy for later communications innovations, but also its distinctiveness—and, in particular, the subtle yet profound ways that it differed from the campaign for cheap postage in Great Britain.

NOTES

For suggestions and advice, I am grateful to Diane DeBlois, Robert Dalton Harris, Nancy R. John, Tom Lera, Jonathan Silberstein-Loeb, and two anonymous referees.

1. Wayne E. Fuller, *American Mail: Enlarger of the Common Life* (Chicago: University of Chicago Press, 1972), chap. 5.

2. Martin J. Daunton, *Royal Mail: The Post Office since 1840* (London: Athlone Press, 1985), p. 339.

3. John Crawfurd, *The Newspaper Stamp, and the Newspaper Postage Compared* (London: J. Reed, 1836), pp. 3–4, 8; A. D. Smith, *The Development of Rates of Postage: An Historical and Analytical Study* (London: George Allen & Unwin, 1917), p. 122.

4. E. L. Woodward, *The Age of Reform, 1815–1870* (London: Oxford University Press, 1938), p. 47.

5. Woodward, *Age of Reform*, p. 47.

6. Cited in Asa Briggs, *Victorian Things* (1988; Phoenix Mill, U. K.: Sutton, 2003), p. 290.

7. David Thompson, *England in the Nineteenth Century, 1815–1914* (1950: New York: Penguin, 1985), p. 81.

8. E. J. Hobsbawm, *The Age of Revolution, 1789–1848* (New York: New American Library, 1962), p. 205.

9. Howard Robinson, *The British Post Office: A History* (Princeton: Princeton University Press, 1948); Briggs, "Stamps—Used and Unused," in Briggs, *Victorian Things*, chap. 9; C. R. Perry, *The Victorian Post Office: The Growth of a Bureaucracy* (Woodbridge: Boydell Press, 1992); "'Send the Letters, Uncle John': Trollope, Penny-Postage Reform, and the Domestication of Empire," in Eileen Cleere, *Avuncularism: Capitalism, Patriarchy, and Nineteenth-Century English Culture* (Stanford: Stanford University Press, 2004), chap. 5; Catherine J. Golden, *Posting It: The Victorian Revolution in Letter-Writing* (Gainesville: University Press of Florida, 2009).

10. Kenneth O. Morgan, ed., *The Oxford History of Britain* (New York: Oxford University Press, 2001); Simon Schama, *A History of Britain*, vol 3: *The Fate of Empire, 1776–2000* (New York: Hyperion, 2002).

11. "The Postage," *Morning Chronicle* (Boston), December 16, 1844.

12. These generalizations are based on a survey of over 40 newspapers for the 1843–1847 period, as well as a personal inspection of the voluminous files of cheap postage petitions in the National Archives.

13. John Bach McMaster, *History of the People of the United States, from the Revolution to the Civil War*, vol. 7: *1841–1850* (New York: D. Appleton & Co., 1910), pp. 106–120, 124–134.

14. Henry Adams, *The Education of Henry Adams*, ed. Ernest Samuels (1906; Boston: Houghton Mifflin, 1974), p. 5.

15. Julian P. Bretz, "Some Aspects of Postal Extension into the West," *American Historical Association Annual Report*, 5 (1909): 143–150; Bretz, "Early Land Communication with the Lower Mississippi Valley," *Mississippi Valley Historical Review*, 13 (June 1926): 3–29.

16. Pauline Maier, et al., *Inventing America: A History of the United States* (New York: W. W. Norton & Co., 2006), vol. 1, chaps. 8, 10; Daniel Walker Howe, *What Hath God Wrought? The Transformation of America, 1815–1848* (New York: Oxford University Press, 2007), chap. 6. Much of the recent interest in the history of the American postal system has been spurred by a recognition that the Post Office Act of 1792 was a landmark in the history of communications in the United States. The first historian to highlight the significance of the Post Office Act of 1792 was Bretz; his conclusions were echoed by Fuller, and elaborated on by myself in a monograph that I published on the early American postal system in 1995: Richard R. John, *Spreading the News: The American Postal System from Franklin to Morse* (Cambridge, Mass.: Harvard University Press, 1995), chap. 1. Since 1995, the significance of the Post Office Act of 1792 has been widely recognized by specialists not only in history, but also in historical sociology, media studies, political science, and law.

17. Fuller, *American Mail*, chap. 5.

18. Fuller, *Morality and the Mail in Nineteenth-Century America* (Urbana: University of Illinois Press, 2003).

19. David M. Henkin, *The Postal Age: The Emergence of Modern Communications in Nineteenth-Century America* (Chicago: University of Chicago Press, 2006).

20. Personal conversation, fall 2009.

21. Hugh Davis, *Joshua Leavitt: Evangelical Abolitionist* (Baton Rouge: Louisiana State University Press, 1990).

22. Daniel R. Headrick, *When Information Came of Age: Technologies of Knowledge in the Age of Reason and Revelation, 1700–1850* (New York: Oxford University Press, 2000).

23. One notable exception to this generalization is David A. Gerber, *Authors of their Lives: The Personal Correspondence of British Immigrants to North America in the Nineteenth Century* (New York: New York University Press, 2006). To a greater degree than any other historian of whom I am aware, Gerber has explored the consequences of cheap postage for letter writing, with an emphasis on its implications for personal identity and social relationships.

24. Joel H. Wiener, *The War of the Unstamped: The Movement to Repeal the British Newspaper Tax, 1830–1836* (Ithaca: Cornell University Press, 1969).

25. George Plitt, *Report*, 26th Cong., 2nd sess., 1841, Sen. Doc. 156 (serial 378); John M. Niles, *Report of the Postmaster General* (1840), pp. 479–484. The Plitt report had originally been commissioned by Niles's predecessor, Amos Kendall. Amos Kendall, *Report of the Postmaster General* (1839), p. 617.

26. *Journal of Commerce* (New York), 5 January 1844; *New York Express*, 3 June 1844.

27. Amos Kendall, *Report of the Postmaster General* (1836), 509; Kendall, "Postage," *Kendall's Expositor*, 3 (13 June 1843): 193–195.

28. "Franklin," *An Examination of the Probable Effect of the Reduction of Postage: As Proposed to be Made by the Bill Introduced into the Senate of the United States by the Hon. Mr. Merrick, of Maryland* (n. p., 1844). This pamphlet can be found in the records of the Post Office Department at the National Archives in Washington, D. C.

29. "Reduction of Postage," *Madisonian*, Feb. 3, 1844.

30. Barnabas Bates, *A Brief Statement of the Exertions of the Friends of Cheap Postage in the City of New York* (New York: New York Cheap Postage Association, 1848), p. xi. The hostility of U.S. postal administrators toward cheap postage was so intense, Bates related, that Postmaster General Wickliffe lobbied for the dismissal from a "paltry office" of an officeholder who had "interested himself in this good cause" (p. xi). The officeholder very possibly was Bates himself.

31. Daunton, *Royal Mail*, pp. 37–38.

32. Daunton, *Royal Mail*, p. 54; Ronald H. Coase, "Rowland Hill and the Penny Post," *Economica*, 6 (November 1939): 423–435.

33. Daunton, *Royal Mail*, pp. 54–55.

34. John, *Spreading the News*, chap. 2.

35. Ronald H. Coase, "Ronald H. Coase," in *Lives of the Laureates: Eighteen Nobel Economists,* ed. William Breit and Barry T. Hirsch (Cambridge: MIT Press, 2004); personal conversation with R. H. Coase, Chicago, Ill., 2007.

BIBLIOGRAPHY

Adams, Henry. *The Education of Henry Adams,* ed. Ernest Samuels. Boston: Houghton Mifflin, 1974.

Bates, Barnabas. *A Brief Statement of the Exertions of the Friends of Cheap Postage in the City of New York.* New York: New York Cheap Postage Association, 1848.

Bretz, Julian P. "Early Land Communication with the Lower Mississippi Valley." *Mississippi Valley Historical Review,* 13:3–29.

———. "Some Aspects of Postal Extension into the West." *American Historical Association Annual Report,* 5:143–150.

Briggs, Asa. *Victorian Things.* Phoenix Mill, U. K.: Sutton, 2003.

Cleere, Eileen. *Avuncularism: Capitalism, Patriarchy, and Nineteenth-Century English Culture.* Palo Alto, Ca.: Stanford University Press, 2004.

Coase, Ronald H. "Ronald H. Coase." In *Lives of the Laureates: Eighteen Nobel Economists,* ed. William Breit and Barry T. Hirsch. Cambridge, Mass.: MIT Press, 2004.

———. "Rowland Hill and the Penny Post." *Economica,* 6:423–435.

Crawfurd, John. *The Newspaper Stamp, and the Newspaper Postage Compared.* London: J. Reed, 1836.

Daunton, Martin J. *Royal Mail: The Post Office since 1840.* London: Athlone Press, 1985.

Davis, Hugh. *Joshua Leavitt: Evangelical Abolitionist.* Baton Rouge, La.: Louisiana State University Press, 1990.

"Editorial." *Journal of Commerce.* 5 January 1844.

"Editorial." *New York Express.* 3 June 1844.

Fuller, Wayne E. *American Mail: Enlarger of the Common Life.* Chicago: University of Chicago Press, 1972.

———. *Morality and the Mail in Nineteenth-Century America.* Urbana, Ill.: University of Illinois Press, 2003.

Gerber, David A. *Authors of their Lives: The Personal Correspondence of British Immigrants to North America in the Nineteenth Century.* New York: New York University Press, 2000.

Golden, Catherine J. *Posting It: The Victorian Revolution in Letter-Writing.* Gainesville: University Press of Florida, 2009.

Headrick, Daniel R. *When Information Came of Age: Technologies of Knowledge in the Age of Reason and Revelation, 1700–1850.* New York: Oxford University Press, 2000.

Henkin, David M. *The Postal Age: The Emergence of Modern Communications in Nineteenth-Century America.* Chicago: University of Chicago Press, 2006.

Hobsbawm, E. J. *The Age of Revolution, 1789–1848.* New York: New American Library, 1962.

Howe, Daniel Walker. *What Hath God Wrought? The Transformation of America, 1815–1848.* New York: Oxford University Press, 2007.

John, Richard R. *Spreading the News: The American Postal System from Franklin to Morse.* Cambridge, Mass.: Harvard University Press, 1995.

Kendall, Amos. *Report of the Postmaster General.* Washington, D. C.: Government Printing Office, 1836.

Maier, Pauline, Merrit Roe Smith, Alexander Keyssar, and Daniel J. Kevles. *Inventing America: A History of the United States,* Vol. 1. New York: W. W. Norton & Co., 2006.

McMaster, John Bach. *History of the People of the United States, from the Revolution to the Civil War.* Volume 7, *1841–1850.* New York: D. Appleton & Co., 1910.

Morgan, Kenneth O., ed. *The Oxford History of Britain.* New York: Oxford University Press, 2001.

National Archives Post Office Department, Washington, D.C. "Franklin." *An Examination of the Probable Effect of the Reduction of Postage: As Proposed to be Made by the Bill Introduced into the Senate of the United States by the Hon. Mr. Merrick, of Maryland.* 1844.

Niles, John. M. *Report of the Postmaster General.* Washington D.C.: Government Printing Office, 1840.

Perry, C. R. *The Victorian Post Office: The Growth of a Bureaucracy.* Woodbridge, U. K.: Boydell Press, 1992.

Plitt, George. U.S. Congress. Senate. 26th Cong., 2nd Sess., 1841. S. Doc. 156.

"Reduction of Postage." *Madisonian.* 3 February 1844.

Robinson, Howard. *The British Post Office: A History.* Princeton: Princeton University Press, 1948.

Schama, Simon. *A History of Britain.* Volume 3: *The Fate of Empire, 1776–2000.* New York: Hyperion, 2002.

Smith, A. D. *The Development of Rates of Postage: An Historical and Analytical Study.* London: George Allen & Unwin, 1917.

"The Postage," *Boston Morning Chronicle.* 16 December 1844.

Thompson, David. *England in the Nineteenth Century, 1815–1914.* New York: Penguin, 1985.

Wiener, Joel H. *The War of the Unstamped: The Movement to Repeal the British Newspaper Tax, 1830–1836.* Ithaca, N. Y.: Cornell University Press, 1969.

Woodward, E. L. *The Age of Reform, 1815–1870.* London: Oxford University Press, 1938.

Introduction to the First Symposium

On November 3–4, 2006, the Smithsonian National Postal Museum and the American Philatelic Society hosted the first symposium in Washington, D.C., with the theme "What Is Postal History?" A seemingly simple question, but when examined by experts from different fields, postal history was found to have divergent meanings. Postal history is the starting point for a philatelic collection, a research project, a museum exhibit, or a future business innovation. Postal history embraces the artifacts, envelopes, stamps, posters, badges, pillar boxes, maps, postal operations records, technology, equipment, and all manner of other philatelic and postal materials.

Over the two days, there were twenty-seven papers, three of which are presented in this book. Sheila A. Brennan, George Mason University, discusses "Consumers, Recreation and the Post" in her paper on "Little Colored Bits of Paper Collected in the Progressive Era." John Kevin Boyle, Benedictine University, discusses "The Mails in Times of War" in his paper "WWI Philatelic Censuses of East Africa." Terence Hines, Pace University, and Thomas Velk, McGill University, discuss "The Gold Mine of *The Official Register* Data" in their paper "Explorations in *The Official Register*: Statistical Analysis of Postmaster Compensation Data from 19th Century New Hampshire."

"Little Colored Bits of Paper" Collected in the Progressive Era

Sheila A. Brennan

Three months ago he did not know
His lesson in geography;
Though he could spell and read quite well,
And cipher, too, he could not tell
The least thing in topography.

But what a change! How passing strange!
This stamp-collecting passion
Has roused his zeal, for woe or weal,
And lists of names he now can reel
Off in amazing fashion.

. . . And now he longs for more Hong Kongs,
A Rampour, a Mauritius,
Greece, Borneo, Fernando Po,—
And how much else no one can know;
But be, kind fates, propitious.[1]

The merits of stamp collecting are applauded in this poem from 1885, as the practice of philately spread throughout the United States at a time when collecting objects of all kinds flourished. Although collecting art and antiques was an elite activity, collecting stamps was common, accessible, and inexpensive. Government-issued "little colored bits of paper" captured the interest of thousands of people including children, middle-class women, and elite businessmen.[2] Beginning in the 1870s American stamp collecting enthusiasts began to act in public ways typical of the progressive era by incorporating scientific language into their pursuit; organizing formal associations; publishing journals; and developing a relationship with the federal government. Stamp collectors redefined the meanings of federally-issued stamps by not using them for postage and collecting them inside their homes or by selling them on the open market. While the postal service promotes philately today, it was not until the World's Columbian Exposition in 1892–1893 that the U.S. Post Office Department acknowledged and capitalized on the growing world of philatelists when it issued the first set of American commemorative stamps. Printing limited-issue collectible stamps generated greater interest in the postal service and for collecting the Department's most popular product.[3]

Nineteenth-century philatelic societies functioned in a world almost completely removed from the producers of American stamps, the U.S. Post Office Department (USPOD), until the World's Columbian Exposition at Chicago in 1892–93. Prior to the 1890s, the USPOD maintained limited contact with stamp collectors. Postmasters General were busy with balancing the duties of the Department with business interests of the press and big business and with morality crusades. Official USPOD records from this time reveal little contact with collectors.[4]

Conversely, philatelic journals did not discuss the USPOD much in their pages. Philatelic societies and journals functioned independently from the federal government. Publishing news releases regarding new issues of stamps was the only role the USPOD played in print until the Columbian Exposition. American stamp collectors were more interested in stamps than the federal agency that produced them.

Retailer John Wanamaker forever changed that relationship during his tenure as postmaster general (1889–1893) by recognizing that collectors were consumers of stamps and that the government should harness their buying power and tap into their well-formed organizations. His administration is remembered mostly for the rural free delivery plan, but Wanamaker also increased the visibility of the USPOD in the philatelic world. Known more as the creator of the modern department store than as a Washington bureaucrat, Wanamaker brought his business acumen and understanding of customer relations to the Department. Additionally, Wanamaker was heavily influenced by the spectacle of the era's great world fairs, making it possible for him to see great potential in promoting the USPOD through a carefully designed exhibit at the Columbian Exposition.[5]

From the early planning stages of the world's fair, Wanamaker envisioned heightening the postal service's visibility by staging an exhibit and issuing the first series of commemorative American stamps. Immediately after securing funding from Congress, the USPOD contacted philatelists who soon heard from renowned dealer C.H. Mekeel that the USPOD would exhibit a complete set of U.S. stamps with the help of the American Philatelic Association (APA). However, the government's display highlighted more than stamps by exhibiting the USPOD's contributions in transportation and communication.[6] The exhibit promoted good will with its patrons—the American people—and emphasized that the department existed for public service. Constantly seeking to balance its

budget, the department looked to the public for continued financial support and the longevity of its agency.

Soon after the announcement of the exposition, the USPOD sought assistance from philatelists to create an exhibit of American and international stamps. Interestingly in 1891, the APA created a committee to develop its own exhibit at the world's fair. Unable to obtain space in a private building, committee members contacted the Third Assistant Postmaster General, A. D. Hazen, asking for help. Hazen obliged their request and offered gallery space in the government building overlooking the USPOD exhibit. Hazen envisioned that collectors from across the country would contribute stamps through the management of the APA. Capitalizing on its national network of state philatelic societies, the APA asked for stamp and monetary donations "to make this exhibit as complete as possible." Encouraging wide participation among its members, the APA emphasized the great "impetus this exhibition will give stamp collecting!"[7]

Identifying themselves as stamp experts and enthusiasts, philatelists reflected many of the main devices of the progressive spirit sweeping across America. Though not seeking to solve social ills, these middle-class and elite collectors brought respectability to their leisure activity by mimicking new professional organizations. They accomplished this through constructing the study of stamps as a scientific pursuit, establishing their own professional associations, and publishing journals.

In the late nineteenth century many Americans searched for order when government and big business expanded, and national institutions consumed local organizations. Robert Wiebe's influential work, *The Search for Order*, details the breakdown of local autonomy in small "island communities" beginning in the 1870s as hierarchical needs of industrial life took hold in the United States With the increased presence of money, workers of all classes produced less inside their homes and began to rely more on stores for consumer goods from necessities to fine goods. Doctors, lawyers, social workers, economists, and psychologists became professional experts who informed the expanding government and the public how to solve social problems in an increasingly urban and industrial America. Professionalization emphasized scientific methods for fixing problems, and those professionals formed associations in the late nineteenth and early twentieth century.[8]

Philatelists also participated in a professionalization process that began by promoting scientific aspects of their hobby. In a popular 1886 book, *The Study of Philately*, Arthur Palethorpe proclaimed that "philately now ranks as a science" as he attempted to distinguish the practice as something different from a mere childhood folly. The *American Journal of Philately* resumed publication in 1888 and its editors wrote about how their readers enjoyed debating "in the field of our sciences," while the subtitle of the *Northwestern Philatelist* noted it was "a monthly magazine devoted to the sciences of philately." Other publications reinforced a connection with a scientific method by writing articles about how to properly classify a stamp collection.[9] This science-laden language offered philatelists an opportunity to become experts in the small bits of paper they collected, traded, or bought.

Stamp collectors organized societies to promote philately as a respectable activity. Following the British lead, the American Philatelic Association (APA) formed in 1886 to promote stamp collecting in the United States. The founders encouraged local groups to form wherever "six philatelists can be brought together." As a national society, the APA connected smaller groups meeting across the country in the pursuit of philatelic knowledge.[10]

Stamp collecting societies were early examples of American middle-class and elite hobby clubs. Many individuals collected various objects inside their homes, but others wanted to connect with like-minded collectors and founded clubs in the late nineteenth century. For instance, the Grolier Club, formed in 1884 in New York City, comprised wealthy male book collectors who also dabbled in poster collecting. Coin collectors started the American Numismatic Association in 1891 and the Collectors Club promoted philately among the elite and middle class beginning in 1896. Many others collected without clubs at this time such as women and children who collected trade cards in scrapbooks kept inside the home, as Ellen Gruber Garvey demonstrates.[11]

Those interested in stamp collecting who did not want to join a club could connect to the emerging philatelic community by participating in the flourishing print culture that emerged in the late nineteenth century. The first serial, *Stamp Collector's Record*, was issued in Albany, New York, by S. A. Taylor in December 1864, and the numbers grew exponentially from there so that between 1864 and 1906 over 900 stamp papers were published in the United States alone. Even though many journals were short-lived, they demonstrate that stamp collecting indeed was a national pastime.[12]

So prolific were philatelic publications that by 1892 they became the subject of separate articles in the *Pennsylvania Philatelist*. Harry Franklin Kantner declared that the "philatelic writer" was "one of the most potent factors in the Philatelic field" fighting for the progression of the hobby. The following year Kantner noted his excitement when reading his first small stamp journal but regretted that there were too many publications available and that "the 'stamp fever' became the 'publishing fever'." His article actively discouraged "all ambitious young men" from starting new papers.[13]

While philatelic associations openly encouraged all to collect stamps, Kantner's comments suggest that lines were beginning to be drawn within the philatelic community. Applying a hierarchical framework to stamp papers and journalists is reminiscent of the post-Civil War tendency to distinguish between high and lowbrow activities. Quite aware of philatelists' place within the greater context of American culture, Kantner commented that it was "not only a progressive age in general affairs but also in philatelic matters."[14]

Federal promotion of stamp collecting at the Chicago world's fair thrilled this growing philatelic community because they believed the fair brought recognition for their pursuit and their associations. Furthermore, philately extended beyond stamp and postal exhibits to the physical presence of stamp collectors who gathered in Chicago for their convention. Just as the American Historical Association held their annual meeting in Chicago, so did the American Philatelic Association. In anticipation of their meeting, the editor of *American Philatelist* grew excited because "the eyes of the entire civilized world" "turned towards Chicago" for the Exposition where their associates met.[15] Believing in the power of this mass cultural gathering, private collectors and the federal government together promoted philately in very public ways for the first time.

To further this relationship, Postmaster General Wanamaker proposed designing and issuing special stamps to appeal to collectors in and outside of the U.S. Wanamaker recognized the stamp collecting "mania" and wanted the USPOD to capitalize on philatelists' desire to acquire new stamps and perhaps attract new collectors amazed by a beautifully-designed set of sixteen stamps depicting the story of Columbus and his journey. Estimating that millions of collectors, from the "school boy and girl to the monarch and the millionaire," kept stamps in collections "never (to) be drawn upon to pay postage," Wanamaker saw great potential for profit. The Columbians' limited issue, combined with a larger size and beautiful design, would attract international dealers and collectors (Figure 1). He also envisioned these stamps stimulating correspondence, private and commercial, because affixing a Columbian stamp brought more attention to what was inside that piece of mail. Not just for collecting, Columbians held value and represented pre-paid postage but did not replace the contemporary issue of stamps from that

FIGURE 1. Landing of Columbus, 2-cent, 1892–1893, Courtesy Smithsonian National Postal Museum. (TMS Object No. 1980.2493.1609).

year. "Though not designed primarily for that object," the profit-making potential of these commemoratives was "of highest importance to the public service," Wanamaker emphasized. He estimated that these stamps would bring in revenues to the federal government of 2.5 million dollars.[16]

Releasing the Columbians turned a spotlight towards collectors in the popular press. Writing one month after their issue, the *New York Times* featured an article on philately claiming that the new stamps gave "extra temporary impetus to the regular trade in stamps which has grown to proportions entirely amazing to persons not informed of its extent and diffusion." This journalist also recognized the profit-making potential of the Columbians that proved "a lucky speculation on the part of the Government." They brought "clean profit," because the stamps would "be locked up in albums and never put upon letters for the Government to carry." E.S. Martin wrote in his *Harper's Weekly* column how the success of the Columbian stamps "called attention to the very lively status of the stamp-collecting mania." So lively, that he noticed the presence of stamps in many homes was as prevalent as soap.[17]

Despite such praises, some criticism surrounded the release of the Columbians. Senator Edwin Oliver Wolcott (R-CO), for example, called for a joint congressional resolution to discontinue the Columbian stamps, exclaiming that he did not want a "cruel and unusual stamp" unloaded on collectors. Wolcott criticized fellow Republican Wanamaker for acting in a mercantilistic manner by profiting from philatelists.[18] Correct about Wanamaker's

retailing instinct, Wolcott's assumptions were slightly flawed because Wanamaker would not profit personally—only the government reaped those monetary benefits. If fiscally successful, the USPOD would require less in appropriations from Congress.

In response to these criticisms, Wanamaker shot back a letter defending his actions. Asserting his domain over postage regulations, he found the special stamps in line with other financial investments contributed by the federal government for mounting the Columbian Exposition. This included "the issue of five million silver souvenir coins," the Treasury Department's production of a collectible related to the fair. He emphasized the Post Office's ability to educate "the people with the story of Columbus." Wanamaker recognized that through stamps, the USPOD "more than any other branch of the Government, comes into familiar contact with all of the people." Citing the popularity of the stamps, Wanamaker referred to a prominent officer in the American Philatelic Society who commended the issuing of the stamp. Moreover, he received letters from private citizens "warmly approving the new stamps." The Senate was unsuccessful in removing the commemoratives from circulation.

Wanamaker's successor, Wilson S. Bissel however, found that the previous administration optimistically predicted stamp sales. According to Bissel, the rate of purchase for the commemoratives fell by mid-1893, and he renegotiated the original order for three billion Columbian stamps down to two because he felt the collectors' purchasing power was not as great as Wanamaker predicted.[19] Prior to his departure, Wanamaker defended himself and the Department, referencing a public-private relationship between the Post Office and the American people that justified the grand issuing of the Columbians.

After the public success of the USPOD's first commemoratives, the government continued to experiment with special-issue stamps celebrating other occasions. World's fairs and historic anniversaries appeared on these stamps, such as the Trans-Mississippi and International Exposition (1898), Pan-American Exposition (1901), and the anniversaries of the Louisiana Purchase Exposition (1904) and of Jamestown Exposition (1907). After projected revenues from the Columbians fell short of Wanamaker's 2.5 million dollar estimate, postal officials commissioned more conservative numbers of commemoratives and shortened the period of availability from a year to a few months. Though not attracting nearly as much publicity, these stamps were successful and collected.[20]

Some philatelists felt uncomfortable with the new role the government played in the stamp market. Outrage and protest came from the editors of the *American Journal of Philately (AJP)* in 1898, who tried stopping the issue of the Trans-Mississippi Exposition commemorative stamp and encouraged other collectors to join them in a letter-writing campaign complaining to the USPOD. Proclaiming that the Columbians "should not be considered a precedent for future issues," the editors lamented that philatelists would endure "a sad blow to (their) hobby if the government of the United States should lend itself to so reprehensible a scheme." Even "The Busy World" columnist at *Harper's Weekly* agreed with the *AJP* but saw the USPOD's role as "going outside its legitimate business in advertising even an enterprise of national moment." In contrast, the *Virginian Philatelist* endorsed the new stamp and revealed that they received only one negative response from a collector. The editor knew that despite the protest of others, "the stamps will be issued nevertheless."[21] Philatelists experienced some growing pains as the USPOD—which prior to Chicago played a minimal role in stamp collecting—now actively influenced the stamp market by issuing special commemorative stamps.

Into the twentieth century, stamp collecting grew in popularity, as did support from the USPOD. The postal service officially supported collecting when it created the United States Philatelic Agency in 1921 to serve American and international collectors exclusively. Currently, the U.S. Postal Service takes an active role in encouraging philately and works to accommodate philatelists even as stamp collecting is on the wane.

The Columbian Exposition forever linked the postal service with stamp collectors after years of traveling on separate paths. The USPOD recognized the public presence of philatelists and spoke to them through promoting philately and issuing a decorative series of commemorative stamps. Philatelists participated in the world's fair and perpetuated a dialog that they had begun decades earlier through buying, trading, and collecting stamps. Because philatelists professionalized by forming associations and publishing journals, Postmaster General Wanamaker recognized their presence and understood that the government needed those private organizations to promote good will and help to maintain the fiscal health of the US Post Office Department.

NOTES

1. Mary L. B. Branch, "The Little Stamp Collector," *St. Nicholas; an Illustrated Magazine for Young Folks* (August 1885): 12. This poem was reprinted in *The Washington Post*, November 11, 1888, 10.

2. "Postage Stamp Collectors: Enthusiasts Who Spend Much Money and Time on Their Hobby," *New York Times*, September 7, 1890: 17. While evidence suggests that nineteenth-century Americans collected many things, little secondary research tells us those stories. To read more about the history of American collecting see: Douglas and Elizabeth Rigby, *Lock, Stock, and Barrel: The Story of Collecting* (Philadelphia: Lippencott, 1949).Thomas J. Schlereth, ed., *Material Culture Studies in America* (Nashville, TN: American Association for State and Local History, 1982). Roy Rosenzweig and Warren Leon, ed., *History Museums in the United States: A Critical Assessment* (Urbana: University of Illinois Press, 1989). Werner Muensterberger, *Collecting : An Unruly Passion: Psychological Perspectives* (Princeton, N. J.: Princeton University Press, 1994). Russell W. Belk, *Collecting in a Consumer Society, Collecting Cultures Series* (London; New York: Routledge, 1995). Susan M Pearce, *On Collecting: An Investigation into Collecting in the European Tradition* (London: Routledge, 1995). Leah Dilworth, ed., *Acts of Possession: Collecting in America* (New Brunswick, N. J.: Rutgers University Press, 2003).

3. Scholarship on stamp collecting is thin, despite its popularity as a hobby in the United States and internationally. Stamp collecting falls between institutional histories of the postal service and material culture studies. A few historians, such as Wayne Fuller and Richard John, recognize the prominent role played by the American postal system in nineteenth-century public policy and communications. Unfortunately, they neglect the explosion of stamp collecting that occurred after the first federally-issued U. S. stamp appeared in 1847. For sources on stamp collecting see: Mauritz Hallgren, *All About Stamps: Their History and the Art of Collecting Them* (New York and London: Alfred A. Knopf, 1940). Rigby, *Lock, Stock, and Barrel: The Story of Collecting*. John Bryant, "Stamp and Coin Collecting," in *Handbook of American Popular Culture*, Vol. 3, ed. M. Thomas Inge (Westport, Conn.: Greenwood Press, 1981); Kenneth Ames and K. Martinez, ed., *Material Culture of Gender/Gender of Material Culture* (Ann Arbor: University of Michigan Press, 1992). Steven M. Gelber, "Free Market Metaphor: The Historical Dynamics of Stamp Collecting," *Comparative Studies in Society and History* 34, no. 4 (October1992). Neil Harris, "American Poster Collecting: A Fitful History," *American Art* 12, no. 1 (Spring 1998). Steven M. Gelber, *Hobbies: Leisure and the Culture of Work in America* (New York: Columbia University Press, 1999).

4. Overall, the USPOD records are very spotty in the late nineteenth century. Archivists from the National Archives told me that federal records often are missing significant amounts of paperwork because there were no requirements to keep files indefinitely. Historians at the U.S. Postal Service concur that few stamp-related records exist from that era. Often records were legally destroyed.

5. Robert Stockwell Hatcher, "United States Postal Notes," *American Philatelist*, Vol. 6, no. 11(November 10, 1892): 185. John Wanamaker began and operated one of the first department stores in the US, Wanamaker's in Philadelphia, Pennsylvania. He forever transformed the retail business and was referred to as

the "greatest merchant in America." As postmaster general he spearheaded postal reform, such as the RFD experiment, which some progressive reformers supported because of its capacity to unify the nation. William Leach argues that Wanamaker's goal was to increase the public's access to goods, subsidized by the government. Since he was a department store merchant, he favored other large-scale retailers, like Sears, Roebuck, and Company's mail order business. See: William Leach, *Land of Desire: Merchants, Power, and the Rise of a New American Culture* (New York: Pantheon Books, 1993), 32–35, 182–184. For Wanamaker's fascination with world fairs, see: Herbert Adams Gibbons, *John Wanamaker* (Port Washington, N.Y.,: Kennikat Press, 1971), 153–180.

6. Mekeel was interviewed in "Postage-Stamp Collectors," *New York Times* September 7, 1890, 17. The government's exhibit included stamped paper, models of postal coaches and mail equipment, photographs, maps, and examples from the Dead Letter Office. USPOD also operated a working post office where Columbians could be purchased at the Fair. United States Post Office Department, *Annual Report of the Postmaster-General of the United States for the Fiscal Year Ending June 30, 1892* (Washington, D. C.: Government Printing Office, 1892): 74. Congress appropriated $40,000 for the postal station and an additional $23,000 for transporting the mail to and from the fairgrounds over the course of the Exposition.

7. American Philatelic Association, *Catalogue of the American Philatelic Association's Loan Exhibit of Postage Stamps to the United States Post Office Department at the World's Columbian Exposition Chicago, 1893*: 3. Albert R. Rogers, "American Philatelic Association's Exhibit of Postage Stamps at the World's Columbian Exposition, Chicago, 1893," *American Philatelist*, Vol. 7, no. 3 (March 10, 1893): 33–35. Memo, "Inventory of Articles turned over to Mr. Tyler," Albert H. Hall, "Letter to Hon. Wilson S. Bissell," in *RG 28, Records of the Post Office Department, Office of the Third Assistant Postmaster General (Stamps and Stamped Envelopes) Correspondence, 1847–1907* (Washington, D. C.: March 2, 1894).There is a slight disconnect between Mekeel's and the APA's version of who asked whom to participate in the exhibition. I represented both here, but tend to believe APA's version since it was their committee. Mekeel may have been discussing what he heard through his network, because APA hadn't formed a committee to deal with the exhibition in 1890.

8. For background information on the post-Civil War and progressive eras see: Robert H. Wiebe, *The Search for Order, 1877–1920*, 1st ed. (New York: Hill and Wang, 1967). Steven J. Diner, *A Very Different Age: Americans of the Progressive Era*, 1st ed. (New York: Hill and Wang, 1998), William Leach, *Land of Desire: Merchants, Power, and the Rise of a New American Culture* (New York: Pantheon Books, 1993), Alan Trachtenberg and Eric Foner, *The Incorporation of America : Culture and Society in the Gilded Age* (New York: Hill and Wang, 1982). Arthur Stanley Link and Richard L. McCormick, *Progressivism* (Arlington Heights, Ill.: Harlan Davidson Inc., 1983).

9. Arthur J. Palethorpe, *The Study of Philately* (Bury S. Edmund's, England: Nunn, Christie & Co., 1886): 6. *American Journal of Philately*, Second Series, Vol. 1, (1888), opening page. *The Northwestern Philatelist: A Monthly Magazine Devoted to the Science of Philately* (Elk Point, South Dakota: J.C. Richard, R.J. Ellis, 1899–1900). American Philatelic Association, *Catalogue of the American Philatelic Association's Loan Exhibit of Postage Stamps to the United States Post Office Department at the World's Columbian Exposition Chicago, 1893* (Birmingham, CT: D.H. Bacon and Company, 1893), 10; James Rees, "Clerk in the Philadelphia Post Office," *Foot-prints of a Letter-Carrier*, (Philadelphia,1866).

10. Hallgren, *All About Stamps*, 185–186. The first permanent organization in the world was the London Philatelic Group in 1869, now known as the Royal Philatelic Society. Letter from Theo. F. Cuno, S. B. Bradt, W. G. Whilden, Jr. to The Philatelists of the United States, June 25, 1886 published in *Official Circular Number 1*, American Philatelic Association, (November 1886): opening page.

11. Neil Harris, "American Poster Collecting," 13–15. Ellen Gruber Garvey, "Dreaming in Commerce: Advertising Trade Card Scrapbooks," in *Acts of Possession: Collecting in America*, ed., Leah Dilworth (New Brunswick, NJ: Rutgers University Press, 2003), 66–85.

12. Edward Denny Bacon, *Catalogue of the Crawford Library of Philatelic Literature at the British Library, Rev. ed.* (Fishkill, N. Y.: Printer's Stone in association with the British Library, 1991). For example of such journals see: *Evergreen State Philatelist* (Hartland, Wash.: R. W. French, 1894–1900), *California Philatelist* (San Francisco, Ca.: E. F. Gambs, 1883–1899), *Southern Philatelist* (Charleston, S. C.: Southern Stamp and Publishing, 1889–1896), *Virginia Philatelist* (Richmond, Va.: Virginia Philatelic Publishing, 1897–1905), *Ohio Philatelist* (Westerville, Ohio: H. W. Keller, 1888–1889), *St. Louis Philatelist* (St. Louis, Mo.: E. F. Gambs, 1876–1882), *Michigan Philatelist* (Detroit: Union Stamp Company, 1877–1879), *Pennsylvania Philatelist*, (Reading, Pa.: C. W. Kissinger, 1891–1898), *Eastern Philatelist* (Fitchburg, Mass.: Eastern Philatelic Publishing, 1887–1899), *Western Philatelist: A Monthly Journal for Stamp Collectors* (Chicago: Western Philatelic Publishing Company, 1887–1888) *Lone Star State Philatelist* (Abilene, Tex.: Bradley,1894–1899). *American Journal of Philately*, Second Series (New York: Scott and Company, 1888–1906), *Mekeel's Weekly Stamp News* (Portland, Maine: Severn-Wylie-Jewett Co, 1891–1996). Mekeel's is still an active publication, but with a different publisher.

13. Harry Franklin Kantner, "The Philatelic Writer," *The Pennsylvania Philatelist*, Vol. 2, no.1 (June 1892): 3. H. Franklin Kantner, "The Philatelic Publisher's Soliloquy," *The Pennsylvania Philatelist*, Vol. 2, no. 1 (June 1892): 3. H. Franklin Kantner, "Philatelic Journalism," *The Pennsylvania Philatelist*, Vol. 3, no. 3 (February 1893): 49–52. His use of "young men" indicates that a majority of the publications were headed by men in the late nineteenth century. Few female writers appeared in the jour-

nals I reviewed, but some like Eva Earl mentioned earlier in the paper encouraged women to collect and participate in philatelic societies.

14. Kantner, "Philatelic Journalism," 52. For a discussion of nineteenth-century cultural hierarchies see: Lawrence W. Levine, *Highbrow/Lowbrow : The Emergence of Cultural Hierarchy in America* (Cambridge, Mass.: Harvard University Press, 1988).

15. "Postage Stamps at the World's Fair," *American Journal of Philately* Vol. 6, (July 31, 1893): 373–374. "Editorial Comment," *American Philatelist*, Vol. 7, no. 5 (May 10, 1893): 73.

16. United States Post Office Department, *Annual Report for 1892*, 77. A. D. Hazen, Third Assistant Postmaster General under Wanamaker echoed those sentiments, 110–111. Marshall Cushing, *The Story of Our Post Office*, Boston: A. M. Thayer, 1893.

17. "Costly Bits of Paper: Extraordinary Prices Paid for Postage Stamps," *New York Times*, February 5, 1893: 20. E. S. Martin, "This Busy World," *Harper's Weekly* (April 14, 1894): 346.

18. "The New Stamps Ridiculed," *New York Times*, January 22, 1893, 1. Senator Wolcott's interest may have influenced his appointment in the 54th Congress to the Committee on Post Office and Post Roads. In one speech, Wolcott referred to a physician's letter suggesting that any unused stamps might have a second life as "chest protectors" due to their unusually large size. "Good as Chest Protectors," *New York Times*, January 23, 1893, 4. This stamp series featured rectangular and longer stamps than previous issues that mostly featured portraits on nearly-square-shaped stamps. The engravings from which the commemoratives were printed from historical painting depicting scenes of Columbus landing in the "new world," his sailing fleet, Columbus in Europe presenting "natives" to the Spanish, and other scenes relating to his life and conquests.

19. Letter from John Wanamaker to Honorable Philetus Sawyer, (February 13, 1893) "Of Interest to Postmasters in Relation to Columbian Postage Stamps—Answer to the Senate Resolution," reprinted in *American Journal of Philately*, Second Series, Vol. 6 (March 31, 1893): 189–193. United States Post Office Department, *Annual Report of the Postmaster-General of the United States for the Fiscal Year Ending June 30, 1892*. (Washington, D. C.: Government Printing Office, 1893), XXX, 473.

20. United States Post Office Department, *Annual Report of the Postmaster-General of the United States for the Fiscal Year Ending June 30, 1901* (Washington, D. C.: Government Printing Office, 1901), United States Post Office Department, *Annual Report of the Postmaster-General of the United States for the Fiscal Year Ending June 30, 1904* (Washington, D.C.: Government Printing Office, 1904), Kenneth A. Wood, *Post Dates: A Chronology of Intriguing Events in the Mails and Philately* (Albany, Or.: Van Dahl Publications, 1985).

21. *American Journal of Philately*, Vol. 9 (January 1898): opening page; and other *AJP* related to the protest included: "Omaha Exposition Stamps—Protest of San Francisco Collectors" (March 1898): 132; "Omaha Stamps at the S. S. S. S." (May 1898): 209; reprinted memo from John A. Merritt, Third Assistant Postmaster General (September 1898): 374–375. "This Busy World," *Harper's Weekly* (January 22, 1898): 79. *The Virginian Philatelist*, Vol. 1, no. 7 (March 1898): 127.

BIBLIOGRAPHY

American Philatelic Association. *Catalogue of the American Philatelic Association's Loan Exhibit of Postage Stamps to the United States Post Office Department at the World's Columbian Exposition Chicago, 1893*, pp. 3, 10. Birmingham, Conn.: D. H. Bacon & Company, Printers, 1893.

Ames, Kenneth, and K. Martinez, ed. *Material Culture of Gender/Gender of Material Cutlure*. Ann Arbor, Mich: University of Michigan Press, 1992.

Annual Report of the Postmaster General of the United States for the Fiscal Year Ending June 30, 1892. Washington, D. C.: Government Printing Office, 1892.

Annual Report of the Postmaster General of the United States for the Fiscal Year Ending June 30, 1901. Washington, D. C.: Government Printing Office, 1901.

Annual Report of the Postmaster General of the United States for the Fiscal Year Ending June 30, 1904. Washington, D. C.: Government Printing Office, 1904.

Bacon, Edward Denny. *Catalogue of the Crawford Library of Philatelic Literature at the British Library*. Rev. ed. Fishkill, N. Y.: Printer's Stone, 1991.

Belk, Russell W. *Collecting in a Consumer Society*. The Collecting Culture Series. New York: Routledge, 1995.

Branch, Mary L. B. "The Little Stamp Collector." *St. Nicholas: an Illustrated Magazine for Young Folks*, (August 1885):12

Bryant, John. "Stamp and Coin Collecting." In *Handbook of American Popular Culture*. Volume 3, ed. M. Thomas Inge. Westport, Conn.: Greenwood Press, 1981.

"Costly Bits of Paper: Extraordinary Prices Paid for Postage Stamps." *New York Times*, 5 February 1893, 20.

Cushing, Marshall. *The Story of Our Post Office*. Boston: A. M. Thayer, 1893.

Dilworth, Leah, ed. *Acts of Possession: Collecting in America*. New Brunswick, N. J.: Rutgers University Press, 2003.

Diner, Steven J. *A Very Different Age: Americans of the Progressive Era*. New York: Hill and Wang, 1998.

"Editorial Comment." *American Philatelist*, 7(5):73.

Garvey, Ellen Gruber. "Dreaming in Commerce: Advertising Trade Card Scrapbooks." In *Acts of Possession: Collecting in America*, ed. Leah Dillworth. New Brunswick, N. J.: Rutgers University Press, 2003.

Gelber, Steven M. "Free Market Metaphor: The Historical Dynamics of Stamp Collecting." *Comparative Studies in Society and History*, 34(4):742–769.

———. *Hobbies: Leisure and the Culture of Work in America*. New York: Columbia University Press, 1999.

Gibbons, Herbert Adams. *John Wanamaker*. Port Washington, N. Y.: Kennikat Press, 1971.

"Good as Chest Protectors." *New York Times*, 23 January 1893, 4.

Hall, Albert H. "Letter to Hon. Wilson S. Bissell." *Records of the Post Office Department, Office of the Third Assistant Post Master General (Stamps and Stamped Envelopes) Correspondence, 1847–1907.* RG 28. Washington, D. C.: National Archives, 1894.

Hallgren, Mauritz. *All About Stamps: Their History and the Art of Collecting Them.* New York: Alfred A. Knopf, 1940.

Harris, Neil. "American Poster Collecting: A Fitful History." *American Art*, 12(1):10–39.

Hatcher, Robert Stockwell. "United States Postal Notes." *American Philatelist*, 6(11):185.

"Inventory of Articles turned over to Mr. Tyler." *Records of the Post Office Department, Office of the Third Assistant Post Master General (Stamps and Stamped Envelopes) Correspondence, 1847–1907.* RG 28. Washington, D. C.: National Archives, 1894.

Kantner, Harry Franklin. "Philatelic Journalism." *The Pennsylvania Philatelist*, 3(3):49–52.

———. "The Philatelic Publisher's Soliloquy." *The Pennsylvania Philatelist*, 2(1):3.

———. "The Philatelic Writer." *The Pennsylvania Philatelist*, 2(1):3.

Leach, William. *Land of Desire: Merchants, Power, and the Rise of a New American Culture*, pp. 32–35; 182–184. New York: Pantheon Books, 1993.

"Letter from Theo. F. Cuno, S. B. Bradt, W. G. Whilden Jr. to The Philatelist of the United States." *Official Circular Number 1.* American Philatelic Association, 1886.

Levine, Lawrence W. *Highbrow/Lowbrow: The Emergence of Cultural Hierarchy in America.* Cambridge, Mass.: Harvard University Press, 1988.

Link, Arthur Stanley, and Richard L. McCormick. *Progressivism.* Arlington Heights, Ill.: Harlan Davidson Inc., 1983.

Martin, E. S. "This Busy World." *Harper's Weekly*, 14 April 1894, 346.

Muensterberger, Werner. *Collecting: An Unruly Passion: Psychological Perspectives.* Princeton, N. J.: Princeton University Press, 1994.

"The New Stamps Ridiculed." *New York Times*, 22 January 1893, 1.

The Northwestern Philatelist: A Monthly Magazine Devoted to the Science of Philately. Elk Point: S. D.: J. C. Richard and R. J. Ellis, 1899.

"Opening Page." *American Journal of Philately*, Second Series, 1(1888).

Palethorpe, Arthur J. *The Study of Philately.* Bury St Edmunds, U. K.: Nunn, Christie & Co., 1886.

Pearce, Susan M. *On Collecting: An Investigation into Collecting in the European Tradition.* London: Routledge, 1995.

"Postage Stamp Collectors: Enthusiasts Who Spend Much Money and Time on Their Hobby." *New York Times*, 7 September 1890, 17.

"Postage Stamps at the World's Fair." *American Journal of Philately*, 6:373–374.

Rees, James. "Clerk in the Philadelphia Post Office." In *Foot-prints of a Letter-Carrier.* Philadelphia: J. B. Lippincott, 1866.

Rigby, Douglas, and Elizabeth Rigby. *Lock, Stock, and Barrel: The Story of Collecting.* Philadelphia: Lippencott, 1949.

Rogers, Albert R. "American Philatelic Association's Exhibit of Postage Stamps at the World's Columbian Exhibition, Chicago, 1893." *American Philatelist*, 7(3):33–35.

Rosenzweig, Roy, and Warren Leon, ed. *History Museums in the United States: A Critical Assessment.* Urbana, Ill.: University of Illinois Press, 1989.

Schlereth, Thomas J., ed. *Material Culture Studies in America.* Nashville, Tenn.: American Association for State and Local History, 1982.

Trachtenberg, Alan, and Eric Foner. *The Incorporation of America: Culture and Society in the Gilded Age.* New York: Hill and Wang, 1982.

Wanamaker, John. "Of Interest to Postmasters in Relation to Columbian Postage Stamps—Answer to the Senate Resolution." *American Journal of Philately*, 6:189–193.

Wiebe, Robert H. *The Search for Order, 1877–1920.* New York: Hill and Wang, 1967.

Wood, Kenneth A. *Post Dates: A Chronology of Intriguing Events in the Mails and Philately.* Albany, Or.: Van Dahl Publications, 1985.

WWI Philatelic Censuses of East Africa

John Kevin Doyle

WORLD WAR I IN GERMAN EAST AFRICA

The Germans were late to the "scramble for Africa"—they were among the last of the European countries to acquire colonies in Africa. The most important German colony was German East Africa (GEA), and it was the colony most nearly self-sufficient. When World War I started in Europe, it began immediately in German East Africa. Within a few months, GEA was invaded by the Allied troops (British, South African, Nigerian, Nyassaland, Indian, etc.) from the north, Belgian from the west, and Portuguese from the south. The largest force was the Allied force, which ultimately chased the Germans around GEA until after the end of WWI—the Germans surrendered in East Africa only after their surrender in Europe.

From a postal history perspective, the Germans began printing all stamps on paper which was watermarked lozenges in 1905, including stamps for the colonies. In late 1905, GEA changed currency from the Pesa/Rupie to Heller/Rupie. All low value stamps were reissued in the new currency (and therefore on the new watermarked paper). The Rupie value stamps, used primarily for internal post office operation (on parcel cards, money orders, etc.), did not need replenishment.

By early 1915, GEA officials requested replenishment of the 1 Rupie stamp, along with other war supplies—ammunition, artillery, medals, '15' and '16' year dates for cancellers, etc. The Germans prepared a blockade breaker, the captured *Dacre Hill*, outfitted as the "Danish" vessel *Nordamerika*. The *Nordamerika* left Wilhelmshaven on January 9, 1916 en route to GEA, with the war supplies and its own pontoon wharf. It successfully avoided the Allied warships in the Atlantic, rounded the Cape, and avoided the Allied blockade off the GEA coast. The *Nordamerika* entered Sudi Bay, just south of Lindi, on March 16, 1916 (see Figure 1). Sudi Bay was the most southerly harbor in GEA for ocean-going vessels.

Capt. Conrad Sörensen rechristened the ship *Marie* (his wife's name) in celebration of the successful voyage. By March 27, 1916, the ship was unloaded, and the cargo (made up in sixty-six pound parcels in Berlin) was on its way via porters. The British discovered the vessel about this time and began shelling her. The *Marie* escaped on April 22 and was interned in Batavia harbor in Indonesia

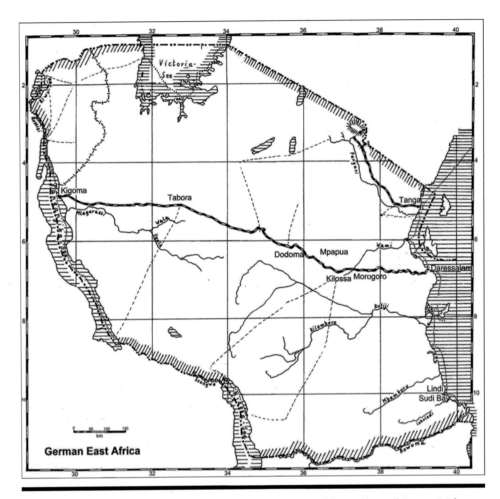

FIGURE 1. German East Africa in 1914.[1] Used by permission of the author and Jürgen Fricke.

on May 13. Sörensen and three crew members escaped. They were captured when attempting to board a U.S. ship in a Japanese harbor. They were interned in the U.S. and repatriated after the war.

Therefore, the 1 Rupie watermarked stamp first arrived in GEA in early 1916, and the use of this stamp, as told by the cancels on surviving copies, gives us information about postal traffic in GEA in 1916. The first known uses of the 1 Rupie watermarked stamp are in June 1916 in Dodoma and Mpapua, both towns along the Mittellandbahn (central railroad)—see Figures 1 and 2. The Allies captured Dodoma on July 29 and Mpapua on August 12, 1916. Table 1 shows the towns from which genuinely used 1 Rupie watermarked stamps have been found with the date they were captured by Allied forces, the number of stamps known, and the period of use of the cancel. Note that the Allied forces, driving from the north,

FIGURE 2. GEA 1 Rupie watermarked, used in DODOMA 19 June 1916. Used by permission of the author and Jürgen Fricke.

TABLE 1. GEA Towns and Central Railway, Capture Date, Number of GEA 1 Rupie Watermarked Stamps, and Period of Use.[1]

Town or Railway	Date of Allied Capture	Number of 1 Rupie Watermarked Stamps	Period of Use
Dodoma	29 July 1916	11	14–30 June 1916
Mpapua	12 August 1916	1	16 June 1916
Kilossa	22 August 1916	3	4–25 July 1916
Morogoro	26 August 1916	8	29 June–10 July 1916
Daressalam	4 Sept. 1916	8	26 June–20 August 1916
Tabora	19 Sept. 1916	2	30 August–1 Sept. 1916
Mittellandbahn	19 Sept. 1916	9	19 June–27 July 1916
Lindi	17 October 1916	2	26 June–7 July 1916

captured Dodoma (the center of the Central Railway–Mittellandbahn) first, then advanced eastward to Dar-es-Salaam and finally westward to Tabora.

WORLD WAR I IN KIONGA

Kionga was a small triangle of land between German East Africa and Mozambique (Portuguese East Africa) south of the Rovuma River and north of the Minengani River (see Figure 3). Various diplomatic agreements between the French, British, Germans, and Portuguese in June and December 1886 disagreed on the possession of this area. The Germans acknowledged that the area had been relinquished to "Portuguese influence" but claimed continued "special interest" in the area. The Portuguese occupied the area in 1887. Five years later, the Germans seized the area back from Portugal.

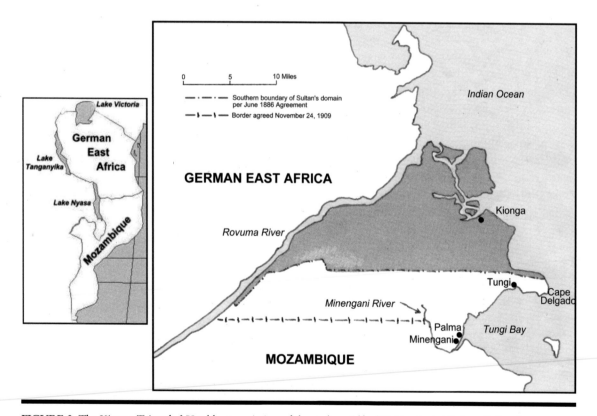

FIGURE 3. The Kionga Triangle.[2] Used by permission of the author, Alfred F. Kugel, and Robert E. Lamb.

FIGURE 4. 5C. Kionga stamp.[2] From the collection of Alfred F. Kugel. Used by permission.

After many more years of "discussions," the British pressured Germany and Portugal to divide the area, giving the northern half to Germany and the southern to Portugal. This was the position when WWI began in August 1914. Portugal was neutral until March 1916 (and in fact permitted mail from GEA through Mozambique to Portugal and then to Germany for some months). Portugal entered the war on March 9, 1916 and occupied the Kionga triangle on April 10. Seven weeks later, on May 29, Portugal issued a set of four stamps overprinted 'KIONGA' for use in its new territory. (See Figure 4)

The underlying stamps depict King Carlos and are from the 1898 issue of Lourenço Marques (a province of Portuguese East Africa). King Carlos was assassinated in 1908, and the Portuguese monarchy was overthrown in 1910. These Lourenço Marques stamps were locally overprinted "REPUBLICA" and issued in 1916. These obsolete stamps were further overprinted "KIONGA" and issued on May 29, 1916.

In 1913, the currency changed from 1,000 Reis = 1 Milreis, to 100 Centavos = 1 Escudo. Kionga stamps are also surcharged with new values in Centavos:

- ½C.—printed matter rate
- 1C.—domestic postal card rate
- 2½C—domestic letter rate
- 5C.—foreign letter rate.

The order of the two overprints and the surcharges is not clear. We presume "REPUBLICA" first, new value surcharges second, and "KIONGA" last, but we have no direct confirmation of this.

There was great interest in "War Stamps" in World War I—stamps issued by the combatants for use in occupied territories. The Kionga stamps were very popular and are quite available even today, both mint and used. There are fifty covers and cards known from Kionga in World War I. Of these, at least thirty went through the mails (they bear appropriate civilian and/or military censor marks, transit cancels, and/or receiving cancels).

The destinations of these covers are shown in Table 2. Of the two covers to Brazil, both went to Rio de Janeiro via Lisbon (see Figure 5). One was censored in Mozambique, and the other in Lisbon. Finally, one bears a Rio receiving cancel, the other does not. The one cover to Denmark (Copenhagen) went via Palma (a border town in northeast PEA) and Lisbon and was censored in Dieppe, France.

The one cover to France (Paris) went via Biera (a town on the PEA coast) was censored both in Biera and Paris and bears a Paris receiving cancel. The three covers to Nyassa are all to Mocimboa da Praia. Two are via Palma, and one is reported as via Tipo, but no censoring or receiving cancels are reported. There are six covers to Portugal (five to Lisbon, one to Coimbra). Three are fieldpost cards, with two censored in Lisbon (August 1918) and one not censored (September 1918). The other three are commercial covers, one censored in Lourenço Marques, one probably in Lisbon, and one at an unknown location. Two of these bear Lisbon receiving cancels.

There are two covers to South West Africa in the census, both to Keetmanshoop. The January 1917 cover was censored in Lourenço Marques; the June 1918 cover was censored in Beira. Both were also censored in Capetown. The January 1917 cover travelled via Lourenço Marques; the June 1918 cover travelled via Palma, Moçambique,

TABLE 2. Destinations of Kionga Covers

Brazil	2	Nyassa	3	Switzerland	7
Denmark	1	Portugal	6	United Kingdom	7
France	1	South West Africa	2	United States	1

FIGURE 5. MAI 16, 1917 Kionga cover to Brazil.[2] Used by permission of the author, Alfred F. Kugel, and Robert E. Lamb.

and Beira. Finally, both covers bear Keetmanshoop receiving cancels.

There are seven covers in the census to Switzerland, all to philatelic addressees (but all of which actually travelled through the mails). Four covers went to Moudon, and three to Basel. Two of the Moudon covers were sent in April 1917—these were both censored in Lourenço Marques, and one was also censored in Capetown. Two other covers to Moudon were sent in October 1917—these were both censored in Lyon, France. All four covers to Moudon bear Moudon receiving cancels. One cover to Basel in January 1918 was censored by the French in London, with Palma, Moçambique, and London transit cancels. Another cover to Basel, sent on February 12, 1918, was censored in Capetown, with a Lourenço Marques transit cancel. Another cover to Basel, sent only two days later on February 14, 1918, was also censored in Capetown, but with Palma and London transit cancels. All three covers to Basel bear Basel receiving cancels.

There are seven covers recorded to the United Kingdom (five to London, one to Nottingham, and one to Oxford). A June 1916 cover to London was censored in Lourenço Marques and bears a London receiving cancel.

Two covers to London in October and November 1916 were censored in Moçambique with Lisbon transit and London receiving cancels. A February 1917 cover to Nottingham was censored in Lourenço Marques and Moçambique (only the front has survived). A February 1917 cover to London was censored in Lisbon (?) and London and bears a London receiving cancel. A June 1917 cover to Oxford was censored in Beira and has Beira and Liverpool transit cancels. Finally, an August 1917 cover to London was censored in Lourenço Marques.

There is one cover recorded to the United States (New York). It was sent April 1917, was censored in Lourenço Marques, bears a New York receiving cancel, and no other censor or transit cancels.

CONCLUSIONS

For the GEA 1 Rupie watermarked stamps, we see that use began in two towns in the middle of the Mittelland-bahn, thence to Morogoro, Daressalam (both farther east on the Mittellandbahn) and Lindi in the far south, then

Kilossa, then Tabora on the Mittellandbahn. Almost all the uses were in towns along the Mittellandbahn. Almost all the uses occurred in less than a month (from June 14 to July 10)—see Figure 2. Given the great importance of the railroad to efficient communications, we suggest that this probably models most of the mid-1916 communication within GEA. Covers are known which were carried by runners in the interior of GEA and others which were carried on dhows along the coast, but we suggest most communication was along the Mittellandbahn as long as possible.

For the covers from Kionga, the routing and censorship was generally predictable—e.g., Kionga to Brazil through Portugal—which makes sense. The local covers (to Nyassa, also in PEA) were not censored. Finally, there are detail differences (in censoring, routes, transit and receiving cancels) even for covers sent on the same day, and certainly for those sent at different times.

A significant amount of information about war-time postal operations is derivable from philatelic censuses.

NOTES

1. John Kevin Doyle and Jürgen Fricke, "The Queen of German Colonial Philately", *The Congress Book 2001*, Chicago (2001): 53–72.

2. John Kevin Doyle, Alfred F. Kugel, and Robert E. Lamb, "The Portuguese in Kionga", *The Congress Book*, Columbus (2003): 149–176.

BIBLIOGRAPHY

Doyle, John Kevin, Alfred F. Kugel, and Robert E. Lamb. "The Portuguese in Kionga." *2003 Congress Book, #69.* Columbus, Oh.: American Philatelic Congress, 2003.

Doyle, John Kevin, and Jürgen Fricke. "The Queen of German Colonial Philately." *2001 Congress Book, #67.* Chicago: American Philatelic Congress, 2001.

Explorations in the Official Register: Statistical Analysis of Postmaster Compensation Data from 19th Century New Hampshire

Terence Hines and Thomas Velk

INTRODUCTION

A continuing problem for economists interested in wealth, income and economic activity in nineteenth century America is a distinct lack of good economic data, especially for the early part of the century. There seems to be no data set that could provide these variables and that is anywhere near complete both geographically and temporally. Thus economists have been forced to reply on measures that are, to say the least, quite removed from the actual economic variables of interest. Worse, the data sets economic historians have used are comparatively crude, happenstance, non-random and irregular "precursor" materials. Probate records, farm books (Mr. Jefferson's is a classic example), village tax records, newspaper reports of prices, merchant inventories, export and import data related to excise tax collections, letters and tax records have all been used. Early American governments often taxed personal as well as fixed wealth. Tax documents can be found that detail taxes paid by households subject to such levies.

For the earliest years, capitalizations of the great trading companies, from the West India Company to the Hudson's Bay Company, as well as other sources, have been used to make indirect, wealth based estimates of income. Excellent examples of this can be found in Coclanis' edited volume.[1] Data sources used include capital investment in the West India Company, wine imports into New York, expenditures on Indians in South Carolina, and average wealth at death of certain persons in New York, Massachusetts, South Carolina, and Jamaica. This last data source focused on estates in which there were significant holdings of wine, especially Madeira. Wines, especially expensive ones such as Madeira, attracted the attention of the tax authorities and thus careful records were kept (or fudged—who knows?) by individuals charged with reporting to the probate courts.

Abramovitz and David point out that "Such measures are neither comprehensive nor unbiased."[2] For example, Jones used probate records to estimate per capita wealth in early America and came up with a figure of seventy-six pounds.[3]

Her nearly forty years of research yielded data on only a very few counties in a few states in colonial America. Hughes and Cain use the seventy-six-pound figure and then note that "dividing this figure by various capital output ratios produces a result that is a measure of output (income) per head. . . . Historic capital output ratios fall somewhere between the boundaries 3/1 and 5/1."[4] Thus, the estimated income per head could be anywhere from fifteen to twenty-five pounds, a rather wide range. According to Abramovitz and David, income estimates for the period before 1870, "are surrounded by particularly wide margins of uncertainty."[5] In this essay, the authors refer to highly aggregated data on the national level. Detailed data at the local level has heretofore simply been unavailable. Most income estimates made by historians who study the eighteenth and nineteenth centuries are built up from such indirect data.

It appears that virtually all of the standard information used by economic historians to estimate income and economic activity in the nineteenth century is either highly aggregated or, when microeconomic, irregular in time and incomplete in geographic extent. This state of affairs has led to at least one highly creative attempt to obtain more comprehensive data. Komlos used the heights and weights of West Point cadets as surrogates for economic variables.[6] The use of such data suggests that scholars in this field are willing to use variables that have at best an extremely distant and at worst an ultimately unknowable relationship to the actual variable(s) of interest.

Economic historians agree that "measurement and analysis of economic growth . . . call for a very large volume of data." Unfortunately, "before 1840 no regular or reasonably complete census of economic activities was carried out in the United States."[7] Even after 1840 data that closely mirrors economic activity at the local level and is available at regular chronological intervals throughout the remainder of the nineteenth century has not been know to economic historians.

In the next section we describe a data set, previously unknown to economic historians, that contains data that we argue provides a measure of economic activity in every town in the United States every two years from 1816 to 1911 and which is much more accurate than anything previously known.

THE OFFICIAL REGISTER

For most of the nineteenth century and the first decade of the twentieth, the federal government published biannually a listing of the salaries of every government employee. While the exact title of this publication changed from time to time,[8] it is generally referred to as the *Official Register*, abbreviated hereinafter as OR. The OR is of special interest to economists and economic historians as it reports the salaries of the postmaster of each post office in the United States and its territories. Postmaster salaries were, during the period the OR was published, a function of the amount of business each post office did. The formulae for deriving total postal income at a given post office from the salary data in the OR are available in the appropriate *United States Statutes at Large*. Happily, they have been summarized in a Congressional report.[9] By "postal income" we mean income generated from the operation of the post office. It is our hypothesis that local postal income can be used as a measure of economic activity at the local level. By examining changes in local postal income over time and space, local, regional and national trends in economic activity can be charted at a level of detail previously impossible. We will test this claim in the next section.

It is important to emphasize the scope and detail of the OR data set. It gives the salaries of the postmaster of each town in every state and territory of the United States every two years from 1816 to 1911. To the extent that local postal income reflects local economic activity, this data set gives an unprecedented opportunity to examine patterns of such activity across space and time in the nineteenth century in a manner never previously possible.

The OR data was first discovered and used by postal historians, generally philatelists who are interested in postal rates, the transportation of the mails, the postmarks and other postal markings used on envelopes (termed "covers" in philatelic jargon), and postal procedures. This is a major portion of modern organized philately and has its own considerable technical literature.

Postal historians have been interested in the OR data as it gives an idea of how rare covers from various post offices are. Generally, one would expect that post offices doing less business would generate fewer covers and covers from such offices would be rarer than those from offices doing more business. Stach has found that the correlations between postmaster compensation and number of known covers from post offices in the Nebraska and South Dakota Territories are, respectively, $r = + .94$ and $r = + .88$.[10]

By far the most sophisticated research using OR data has been done by Harris, who first realized the importance of this data for historical and economic analysis.[11] Harris' research has been mostly aimed at using OR data to show the effects of local economic activity on post office receipts. DeBlois and Harris analyzed the postal receipts of small post offices in Rensselaer County, N.Y., and found examples of the exquisite sensitivity of the OR data to local events.[12] For example, for the period 1827 to 1833 the receipts of the Sand Lake post office grew at more than the national average. When other post offices were opened in the vicinity of Sand Lake, that office's receipts dropped. The receipts of the Sand Lake post office showed a sharp drop between 1851 and 1853, a drop not seen to any great extend in the other regional offices. DeBlois and Harris note that on December 25, 1852, a glass factory in Sand Lake was destroyed by fire. They argue that since the factory was the major industry in the town, this loss can explain the greater decline in revenues from this office.

The original printed volumes of the Official Register are extremely rare. Even the largest institutional libraries do not have anything approaching a complete set. Such a set does exist in the collection of the Library of Congress. However, efforts are now under way to digitize the OR data through the 1871 volume.[13]

OR DATA AND ECONOMIC VARIABLES

This section provides a preliminary analysis, using the data from New Hampshire post offices, of the relationships between postmaster compensation data and economic and demographic variables. New Hampshire was chosen because one of us (TH) has copies of the New Hampshire date from all the ORs and because New Hampshire is the only state for which census data is available on-line. This data can be found at the web site of the New Hampshire Historical Society, www.nhhistory.org.

The specific date reported in the OR varied over the almost one hundred years of this title's publication. For the entire period, 1816 through 1911, compensation for each postmaster is reported. For the years 1841 through 1869, in addition, the "net proceeds" at each office are reported. Adding the compensation to the proceeds results in the total postal income for the post office that year.[14]

While it was always the case that as postal income increased, postmaster compensation increased, this relation was not a simple one but an incremental one. That is, as income increased, postmasters received a decreasing percentage of incremental income. Further, the exact formula for compensation varied over the years as Congress altered the way postmaster compensation was computed. The details of these changes in compensation rates are beyond the scope of this paper but can be found in Joint Commission on Postal Salaries.[15] As an example, under

the Act of June 22, 1854, postmasters received sixty percent of the first $100 of income, fifty percent of the next $300, forty percent of the next $2,000 and fifteen percent on all income over $2,400.

The incremental nature of the compensation formulae presents a problem for some statistical analyses. This is because the formulae result in distributions of compensation values that have smaller variances than the distributions of actual income values. In other words, the distributions of compensations are compacted relative to the distributions of actual incomes. Especially for correlational analyses, the restricted range of the compensation data may cause one to miss effects that would be found were the total postal income data, with its greater variance, to be used. This, of course, isn't a problem for those years when both compensation and net proceeds are provided as one may simply add the two (but see below). However, for years where only compensation is provided, it is necessary to calculate the income based on the compensation schedules provided in the Joint Commission on Postal Salaries publication.[16] Happily, for most years this is rather straightforward.

PRELIMINARY ANALYSES

Before undertaking an analysis of the compensation data, it is important to establish that the basic data of postal income is economically relevant. One way to approach this question is to examine postal income data at the national level and see if it is correlated with important economic variables. The 1911 Annual Report of the Postmaster General gives the audited postal revenues for each fiscal year from 1837 through 1911.[17] These figures were correlated with the nominal Gross Domestic Product of the corresponding years taken from the on-line economic history database at www.eh.net. The resulting Pearson product-moment correlation is $r = +.976$ ($p < .001$). This very high correlation shows that, at least at the national level, postal revenues do correlate impressively with GDP and thus suggests that postal revenues do reflect economic activity. For even earlier years, the 1831 Annual Report of the Postmaster General reported total postal receipts for 1789 through 1830.[18] Correlating these numbers with nominal GDP (starting with 1790–nGDP is not available for 1789) resulted in another high correlation: $r = +.84$ ($p < .001$). These high correlations gave us some confidence that postal data have some relationship to economic factors and spurred further analyses.

As noted above, for some years the OR reported only the postmasters' compensation. Using the formulae published in the statutes relating compensation to total postal income, it should be possible to derive total postal income from the compensation data. For example, in 1859 the Concord NH postmaster received $1,783 (rounded to the nearest dollar) in compensation. But for the year 1859 the OR reports not only the compensation but also the net income. Adding the two together produces total postal income of $5,424.[19] If compensation were based only on postal income, a calculation of the 1859 Concord post office income using the compensation rates in effect at the time should result in a figure of approximately $5425. This calculation actually yields a figure of $7,553, a difference of $2,129, or thirty-nine percent (Table 1).

This calculated figure is higher than the actual income because postmaster compensation included monies for things other than postal income such as box rents, extra pay for delivery of late mails, delivery of newspapers, and the like. One would expect that the discrepancy between the actual reported income and estimated income would be in the positive direction. Further, the discrepancy should be larger for larger post offices where the postmaster would have greater opportunities for earning additional compensation not directly related to the amount of money his office received. To test this hypothesis and to get an idea of how generally reflective of true total postal income the reported compensation figures were, a total of twenty-five New Hampshire post offices varying in size were selected from the 1859 OR. For each office, the compensation due based on the reported compensation plus net income figure was calculated. The difference was then expressed as a percentage with positive percentages indicating the

reported compensation was greater than the calculated compensation. The average difference was twelve percent with a standard deviation of twenty-two. Of the twenty-five offices, nineteen had positive differences and six had negative differences.

Positive differences are fairly easy to explain. Postmaster compensation included monies for things other than postage paid at the office. Depending on the specific compensation rules in effect, these included extra compensation for such things as receipt of newspapers, post office box rents, onward routing of letters, receipts of mails after a certain time at night. These extra sources of compensation a postmaster earned would be more likely to occur at the larger post offices. This supposition is supported by the significant correlation of reported compensation with the percentage difference between reported and calculated compensation and is significant with $r = +.40$ ($p < .047$).

The negative differences may have been due to fines for various infractions, but additional research will be needed to investigate the rules for such fines and the characteristics of post offices with negative differences.

Two other variables had some effect on compensation. Postmasters received extra compensation (usually ten percent) of the first compensation increment if they had to open their office at late hours to receive or dispatch the mail. Postmasters at "distributing offices" which received and then sorted mail bound for other offices also received extra compensation. There were no distributing offices in New Hampshire after 1842. In earlier years only Hanover (until 1837 or 1838), Portsmouth (until 1837 or 1838) and Walpole (until at least 1831) were distributing offices in the state.

POPULATION EFFECTS

In the previous section the general validity of calculating estimated post office income from the published postmaster compensation data was established. This being the case, it is appropriate to investigate further the factors that correlate with the estimated income variable. An obvious candidate is population. A simple prediction is that as the population of a town or city increases, so will the amount of business its post office does, resulting in a higher postal income for that town. There are two ways to examine the relationship between population and estimated income. The first is to examine the relationship for each census year for which data is available. Here this means the decennial census years of 1820 to 1910. The year 1880 is not included in the percent analysis as the law in effect

TABLE 1. Calculation of estimated income for Concord, NH 1859.

Actual Compensation	Net	Sum
$1783	$3641	$5424

Calculation:

Range	Income Amount	Compensation Percent	Compensation	Remainder
				$1783
$0–$100	$100	60%	$60	$1723
$100–$400	$300	50%	$150	$1573
$400–$2400	$2000	40%	$800	$773
$2400+	$5153	15%	$773	$0
Sum	$7553		$1783	

TABLE 2. Population versus Postmaster Compensation for Census Years 1820 To 1910.

Census Year	Correlation	Significance	N
1820	0.88	0.001	12
1830	0.85	0.001	19
1840	0.91	0.001	19
1850	0.96	0.001	19
1860	0.97	0.001	19
1870	0.97	0.001	19
1880	not calculated—see text.		
1890	0.92	0.001	19
1900	0.96	0.001	19
1910	0.97	0.001	18

TABLE 3. Correlations between Population and Estimated Income for Individual Post Offices.

Post Office	Correlation	Significance	Change in Population (%)	Period
Bethlehem	0.91	0.002	78	1830–1910
Brookline	–0.77	0.026	–20	1830–1910
Center Harbor	–0.73	0.026	–1	1820–1910
Concord	0.90	0.001	657	1820–1910
Dover	0.87	0.002	361	1820–1910
Goshen	–0.60	0.120	–57	1830–1910
Hanover	–0.44	0.240	–7	1820–1910
Keene	0.94	0.001	431	1820–1910
Kingston	0.23	0.555	20	1820–1910
Lebanon	0.97	0.001	234	1820–1910
Middleton	–0.09	0.840	–47	1830–1900
Portsmouth	0.48	0.191	54	1820–1910
Randolph	0.34	0.414	–4	1830–1910
Sanbornton	–0.64	0.064	–74	1820–1910
Springfield	–0.48	0.234	–65	1830–1910
Strafford	0.74	0.023	152	1820–1910
Walpole	0.80	0.010	32	1820–1910
Whitefield	0.82	0.012	139	1830–1910
Windham	–0.41	0.276	–34	1820–1910

in 1880 relating to postmaster compensation is extremely unclear as to how compensation was calculated. Thus, it has not yet been possible to calculate estimated postal incomes for 1880. For the other years, however, the correlations between estimated income and population are consistently high and positive, as shown in Table 2. All correlations reported in this paper are Pearson Product-Moment correlations.

It was not feasible to calculate the estimated income for all the several hundred post offices in New Hampshire every census year. To simplify matters, a quasi-random sample of nineteen post offices was chosen from the list of New Hampshire post offices operating in 1850. This resulted in the year 1820 having fewer than nineteen offices in the sample, as seven offices that were operating in 1850 had not yet opened in 1820. By 1910, one office, Middleton, had closed, thus reducing the 1910 sample to eighteen offices. In order to assure that the obtained correlations would not be artifactually small due to range restriction effects, all the largest post offices were included in the sample as well as a range of other sizes from medium to small (Table 2).

Correlations were also calculated between population and the uncorrected "raw" compensation data. Since comparisons were being made within a given year when the compensation formula was the same across all postmasters, it was not felt necessary to calculate estimated postal income. These correlations were consistently high and positive. As would be expected based on the argument above that the compensation figures truncate the actual distributions of income, these correlations were generally somewhat smaller than those reported in Table 2. The correction for 1880 was $r = + .90$ ($p < .001$).

It is also possible to examine the correlations between population and estimated postal income by examining this relationship at individual post offices over the period 1820 (or 1830 in the case of offices not open in 1820) to 1910. Table 3 shows these correlations for the nineteen post offices in the sample.

The pattern of correlations in Table 3 is clearly far from consistently positive. Of the nineteen, seven are significantly positive, two are significantly negative and one almost so. The others are not significant. This hardly seems to be the pattern expected based on the results of the analyses of the correlations between population and estimated income seen in Table 2.

What characteristics of the different towns could account for this pattern of correlations? Inspection of the data suggested that in cases where the population of a town increased over the period in question, the correlation between population and estimated income was positive. But if the population of a town declined, the correction was negative. To test this, the percentage change in population (also shown in Table 3) of each town for the period in question was correlated with the correlation between estimated income and population. This resulted in a highly significant correlation of $r = + .89$ ($p < .001$).

This correlation indicated that when a town's population increased, so did estimated postal income. The correlation further shows that even when a town's population decreased, income increased. What could account for this seemingly odd result? It appears that over the course of the nineteenth and into the twentieth centuries, there was a dramatic and pervasive increase in the use of the postal service. Certainly over this period, postal rates decreased, both in nominal and real terms. For example, in 1820, when postal rates were determined by the distance even a domestic letter would travel, it cost 18.5 cents to send a letter between 150 and 400 miles. That corresponds to $3.07 in 2005 dollars. In 1920, sending the same letter cost two cents ($.41 in 2005 dollars). Early in the nineteenth century, because of the high cost of postage, the mails had been primarily used for business correspondence. As the century progressed postage rates decreased considerably while literacy rates increased. Both these factors led to more correspondence. In addition, the country grew in size and, especially in northern New England, young people moved west where much better land was available. This great westward migration also led to greater correspondence as family members staying in the east corresponded with relatives who had moved west. The finding that local postal incomes increased whether population of a town increased or decreased strongly supports the argument made by Henkin that the post office emerged as a, if not the, major source of personal communication in the nineteenth century.[20]

In economic terms the data in Table 3 suggest that even when population shrinks in a town, if per capita income grows sufficiently and if per capita usage of capital grows as well, postal revenue may well expand, demonstrating not only economic growth but development as well. This further suggests that postal efficiency closely parallels a general trend of increasing efficiency of capital. A question for further analysis is whether there is a difference between "public" capital efficiency (the post office) and private capital efficiency in allied communication and transportation systems such as railroads and telegraph companies. It should be realized, of course, that both these systems did receive government support in the nineteenth century.

The correlations between population and estimated postal income may be modified by a factor not mentioned previously. And this factor may actually add to the usefulness of the Official Register data for economic analyses. The published census data reports the total population for a given political entity such as Hanover, New Hampshire.

But the town of Hanover has had, at different times, three different post offices—Hanover itself (1792 to date), Hanover Center (1828–1918) and Etna (1882 to date). The Official Register reports data for each post office individually, permitting a more fine grained analysis than the census data both in place and in time, since the Official Register data is available every two years and the census data only every ten years.

RECESSION OF 1837

The Official Register data may be useful for examining more directly economic variables. The National Bureau of Economic Research (NBER) supplies a list of generally accepted dates for the economic ups and downs of the national business cycle. One well-known data phase was the recession of 1837. Does evidence of this recession appear in OR data? To examine this question with regard to New Hampshire, the estimated postal incomes for the six largest towns in New Hampshire (Concord, Dover, Hanover, Keene, Nashua, and Portsmouth) for the years 1835 to 1845 were submitted to a one-way analysis of variance. The mean income data is shown in Table 4. Examination of the data shows that while there was an increase from 1837 to 1839, from 1839 to 1845 there was a consistent decrease. However, the variance among the six different towns was so great that this trend did not even approach significance ($F (3, 23) = .383$) (Table 4).

New Hampshire was then, admittedly, a small state removed from the main centers of economic activity in the nation. It is perhaps thus not surprising that the recession of 1837 had no noticeable effect on postal income even in its largest cities and towns. Examination of Official Register data from other larger states and with more sophisticated analytical tools may well reveal the effects of recessions and recoveries. To the extent that this is the case, it may be possible to examine the time course of recessions and recoveries in different parts of the country. A recession is not like an explosion that happens suddenly. Rather, the business cycle is a dynamic process that affects

TABLE 4. Mean Estimated Income, 1835 to 1845.

1835	1837	1839	1841	1843	1845
8234	7363	8294	7736	7146	6323

different geographic and demographic areas differently in both time and intensity. It is our hope that careful analysis of regional and nationwide OR data will reveal these temporal and spatial changes in the business cycle at a level of detail heretofore unavailable.

CONCLUSIONS

Our analysis of the OR data from the State of New Hampshire has shown that these data hold considerable promise as a source of previously unavailable insights into economic and demographic variables during the nineteen century. We have specifically examined population effects and the effects of one recession on postal income. The OR data can be used to examine a number of other interesting historical trends. For example, how does the use of the postal service change with the advent of improved transportation and other communication systems such as railroads, telegraph lines, and road construction? Does the integration of the frontier and the re-integration of the South following the Civil War manifest in the OR data?

It should be mentioned here that similar data are available from Canada. In Canada, from at least Confederation until 1948, local postmaster compensation was based on the income accruing to each individual post office.[21] This compensation data is found in the annual report of the postmaster general printed each year in the Sessional Papers of Parliament. The reports of the postmaster general also give very valuable statistical data not found in any US official document. For every post office issuing money orders, the annual report gives the total value of money orders issued and cashed by that office. Further, for at least some years (neither of us have yet been able to examine a complete run of the postmaster general reports), data on the number and value of money orders issued in one province destined for another province is given, as well as the number and value of money orders issued in the second province that were paid in the first province. The postmaster general reports also give, for at least some years, information on the number and value of money orders issued to and received from other countries.

Returning to the compensation data, given that in Canada postmaster compensation was based on postal business, it might be suspected that a similar practice was followed in Great Britain. This is not the case. In Britain, at least during the nineteenth century, postmaster salary was based on the individual's grade and not on the amount of business done by the office.

STATISTICAL APPENDIX

THE PEARSON PRODUCT MOMENT CORRELATION COEFFICIENT

The Pearson product moment correlation coefficient is one of a family of correlational techniques and probably the one most commonly used in research. A correlation is a number between negative one and positive one that indicates the strength of the relationship between two variables. A positive correlation indicates that when the value of one variable increases (or decreases), the value of the other variable changes in the same direction. A negative correlation indicates that a change in one variable is associated with a change in the opposite direction of the other variable. In the text, the value of the Pearson correlation coefficient is indicated by the symbol lower case r, as in "$r = 0.66$."

NOTES

1. P. A. Coclanis, ed., *The Atlantic Economy During the Seventeenth and Eighteenth Centuries: Organization, Operation, Practice and Personnel* (Columbia, S. C.: University of South Carolina, 2005).

2. M. Abromovitz, and P. A. David, "American macroeconomic growth in the era of knowledge-based progress: The long-run perspective." In *Cambridge Economic History of the United States,* Vol. III, ed. S. L. Engerman and R. E. Gallman (Cambridge, U. K.: Cambridge University Press, 2000), 6.

3. A. H. Jones, *Wealth of a Nation to Be: The American Colonies on the Eve of the Revolution* (New York: Columbia University Press, 1980).

4. J. Hughes and L. P. Cain, *American Economic History* (Boston: Addison Wesley, 2007), 50–51.

5. Abramovitz and David, "American macroeconomic growth," 66.

6. J. Komlos, "The height and weight of West Point cadets: Dietary change in antebellum America," *Journal of Economic History*, 47:897–927, 1987.

7. L. E. Davis, American Economic Growth: An Economist's History of the United States (New York: Harper and Row, 1972), 16.

8. R. D. Harris, "The Official Register. Part 1," *Post Script*, 2:12–20, 1977; A. Hecht, "Official Register of the United States," *American Philatelist*, 74(12):891–894, 930–931, 1961.

9. Joint Commission of Postal Services, "Memorandum concerning compensation of postmasters and method of determining same, etc." In *Postal Salaries: Final Report of the Joint Commission on Postal Salaries* (66th Congress, 3rd Session, Senate Document No. 422, Vol. 1, 1921), 102–118.

10. K. Stach, "A statistical analysis of Nebraska Territorial postal history," *La Posta*, 33(6):15–19, 2003; K. Stach, "A

statistical analysis of South Dakota Territorial postal history," Unpublished manuscript.

11. Harris, "The Official Register."

12. D. DeBlois and R. D. Harris, "Using the Official Registers: Local Sources of Postal Revenue." Presented at the First Annual Winton M. Blount Postal History Symposium, Washington, D. C., Smithsonian National Postal Museum, 4 November 2006.

13. M. C. O. O'Reilly, "Providing Access to the Official Register Data." Presented at the First Annual Winton M. Blount Postal History Symposium, Washington, D. C., Smithsonian National Postal Museum, 4 November 2006.

14. Harris, "The Official Register."

15. Joint Commission of Postal Services, "Memorandum concerning compensation."

16. Joint Commission of Postal Services, "Memorandum concerning compensation."

17. *Annual Report of the Postmaster General* (Washington, D. C.: Government Printing Office, 1911), 387.

18. *Annual Report of the Postmaster General* (Washington, D. C.: Government Printing Office, 1831).

19. Harris, "The Official Register."

20. D. M. Henkin, *The Postal Age: The Emergence of Modern Communications in Nineteenth-Century America* (Chicago: University of Chicago Press, 2006.)

21. C. Amyot and J. Willis, *Country Post: Rural Postal Service in Canada, 1880 to 1945* (Gatineau, Qc., Canada: Canadian Museum of Civilization, 2003).

BIBLIOGRAPHY

Abramovitz, M. and P. A. David. "American Macroeconomic Growth in the Era of Knowledge-Based Progress: The Long-Run Perspective." In *Cambridge Economic History of the United States,* Vol. III, ed. S. L. Engerman and R. E. Gallman, pp.–92. Cambridge, England: Cambridge University Press, 2000.

Amyot, C. and J. Willis. *Country Post. Rural Postal Service in Canada, 1880 to 1945.* Gatineau, Qc., Canada: Canadian Museum of Civilization, 2003.

Annual Report of the Postmaster General. Washington D. C.: Government Printing Office, 1831.

Annual Report of the Postmaster General. Washington D. C.: Government Printing Office, 1911.

Coclanis, P. A., ed. *The Atlantic Economy During the Seventeenth and Eighteenth Centuries: Organization, Operation, Practice and Personnel.* Columbia, S. C.: University of South Carolina, 2005.

Davis, L. E. *American Economic Growth: An Economist's History of the United States.* New York: Harper and Row, 1972.

DeBlois, D. and R. D. Harris. Using the Official Registers: Local Sources of Postal Revenue. Presented at the First Annual Winton M. Blount Postal History Symposium. Washington, DC: Smithsonian National Postal Museum, Nov. 4, 2006.

Harris, R. D. The Official Register. Part 1. *Post Script*, # 2:12–20, 1977.

Henkin, D. M. *The Postal Age. The Emergence of Modern Communications in Nineteenth-Century America.* Chicago: University of Chicago Press, 2006.

Hecht, A. Official Register of the United States. *American Philatelist*, 74(12):891–894, 930–931, 1961.

Hughes, J. and L. P. Cain. *American Economic History.* Boston: Addison, Wesley, 2007.

Joint Commission of Postal Services. "Memorandum Concerning Compensation of Postmasters and Method of Determining Same, etc." In *Postal Salaries: Final Report of the Joint Commission on Postal Salaries.* 66th Congress, 3rd Session, Senate Document 422, Vol. 1, pp. 102–118, 1921.

Jones, A. H.. *Wealth of a Nation to Be: The American Colonies on the Eve of the Revolution.* New York: Columbia University Press, 1980.

Komlos, J. "The Height and Weight of West Point Cadets: Dietary Change in Antebellum America." *Journal of Economic History*, 47:897–927, 1987.

O'Reilly, M. C. O. Providing Access to the Official Register Data. Presented at the First Annual Winton M. Blount Symposium on Postal History. Washington, D. C.: Smithsonian Institution National Postal Museum, Nov. 4, 2006.

Stach, K. A Statistical Analysis of Nebraska Territorial Postal History. *La Posta*, 33(6):15–19, 2003.

Stach, K. (undated). A Statistical Analysis of South Dakota Territorial Postal History. Unpublished manuscript.

Introduction to the Second Symposium

The second annual postal history symposium, sponsored by the Smithsonian National Postal Museum, the American Philatelic Society, and the American Philatelic Research Library, was held in Bellefonte, Pennsylvania, at the American Philatelic Center on October 21–22, 2007. The theme was "Further, Farther, Faster: Transportation Technology and the Mail," the exploration of how, through the application of new technologies for transporting the mail, the post office and the transportation industry have encouraged, supported, and benefited from each other's growth and development.

The symposium featured scholars of a variety of postal and transportation technologies who presented nine papers, which explored the postal-transportation nexus in three moderated panels—Land, Sea, and Air. Cheryl R. Ganz, Philatelic Curator at the Smithsonian National Postal Museum, discusses "Air Transportation" in her paper "Zeppelin Posts at the 1933 Chicago World's Fair: Integrating Collector and Historian Methodologies."

Zeppelin Posts at the 1933 Chicago World's Fair: Integrating Collector and Historian Methodologies

Cheryl R. Ganz

INTRODUCTION

Philatelists study postage stamps from concept through design and production to use. Stamp collectors also study mail as postal history, especially markings, rates, transportation, and routes. In recent years, they have eagerly sought the untapped wealth hidden in philatelic-related ephemera and in this way have added richness and depth to the body of philatelic knowledge. I have no doubt that philatelists are the most prolific authors of any hobby, and many philatelic libraries around the world are a testament to their voluminous output.

Archives are expanding ephemera holdings to meet the needs of scholars and to distinguish holdings. Online auctions, which collectors, libraries, and authors regularly peruse, have made many hitherto obscure items accessible. Wanting to fill gaps in a narrative, scholars sometimes purchase original ephemera that offer information different from that offered by books and manuscripts. The bonus is often images without reproduction restrictions and the high costs for use in publications.

As a professional historian, museum curator, and a zeppelin collector of posts and ephemera, I have striven to bring the very distinctive approaches of each discipline together in my life, my hobby, and my career. By sharing my experience, I hope that other historians will realize the untapped potential of philately and ephemera. Further, I hope that other collectors will rethink their approaches to collecting, exhibiting, researching, writing, and judging/critiquing to expand their perspectives, ask new questions, and, as chef Emeril Lagasse says, "Kick it up a notch."

This essay discusses my holistic approach to collecting and includes an example from my own research that integrates the story of zeppelin mail, ephemera, the 1933 Chicago World's Fair, and the diplomacy that stabilized a potentially volatile situation. The article illustrates ways in which philately and ephemera souvenirs from one day at the fair, when put in context, can touch people's lives and inspire collectors, seasoned and novice alike.

As a collector of philately and related ephemera and artifacts, I relish each detail and thrill to each newly discovered fact. A descriptive approach identifies each object collected and, often through exhibiting and writing, relates objects to each other, all celebrated because they exist and because I have collected them for some reason.

As a historian, however, I place objects, details, and facts into a larger framework, asking how each relates to the historical process. In other words, I put the research in context and interpret it.[1] I must answer what historians call the "So what?" question, and I must develop a thesis that presents a fresh perspective. Further, as a curator, I must seek strong stories that touch visitors' lives and make the onsite and online experience engaging and rewarding.

By reading the current literature in both fields—collecting and history—I am able to apply ideas from other philatelists, paper collectors, and historians to my own work, even if their topics do not relate specifically to my own focus, that being zeppelins, aerophilately, and the juxtaposition of art and industry during the Great Depression. For example, in his book *The Postal Age*, David Henkin examines mail users rather than the state postal system or the envelopes themselves.[2] As a result, he makes new discoveries about how mail changed lives and how lifestyles changed mail handling in the nineteenth century.

Henkin inspired me to examine the mail in my collection that the LZ127 *Graf Zeppelin* had flown from Germany to Brazil to the United States and back to Germany on the 1933 Chicago flight.[3] I was stunned to discover that forty of sixty covers in my United States dispatches had names of Germanic origin for either the American sender or American addressee. Of course, German language immigrants comprised the largest ethnic group in Chicago, almost thirteen percent of the city's population in 1930. Even Ernst J. Kruetgen, the city's postmaster, was of German heritage. So while other collectors also serviced mail, the *Graf Zeppelin's* visit was a source of especial pride for the German American community. This evidence proved significant when I studied the German American community's reaction to the zeppelin visit.[4]

CASE STUDY: FIFTY-CENT *GRAF ZEPPELIN* A CENTURY OF PROGRESS STAMP

Germans had been celebrating the progress of zeppelins since Count Ferdinand von Zeppelin flew his first design, the LZ1, on July 2, 1900. The zeppelin had become a symbol not only of German nationalism, but also of the nation's economic resurgence. Zeppelin fever, reflecting the pride and awe of the Germans for these masterpieces of airship technology, ran rampant. German airship

technology first linked to nationalism in 1908 when a spontaneous public outpouring of funds followed the destruction of Zeppelin's fourth dirigible, the LZ4. After World War I, the Zeppelin Company and many aviation supporters promoted airships as the vehicles of the future for long distance travel and transport, connecting the airship routes to local airline routes. Air-minded Americans also caught zeppelin fever, a contagious enthusiasm sweeping the country as airships floated overhead.[5]

Approaching Chicago at daybreak on October 26, 1933, Commander Hugo Eckener ordered the *Graf Zeppelin*, a 775-foot long German airship, to fly west beyond the city and then to circle clockwise, although a northerly route from Indiana with an approach to Chicago from the east over Lake Michigan would have been more expeditious. After circling above the city for about an hour, the *Graf Zeppelin* flew north to suburban Glenview for a brief exchange of passengers and mail.

Adolph Hitler, leader of the National Socialist party, had become Chancellor of Germany earlier that year. The German government had required the Zeppelin Company to paint the National Socialists' swastika banner, which was one of the two official German flags, on the port side of the upper and lower tail fins (Figure 1).[6] Rather than display the two red billboards featuring twenty-foot swastikas, Eckener preferred to show Chicagoans the starboard side of the craft, which featured the traditional tri-color German flag.[7]

Willy von Meister, the United States special representative of Luftschiffbau Zeppelin G.m.b.H., the Zeppelin Company, was in the control car with Eckener during the approach to Chicago. He asked why Eckener had not taken the shorter circle. "And let my friends in Chicago see the swastikas?" asked Eckener, who had a doctorate in psychology and was sensitive to the German community's reaction.

As a result of the arrival time, the choice of the flight path, and the press's selections of which photographs to publish to represent this flight, the local population saw more images of the *Graf Zeppelin* with the swastika than without it. In flying a route that brought the airship over Lake Michigan, parallel to and east of Chicago at daybreak, the *Graf Zeppelin* became a silhouette against the sunrise. Photographers either could take photographs of the shadow side of the airship over the lake or, as it made its circle over the fairgrounds and central business district, the sunlit side with the photogenic elements of the city in the background. In order to photograph the *Graf Zeppelin* with the fairgrounds in the same image, one newspaper photographer shot his images from an airplane. He was

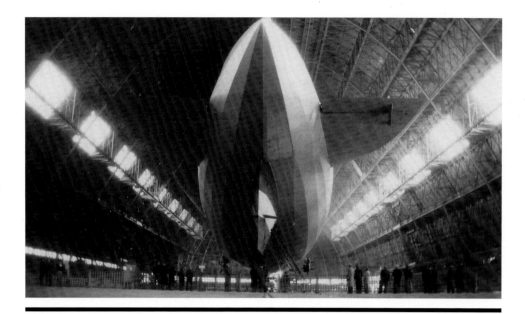

FIGURE 1. The LZ127 *Graf Zeppelin* in the Akron airship hangar, mooring site before and after its flight to Chicago. Both German flags, the swastika on port side (left) and the traditional tri-color on starboard side (right), are nearly visible from this perspective of the lower tail fin. Bill Schneider, photographer. From the collection of Cheryl R. Ganz.

able to capture the sunlit side of the *Graf Zeppelin* over the Chicago World's Fair, and consequently his photograph showcased the swastika. The *Chicago Daily News* and the *New York Times* published these images, reaching yet a larger audience than the eyewitnesses.[8]

Germany's *Graf Zeppelin* became the fair's most powerful and divisive emblem of national identity. As a symbol of Germany and its technological progress, the *Graf Zeppelin* captured the public's imagination and ultimately became an international symbol of goodwill and cooperation. On the other hand, the swastika broadcast anti-Semitism and Hitler's National Socialist policies. The swastika clearly inspired racial pride and patriotic obedience in Nazi followers, but it antagonized or embarrassed many German Americans.

On August 1, 1933, the Zeppelin Company had responded to an official invitation from Rufus Dawes, president of A Century of Progress. Hugo Eckener had accepted the invitation, saying that the LZ127 would visit Chicago as an extension of the final trip of the 1933 season to Brazil if the United States Post Office Department would issue a zeppelin postage stamp. Eckener had requested the stamp because he needed to secure adequate financing before committing to the special flight. He had proposed sharing profits from the sale of the zeppelin postage stamp. The plan was not unique. Philatelists in Germany, Europe,

and the United States had already financed several special flights of the *Graf Zeppelin* by purchasing special postage stamps and by sending mail for flights to the Arctic, South America, and around the world.

President Franklin D. Roosevelt's lack of support for the stamp threatened to bury the idea and create diplomatic problems with Germany. The Bureau of Engraving and Printing, which designed and printed postage stamps for the Post Office Department, had prepared three designs of the stamp to be presented to Roosevelt for his final approval. The president immediately protested, "This zeppelin is just toddling back and forth across the ocean. I don't see why a stamp should be issued again for it," and he rejected the issue.[9] Negotiations followed, and Secretary of State Cordell Hull advised that the breach of diplomacy resulting from the rejection of the stamp issue would be a disaster.[10] The argument swayed Roosevelt, and the new zeppelin stamp was available at the New York City post office just ten days after approval.

As printed, the fifty-cent green stamp depicted the *Graf Zeppelin* without the swastika, the Federal Building at the Chicago fair, and one of the zeppelin hangars in Friedrichshafen, Germany.[11] The United States Post Office Department would receive fifteen percent or 7.5 cents of the fifty-cent rate. The remaining 42.5 cents would be paid to the German Postal Administration to help offset the

FIGURE 2. Following a bomb threat, Commander Hugo Eckener ordered an earlier arrival than reported in the press. The clock inside the control car indicates it was shortly after seven AM. That clock, however, was set for Eastern Standard Time, thus it was actually just after six AM in Chicago. From the collection of Cheryl R. Ganz.

expenses of the Zeppelin Company for operating the *Graf Zeppelin* at a cost of about $300 an hour.[12] The Zeppelin Company expected to realize $10,000 from the United States stamp sales, but it actually realized several times that amount. Over 100,000 American stamps on souvenir envelopes were flown in addition to mail carried from Germany, Brazil, and over sixty other countries.[13]

Meister informed fair president Rufus Dawes that the *Graf Zeppelin*, operating under the auspices of the German government, would fly the flags of the German government, including the swastika. He then posed the issue of possible protests by Jewish citizens in response to Nazi harassment of German Jews and laws that stripped them of German citizenship. Dawes wanted to be prepared for a possible demonstration against either the swastika emblem or the arrival of the pro-Nazi German ambassador and former chancellor, Hans Luther. The Post Office Department made special arrangements to examine all mail and parcels intended for delivery to the zeppelin. Postmaster

General Farley also requested that local authorities cooperate to assure proper protection for passengers and the crew.[14]

Because of a bomb threat, Eckener altered his flight plans slightly. He decided to fly to Chicago and make a short landing in a closed field. The day before the *Graf Zeppelin*'s arrival in Chicago, the press announced that the great airship would arrive at about nine o'clock the next morning. In fact, the *Graf Zeppelin* arrived three and a half hours earlier. Because of the misinformation provided to the press and the sheriff's order to close the airport to those without passes, only a few hundred spectators were on hand at the landing field besides the landing crew, press, and welcoming officials (Figure 2).[15]

Following a busy day of touring the fairgrounds and luncheon and dinner events, Eckener attended the Zeppelin Day evening event at Chicago's Medinah Temple (Figures 3 and 4). Thousands of enthusiastic German Americans filled the hall, many wearing the Zeppelin Tag lapel pin

FIGURE 3. The program for the Zeppelin Day evening reception listed patriotic music and speakers, including German Ambassador Hans Luther and Commander Eckener. The image of the *Graf Zeppelin* lacked either flag symbol on the tail fins. From the collection of Cheryl R. Ganz.

FIGURE 4. The postcard sold at the Zeppelin Day evening reception illustrated the *Graf Zeppelin* with swastikas on the port side tail fins, the Travel and Transport building at the 1933 Chicago World's Fair, and a portrait of Commander Hugo Eckener. From the collection of Cheryl R. Ganz.

sold at the door for fifty cents. The program included patriotic German music with speeches by the mayor, representatives of the German community, Eckener, and Luther. Postmaster Kruetgen, president of the German Group of the World's Fair, had refused to attend what he saw as a Nazi reception.[16]

News of the gathering had, of course, reached the general public. Theodore Light, a twenty-year-old stamp collector, went with a friend to Medinah Temple that evening, hoping to get Eckener's autograph on some letters he had mailed himself via the *Graf Zeppelin* using the special

zeppelin stamp (Figure 5). Upon arriving home from work he found that his mail delivery included envelopes transported by airship from Miami and Akron to Chicago. Meanwhile at Medinah Temple, limousines dropped off local politicians and members of the diplomatic corps. Delighted to discover that the public was permitted to enter, Light and his friend joined the crowd. Once inside, however, they "found ushers all in storm trooper uniforms and across the stage was the biggest flag I have ever seen and it was the swastika." The astonished young men looked at one another, thinking that this was the wrong place for

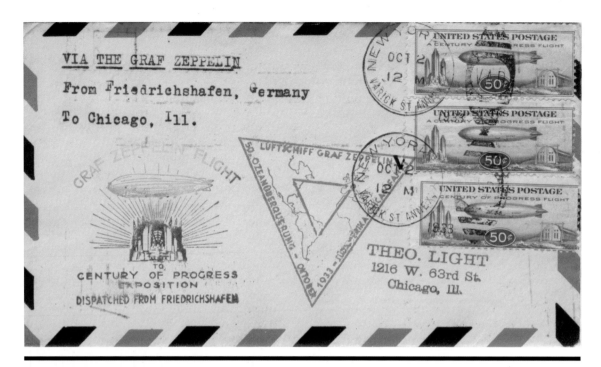

FIGURE 5. Stamp collector Ted Light prepared this envelope for the first day of issue of the zeppelin stamp in New York. The New York post office forwarded it by sea post to Germany, from where the *Graf Zeppelin* then flew it to Chicago via Brazil. The presence of National Socialists at the German American reception for Eckener prevented Light from obtaining an autograph. From the collection of Cheryl R. Ganz.

Jewish men to be at that moment, and said, "Let's forget about autographs and get out of here."[17]

The swastika experiences at the exposition forced German Americans, Chicago's largest ethnic group, to face difficult choices of national allegiance even before the outbreak of the Second World War, to reassess their identity, and to act on their convictions. The German Group of the World's Fair had tied its nationalism to the proud display of German accomplishments, both cultural and technological. It had fought the display of the swastika at all fair events because it represented a political party and anti-Semitism.

When the *Graf Zeppelin* arrived with swastikas on its fins, there was no way to prevent the Consul General in Chicago and the German ambassador from displacing the German Group of the World's Fair as the welcoming leadership of the community. German Americans in Chicago were forced to make choices, not only of their political alliance but also of their identity as Germans or Americans. By the time the fair closed in November, Chicago's German societies had divided over Nazi policy and the Jewish question. They had been able to distinguish the differences between the symbols of the *Graf Zeppelin* and the swastika. German Jews in America and German Christians in America would, however, find themselves no longer unified as 'German Americans.'[18]

CONCLUSION

By placing the fifty-cent *Graf Zeppelin* stamp in the context of its philatelic story as well as its social and cultural story, the significance of this issue is enhanced and has a stronger appeal to larger audiences without diminishing the philatelic study aspects. While many collectors research and study the subject depicted on a stamp, the production of a stamp, or the uses of a stamp, fewer collectors ask, "Why was this particular stamp or series issued at this time (beyond fulfilling a rate need) and what impact did it have on senders, recipients, and society?" Further, while the postage stamp was a product of the federal government, the study of ephemera can reveal information about the organizations, corporations, or individuals who produced these paper objects intended for brief use before being discarded.

Examining cause and effect can inspire collectors and researchers to ask new questions and, as a result, can offer new insights. As for me, thinking outside the traditional philatelic and collector box has allowed me to understand not only how the United States government and post office helped subsidize this 1933 flight but also the role of the *Graf Zeppelin* and the fifty-cent stamp as symbols of progress and goodwill during tough political times and economic strife.

NOTES

1. For an understanding of ways to study a subject internally, externally, or in context, see John M. Staudenmaier, *Technology's Storytellers: Reweaving the Human Fabric* (Cambridge: Society for the History of Technology and MIT Press, 1985).

2. David M. Henkin, *The Postal Age: The Emergence of Modern Communications in Nineteenth-Century America* (Chicago: University of Chicago Press, 2007).

3. This special triangular flight to Chicago was an extension of the ninth and final 1933 transatlantic crossing of the *Graf Zeppelin*. After flying from Germany to Brazil, the *Graf Zeppelin* made stops in Miami, Akron, Chicago, and Akron before returning to Friedrichshafen, Germany by way of Seville, Spain. Although the *Graf Zeppelin* was the 127th design of the Zeppelin Company, it was their 117th airship constructed.

4. For an expanded study of this story, see: Cheryl R. Ganz, *The 1933 Chicago World's Fair: A Century of Progress* (Champaign, Ill: University of Illinois Press, 2008).

5. Peter Fritsche, *A Nation of Fliers: German Aviation and the Popular Imagination* (Cambridge: Harvard University Press, 1992); Henry Cord Meyer, *Airshipmen, Businessmen and Politics, 1890–1940* (Washington: Smithsonian Institution Press, 1991); and Guillaume de Syon, *Zeppelin! Germany and the Airship, 1900–1939* (Baltimore: Johns Hopkins University Press, 2002). For "airmindedness" see Joseph J. Corn, *The Winged Gospel: America's Romance with Aviation* (Baltimore: Johns Hopkins University Press, 1983, 2001), 12.

6. "Hoheitszeichen der Luftschiffe," *Reichsgesetzblatt* 77(8 July 1933):457, *Graf Zeppelin* files, Dieter Leder collection, Meersburg, Germany.

7. *Chicago Tribune*, 26 Oct. 1933, 4; and LZA 016/385-6 Fahrtberichte LZ127 [logbook], 1933, Archiv der Luftschiffbau Zeppelin G.m.b.H., Friedrichshafen. Wilhelm von Meister, interview with author, Peapack, N. J., July 1976. *Chicago Daily News*, 26 Oct. 1933, 4–5; and "Mid-Week Pictorial," *New York Times*, 4 November 1933, 7.

8. *Chicago Daily News*, 26 Oct. 1933, 4–5; and "Mid-Week Pictorial," *New York Times*, 4 November 1933, 7.

9. Meister interview.

10. Memorandum of conversation between Secretary Hull and the German Chargé, Herr Rudolf Leitner, 14 September 1933. Acting Postmaster General to Cordell Hull, 18 September 1933, National Archives, College Park, Maryland.

11. The artists at the Bureau of Engraving and Printing used a 1929 photograph of the *Graf Zeppelin* from its landing at Mines Field in Los Angeles on the World Flight. At that time the zeppelin carried no government flag on its fins. Stamp Design File, National Postal Museum Library, Smithsonian Institution Libraries, Washington D. C.; *Graf Zeppelin* postage stamp files, Bureau of Engraving and Printing, Washington, D. C.

12. *Chicago Daily News*, 26 Oct. 1933, 1. On 26 March 1931 the Reichspost and Luftschiffbau Zeppelin agreed to the Zeppelin Company's share of the postal revenue: 5/6 of the total fees paid for mail carried by the airship. John Duggan, "Income from Carrying the Zeppelin Mail," *Zeppelin* 12(February 1997):12. For arrangements of the United States fees for this flight, see E. R. White to F. W. von Meister, Stamp Design File, National Postal Museum Library, Smithsonian Institution Libraries, Washington, D. C.

13. For further information on *Graf Zeppelin* postal flights, see John Duggan and Jim Graue, *Commercial Zeppelin Flights to South America* (Valleyford, Wash.: J. L. Diversified, 1995); *Michel Zeppelin Specialized Catalogue* (Germany: 2003); and *Sieger Zeppelinpost Spezial-Katalog*, 22nd edition (Germany: 2001).

14. James Farley, Postmaster General, to Cordell Hull, Secretary of State, 23 October 1933, National Archives, College Park, Maryland.

15. For further information about the security issues, see Hugo Eckener, *Im Zeppelin Über Länder und Meere: Erlebnisse und Erinnerungen* (Flensburg, Germany: Verlagshaus Christian Wolff, 1949); Ganz, The 1933 Chicago World's Fair; and J. Gordon Vaeth, *Graf Zeppelin: The Adventures of an Aerial Globetrotter* (New York: Harper & Brothers, 1958), 161–162.

16. Invitation and *Zeppelin Tag Fest Programm*, Cheryl R. Ganz collection, Chicago, Ill.: (Chicago) *Sentinel*, 9 November 1933, 13.

17. Theodore Light, interview with author, tape recording, Morton Grove, Ill., 25 October 1993.

18. The swastika clearly inspired racial pride and patriotic obedience in Nazi followers, but it antagonized or embarrassed many German Americans, who, in 1933, formed one of the largest ethnic groups in Chicago. For further information on the German American reaction to the *Graf Zeppelin* visit to Chicago, see Ganz, *The 1933 Chicago World's Fair*. For more information on German Americans, see John A. Hawgood, *The Tragedy of German-America: The Germans in the United States of America during the Nineteenth Century – and After* (New York: G. P. Putnam's Sons, 1940); Melvin G. Holli, "German American Ethnic and Cultural Identity from 1890 Onward," in *Ethnic Chicago: A Multicultural Portrait*, ed. Melvin G. Holli and Peter d'A. Jones (Grand Rapids, Mich.: William B. Eerdmans Publishing, 1995); and Leslie V. Tischauser, *The Burden of Ethnicity: The German Question in Chicago, 1914–1941* (New York: Garland, 1990).

BIBLIOGRAPHY

Acting Postmaster General to Cordell Hull. Memorandum of conversation between Secretary Hull and German Chargé Herr Rudolf Leitner. College Park, Md.: National Archives, 18 September 1933.

Corn, Joseph J. Corn. *The Winged Gospel: America's Romance with Aviation.* Baltimore, Md.: Johns Hopkins University Press, 2001.

de Syon, Guillaume. *Zeppelin! Germany and the Airship, 1900–1939.* Baltimore, Md.: Johns Hopkins University Press, 2002.

Duggan, John. "Income from Carrying the Zeppelin Mail." *Zeppelin,* 12:12, 1997.

Duggan, John, and Jim Graue. *Commercial Zeppelin Flights to South America.* Valleyford, Wash.: J. L. Diversified, 1995.

Eckener, Hugo. *Im Zeppelin Über Länder und Meere: Erlebnisse und Erinnerungen.* Flensburg, Germany: Verlagshaus Christian Wolff, 1949.

Fritsche, Peter. *A Nation of Fliers: German Aviation and the Popular Imagination.* Cambridge, Mass.: Harvard University Press, 1992.

Ganz, Cheryl R. *The 1933 Chicago World's Fair: A Century of Progress.* Champaign, Ill.: University of Illinois Press, 2008.

Graf Zeppelin Visits City. *Chicago Daily News.* 26 October 1933.

Hawgood, John A. *The Tragedy of German-America: The Germans in the United States of America during the Nineteenth Century—and After.* New York: G. P. Putnam's Sons, 1940.

Henkin, David M. *The Postal Age: The Emergence of Modern Communications in Nineteenth-Century America.* Chicago: University of Chicago Press, 2007.

"Hoheitszeichen der Luftschiffe." *Reichsgesetzblatt* 77:457. *Graf Zeppelin* Files. Dieter Leder Collection, 1933.

Holli, Melvin G. "German American Ethnic and Cultural Identity from 1890 Onward." In *Ethnic Chicago: A Multicultural Portrait,* ed. Melvin G. Holli and Peter d'A. Jones. Grand Rapids, Mich.: William B. Eerdmans Publishing, 1995.

Light, Theodore. 1993. Interview with author. Tape recording. Morton Grove, Ill. 25 October 1993.

LZA 016/385-6 Fahrtberichte LZ127 [logbook]. Friedrichshafen, Germany: Archiv der Luftschiffbau Zeppelin G.m.b.H., 1933.

Meyer, Henry Cord. *Airshipmen, Businessmen and Politics, 1890–1940.* Washington, D. C.: Smithsonian Institution Press, 1991.

"Mid-Week Pictorial." *New York Times.* 4 November 1933, 7.

Michel Zeppelin Specialized Catalogue 2003. Unterschleißheim, Germany: Schwaneberger Verlag GmbH, 2003.

Mullin, Earl. "Fair President Says Thank You to Police Today: Eckener and His Crew to Be Welcomed." *Chicago Tribune,* 26 October 1933, 4.

Sieger Zeppelinpost Spezial-Katalog, 22nd Ed. Lorch, Württemberg, Germany: Sieger-Verlag, 2001.

Staudenmaeir, John M. *Technology's Storytellers: Reweaving the Human Fabric.* Cambridge, Mass.: Society for the History of Technology and MIT Press, 1985.

Tischhauser, Leslie V. *The Burden of Ethnicity: The German Question in Chicago, 1914–1941.* New York: Garland, 1990.

Vaeth, J. Gordon. *Graf Zeppelin: The Adventures of an Aerial Globetrotter.* New York: Harper & Brothers, 1958.

von Meister, Wilhelm. 1976. Interview with author. Peapack, N. J., July, 1976.

Introduction to the Third Symposium

The 2008 Winton M. Blount Postal History Symposium, jointly sponsored by the Smithsonian National Postal Museum, the American Philatelic Society, and the American Philatelic Research Library, was held in Washington, D.C. on September 26–27, 2008. It was the third annual national conference for academic scholars, philatelists, and industry experts on the discussion of research into the history of postal organizations and systems.

The theme was "When the Mail Goes to War," broadly interpreted to include everything related to defense and the postal system in all countries and eras. Postal topics are usually framed in peaceful terms: mail "binds the nation together" by enabling commerce and encouraging technological development, while stamps are "works of art in miniature" or "little paper ambassadors" of national cultures and achievements. Often overlooked is the fact that when a nation goes to war, its stamps and postal system are always an integral part of the mobilization as well as the relief effort.

There were twenty papers presented, four of which are included here. Robert Cullen discusses "Winning on the Home Front" in his paper "Food Will Win the War: Motor Trucks and the Farm-To-Table Postal Delivery Program 1917–1918." Ann Phau, New York State Museum, discusses "Examining Censorship Due to War" in her paper "Postal Censorship and Military Intelligence during World War II." Janet Klug, past president of the American Philatelic Society, discusses "Analyzing Logistics and Systems in Adversity" in her paper "Picking Up the Pieces: The Aftermath of Hiroshima." Robin Gates Elliott, National Postal Museum, discusses "Interpreting Propaganda and the Post" in her paper "Philatelic Propaganda: A Case Study—Border Changes in Eastern Europe, 1938–1941."

"Food Will Win the War": Motor Trucks and the Farm-To-Table Postal Delivery Program, 1917–1918

Robert G. Cullen

It was a Wednesday night in March 1918. The United States was at war in Europe and, while many of the nation's soldiers were overseas fighting in that conflict, the Motor Truck Club of America gathered in New York City for its largest-ever annual dinner meeting. James I. Blakslee, the Fourth Assistant Postmaster General, addressed that group. While doing so, he made a surprise announcement about a town 180 miles away called Lancaster, Pennsylvania. The U.S. Post Office Department, Blakslee informed the 200 Motor Truck Club members in attendance, had just put that town in southeastern Pennsylvania on the map of suburban New York.[1]

Blakslee's news about Lancaster was not the result of some Houdini-worthy magic nor did it stem from a farfetched redistricting of state lines. As Blakslee further explained in his remarks that night, a motor truck carrying about 2,900 pounds of farm produce had left Lancaster at 4:14 that morning. That vehicle made its way to New York City's post office building at 23rd Street and Eighth Avenue at 4:17 that afternoon.[2] Blakslee could not stress enough the significance of that 12-hour trek from the heart of Pennsylvania Dutch Country to America's largest city. That mail-delivery experiment, he told his audience, was, "a convincing illustration of improved efficiency which the Post Office Department is endeavoring to establish in the farm-to-table food movement."[3]

That farm-to-table movement was an ambitious postal initiative that took place during President Woodrow Wilson's administration, seeking to transport produce directly from rural areas to cities. The program entailed picking up farm-fresh products—butter, eggs, poultry, vegetables, to name a few—and taking them as directly and quickly as possible to urban destinations. It was conceived and launched in peacetime, but it took on additional significance during America's eighteen-month involvement during what we know today as World War I. In the course of that bloody conflict, the experimental motor truck routes set up as part of that program were seen by many as important to the nationwide food conservation campaign.[4]

The origins of the farm-to-table postal delivery initiative took shape about two decades earlier. Rural Free Delivery, which started out on a trial basis in 1896 and became permanent in 1902, proved to be a widespread and welcome

FIGURE 1. Individuals in a city post office checking out the list of goods available through the farm-to-table program, which sought to match rural produce with urban demand. Courtesy of the National Postal Museum Library, Smithsonian Institution Libraries.

service that brought mail directly to rural residents. During President William Howard Taft's time in the White House, Rural Free Delivery was enlarged to include Parcel Post Service. That service, officially launched in the waning days of the Taft Administration in early 1913, allowed the shipment of packages that could not be delivered through regular mail within rural communities. The service turned out to be highly popular; in its first six months alone, approximately 300 million parcels were handled.

Albert S. Burleson, postmaster general for the fledgling Wilson Administration, sought to capitalize even further on Rural Free Delivery's dramatic success. One way to accomplish that was an experiment, implemented in 1914, encouraging farmers to export more of their goods via the mail to consumers in the city. This experiment focused on a perceived gap in the existing Rural Free Delivery system: while farm families extensively used the parcel post service to request and receive such items as newspapers, magazines, and mail-order merchandise, there was

unmet marketing possibility in the goods that could just as easily flow from the country to the city.[5] As a department spokesman explained, "The Postmaster General has the firm conviction that this plan is the one thing necessary to enable the people of this country to enjoy the potential benefits of the parcel post."[6]

The program's first year was on the whole promising, with 26 large cities selected for experimental delivery routes. Basically, postmasters in rural areas compiled lists of farmers and others wishing to sell their products to city residents by way of parcel post. Those postmasters would then forward the lists to their urban counterparts, who in turn shared the information through such means as letter carriers going door to door and posted advertisements (Figure 1). Ultimately, the urban consumer could place orders with his or her local post office and then await the arrival of farm-fresh products at home.[7]

The Post Office Department, by serving as the conduit between producers and buyers, hoped to profit from business that most likely otherwise would have gone to such middlemen as general stores, express companies, and railroads. A lot of emphasis, though, was placed on how the farmers themselves could benefit from this mail-delivery undertaking. "Every possible thing has been done to give the farmer an equal chance to compete with the corner grocery store on equal terms," reported an April 1915 article entitled "Butter from the Post Office" in *The Independent*. "Special fast auto service is used in many cities to effect immediate delivery of perishable goods."[8] An example of this transportation service could be seen in Cleveland, Ohio, where in the fall of 1914 the postmaster obtained five new automobiles to facilitate deliveries from farms in the region.[9]

By 1916, the groundwork was laid for the program's enlargement. A joint congressional resolution that summer authorized new routes, and postal officials began planning accordingly. Meanwhile, however, the United States found itself being drawn more deeply into the war in Europe. The nation formally entered that brutal conflict on April 6, 1917, when Congress declared war on Germany.[10] President Wilson, in a subsequent address to the American people, appealed to the nation's farmers for help with food conservation efforts. He asserted, "Without abundant food, alike for the armies and the peoples now at war, the whole great enterprise upon which we have embarked will break down and fail . . . Upon the farmers of this country, therefore, in large measure, rests the fate of the war and the fate of the nations."[11]

With those words, Wilson voiced the need to produce and preserve ample food for the duration of the war. The conservation of food became one of the most crucial goals on the homefront and, in terms of wartime mobilization efforts, among the most far-reaching. U.S. Food Administrator (and future president) Herbert Hoover firmly and consistently exhorted his fellow Americans not to waste food so that enough of it could be shipped overseas to feed American troops and others.

Under Hoover's leadership, the Food Administration used every means, medium, and method possible to promote its message to the public and make sure that everyone did what they could to ensure the availability of adequate rations abroad. "Meatless Mondays" and "Wheatless Wednesdays" became a regular part of each person's calendar. "Food Will Win the War" was a familiar rallying cry, and posters and signs carrying that mantra and others blanketed the nation. A host of likeminded slogans, which regularly showed up in newspapers, included: "Don't let your horse be more patriotic than you are—eat a dish of oatmeal!;" "Wheatless days in America make

sleepless nights in Germany;" "U-boats and wastefulness are twin enemies;" "Serve beans by all means;" and "The Battle Cry of Feed 'Em."

As Wilson underscored, however, a special burden was placed on farmers when it came to this entire campaign. They were under pressure, stronger than ever before, to not only produce enough food but also make sure that as much of it as possible went to market without rotting or simply going unused.[12] The Post Office Department, having already received authorization for more farm-to-table routes, stood ready to help accomplish those aims. Fourth Assistant Postmaster General Blakslee, who both dreamed and talked big anyway when it came to motorized transportation's potential role in mail delivery, pushed for motor trucks rather than automobiles on those new routes.

A total of eight motor truck routes came into existence after postal officials wrestled extensively with logistics and unsuccessfully sought to secure additional funds for the endeavor. The routes, located mostly in the Middle Atlantic region, took effect between December 1917 and June 1918. They were specifically situated between Philadelphia, Pennsylvania, and Atlantic City, New Jersey; Baltimore, Maryland, and Solomons Island, Maryland; Washington, D. C., and Leonardtown, Maryland; Washington, and Baltimore; Baltimore and Lancaster; Philadelphia and Washington; Savannah, Georgia, and Statesboro, Georgia; and Columbus, Ohio, and Zanesville, Ohio.

The Post Office Department, which kept thorough records of all expenses for this part of the farm-to-table program, announced that the net profit for these routes in their first few months of operation was substantial.[13] In addition, Blakslee stressed how at least some of these routes provided essential transportation services that could not be easily duplicated. "There is no rail or water transportation possible between Baltimore and Solomon's Island nor between Washington and Leonardtown," he offered as an example of this, "and there are over 1,000 similar localities east of the Mississippi River."[14]

Overall, though, the most salient feature of these motor trucks was how they could pick up and deliver larger-than-before quantities of farm goods for city residents. The Lancaster–New York City test run during this time further confirmed that advantage. That shipment was taken, within 45 minutes after reaching the New York City post office, to the customer—a produce dealer named Harry Atlas. His order, incidentally, included 400 newly hatched chicks, 18,000 fresh eggs, 200 pounds of honey, 500 pounds of butter, and 500 pounds of smoked sausage.

This experimental trip was the longest postal run of its kind up to that time. The trip was also noteworthy due

FIGURE 2. The Autocar screen-side truck used for the historic postal test run between Lancaster, Pennsylvania, and New York City on March 20, 1918. This vehicle transported about 2900 pounds of farm produce in what was the longest mail-delivery trip of its kind up to that time. Courtesy of the National Postal Museum Library, Smithsonian Institution Libraries.

to the truck's comparatively few stops in transit while delivering the produce to New York City from a rural area over 100 miles away (Figure 2).[15] That night at the dinner meeting of the Motor Truck Club of America, New York's Secretary of State Francis Hugo called the test run, "an epoch in the history of the United States and the world."[16] Epoch or not, that test run and other aspects of the motor truck farm-to-table routes did receive positive public notice. This was because the whole enterprise fit in well with the food-conservation ethos that dominated the war.

The service, to be sure, was far from perfect. It could be expensive, first of all. Other periodic drawbacks included trucks breaking down and food getting spoiled in transit. Farmers nonetheless embraced the service, and not just because of how much produce the motor trucks could carry. Many farmhands who normally might take produce elsewhere were serving in the military or performing other wartime duties, and the Post Office Department's program helped mitigate that manpower shortage.[17]

Blakslee emphasized those linkages with the larger war effort. As he noted in an April 1918 *New Times* article, "Government profit in any branch of the postal service is a good thing, but at the present time that takes second place when compared to the necessity for food production on the biggest possible scale. And do not forget that we have less men than ever to produce the food."[18] Throughout the U.S. involvement in World War I, the Farm-to-Table postal delivery service was widely praised in the press. Hoover hailed the service as an important means of saving food.[19]

Blakslee, trying to seize this momentum, promoted a nationwide network of profitable motor truck routes. He reasoned that the surplus he felt would surely result from those routes could be used to improve the roads on which the vehicles traveled. Virginia's Senator Claude Swanson, in fact, introduced a bill authorizing the Postmaster General to establish such routes and to use half the gross revenues from those routes for road improvements. That bill died in a Senate committee, but in July 1918 Congress did appropriate a smaller amount for a few more experimental routes. Just a few months later, however, the armistice with Germany was signed. The Treaty of Versailles in June of the following year would officially end the state of war, but the armistice halted the actual fighting.[20]

In the post-armistice atmosphere, Blakslee and others in the department found it tougher to extend—let alone maintain—the farm-to-table postal delivery program and in particular its motor truck routes. The once solid public

"Farmers Want Better Parcel Post System in Entire Country," *Cedar Rapids Evening Gazette*, 19 February 1920.

Federal Highway Administration. *America's Highways, 1776–1976*. Washington, D. C.: Government Printing Office, 1977.

"Food by Parcel Post," *Washington Post*, 23 March 1914.

"Food from Farm to City by Postal Truck Plan," *New York Times*, 23 September 1917.

"Fords for Postoffice," *Washington Post*, 3 January 1915.

Fuller, Wayne E. *RFD: The Changing Face of Rural America*. Bloomington, Ind.: Indiana University Press, 1964.

Guffey, A. S. Letter to James I. Blakslee. 11 April 1919. Box 1, Entry 185, RG 28. Washington, D. C.: National Archives and Records Administration.

Hagedorn, Ann. *Savage Peace: Hope and Fear in America, 1919*. New York: Simon & Schuster, 2007.

"Herbert Clark Hoover: A Biographical Sketch." Herbert Hoover Presidential Library and Museum. http://hoover.archives.gov/education/hooverbio.html.

Ho, Szu-Han. "From Farm to Table: Mailman As Middleman." thenorthroom. http://www.thenorthroom.org/FTT.pdf.

Holley, I. B. Jr. *The Highway Revolution, 1895–1925: How the United States Got Out of the Mud*. Durham. N. C.: Carolina Academic Press, 2008.

"J. I. Blakslee Praises Auto Trucks in Service of the P. O. Department; Stimulate the Production of Food," *Washington Post*, 7 April 1918.

Jacob, E. H. Letter to Albert S. Burleson, 1 January 1919. Box 2, Entry 185, RG 28. Washington, D. C.: National Archives and Records Administration.

"Mail by Motor." Smithsonian National Postal Museum. http://www.postalmuseum.si.edu/exhibits/2b1c3_motor.html.

"Mail Carrying Motor Trucks Prove Success," *The Daily Tribune* (Logansport, Ind.), 5 November 1918.

McNichol, Dan. *The Roads That Built America: The Incredible Story of the U.S. Interstate System*. New York: Sterling Publishing Co., 2006.

"Motor Mail Is Making Money," *The Gettysburg Times*, 17 April 1918.

"Motor Trucks for Mail," *New York Times*, 14 April 1918.

"Motor Trucks Pay for Parcel Post," *New York Times*, 30 June 1918.

Nash, George H. *The Life of Herbert Hoover: Master of Emergencies, 1917–1918*. Vol. 3. New York: W. W. Norton & Company, 1996.

"Never Such Need for Motor Trucks," *New York Times*, 6 January 1918.

"Parcel Post Ready by January Next," *New York Times*. 26 August 1912.

"Post Office Aid for Farmers," *Christian Science Monitor*, 19 February 1920.

"The Post Office Rides the Highway," *Indianapolis Star*. Magazine. 14 September 1952.

"Postal Truck Brings Produce 180 Miles," *New York Times*, 21 March 1918.

"Record Year in the Mail Department," *Christian Science Monitor*, 6 December 1918.

"Rouses Senator's Ire," *Washington Post*, 28 May 1916.

"Rural Delivery Waste Charged," *Christian Science Monitor*, 19 February 1920.

"Rural Mail Service Policy Under Attack," *Christian Science Monitor*, 18 August 1916.

Schlesinger, Arthur M. Jr., ed. *The Almanac of American History*. Greenwich, Conn.: Brompton Books, 1993.

The United States Postal Service. *The United States Postal Service: An American History, 1775–2006*. Washington, D. C.: USPS, 2007.

The United States Statutes at Large, December 1915 to March 1917.Volume 39, Part 1.Washington D. C.: Government Printing Office, 1917.

U.S. Post Office Department. *Annual Report of the Postmaster General for the Fiscal Year Ended June 30, 1917*. Washington, D. C.: Government Printing Office, 1917.

———. *Annual Report of the Postmaster General for the Fiscal Year Ended June 30, 1918*. Washington, D. C.: Government Printing Office, 1919.

———. *Annual Report of the Postmaster General for the Fiscal Year Ended June 30, 1919*. Washington, D. C.: Government Printing Office, 1919.

———. *Annual Report of the Postmaster General for the Fiscal Year Ended June 30, 1951*. Washington, D. C.: Government Printing Office, 1951.

"War's Effect on Automobile Trade," *New York Times*, 17 November 1918.

"Wider Use of Parcel Post in U.S. Now Seen," *Christian Science Monitor*, 5 October 1914.

Wilson, Woodrow. "Address to the Nation. 16 April 1917." The American Presidency Project. http://www.presidency.ucsb.edu/ws/print.php?pid=65399.

Philatelic Propaganda: A Case Study—Border Changes in Eastern Europe, 1938–1941

Robin Gates Elliott

The purpose of postage stamps, first introduced in Great Britain in 1840, is to pay to send an item, usually a letter or package, through the mail. Since then, governments have realized that postage stamps could serve additional functions. This awareness, in turn, has influenced stamp design since the early twentieth century, when philately became a well-established hobby. Once governments realized that collectors were prepared to spend considerable sums of money on stamps which would never be used as postage—and therefore constituted pure profit—stamp design began to evolve beyond the simple monochromatic portraits of reigning monarchs, founding fathers, allegorical figures, and coats of arms typical of the nineteenth century. The purpose, of course, was to appeal to collectors and, by so doing, generate income. During the inter-war period many governments developed another additional use for postage stamps: the dissemination of propaganda.

Propaganda is material produced and circulated to influence public opinion, to persuade people to think, and sometimes to act, in a certain way. It has taken various forms over time, such as posters and pamphlets, and has been utilized by governments over time to promote attitudes, values, and behaviors which they wish their citizens (and, in some cases, foreign governments and foreign nationals) to adopt. Government propaganda, therefore, is nothing new; but the use of postage stamps to disseminate it is a twentieth-century phenomenon. A postage stamp lends itself to propaganda surprisingly well for something so small and seemingly innocuous, for several reasons. First, the issuing government has complete control over stamp design; it can use postage stamps to send any kind of message it wants. Furthermore, that message will be widely disseminated, since stamps are produced in large quantities, are inexpensive, and pass through many hands (including those of collectors) as they travel domestically and abroad.[1]

Stamp design consists of three component parts: format, textual message, and iconic content. The format is the size and shape of the stamp, traditionally a small square or rectangle, which sets the parameters for the textual message and iconic content. The textual message consists of linguistic or numerical elements—numbers, letters, names, or acronyms—that identify the country of origin and the amount of postage paid. Iconic content consists of graphic pictorial representations (icons) such as pictures and designs (drawings, engravings, photographs, or other graphics). Iconic content is of paramount importance in a stamp design that is to carry a propaganda message. The old saying that one picture is worth a thousand words is particularly true for postage stamps, since they are so small; whatever message is to be conveyed has to fit into a miniscule format. Pictures also can have an immediate emotional impact invaluable for effective propaganda. A brief textual message, such as a slogan, can be used to reinforce the message conveyed by the stamp's iconic content.[2]

The first countries to appreciate and utilize the propaganda potential of postage stamps were the major European dictatorships of the 1930s: Hitler's Germany, Mussolini's Italy, and Stalin's Soviet Union. Philatelic literature has noted the propaganda function of the stamp designs of these three countries; the stamps of Nazi Germany, along with its cancellations and postal cards, have been studied in depth. In addition, David Scott has studied the history of stamp design in several western European countries, including stamps issued during the 1930s and World War II.[3] The literature has had little, if anything, to say about stamp design and its propaganda function in the countries of eastern Europe during this period. Yet by the 1930s, most of the countries of eastern Europe were dictatorships, and their governments felt the same need to influence public opinion (if not to the same degree) as those of Germany, Italy, and the Soviet Union. The purpose here is to study the stamp designs of a small subset of eastern European stamps: stamps issued by countries that had annexed territory between 1938 (the Munich crisis) and 1941 (the Nazi invasion of the Soviet Union) and which celebrate (and seek to justify) their territorial acquisitions.

From the Munich crisis in the fall of 1938 to V-E Day in May, 1945, the borders of all of the countries in eastern Europe underwent changes. Countries gained territory from or lost territory to their neighbors. Several countries entirely disappeared—occupied, partitioned, or dismembered—and two new ones (Croatia and Slovakia) emerged. These changes had their roots in the peace settlements following World War I, which redrew the map of central and eastern Europe. The old empires—German, Austro-Hungarian, Russian, and Ottoman—had collapsed and were replaced by successor states, and the previously existing states in the area either gained or lost territory. Given the multitude of competing territorial claims based on historic, cultural, ethnic, economic, and strategic arguments, no settlement could satisfy everyone, and resentment of the results was widespread.[4]

Starting with Munich and continuing into World War II, countries occupied neighboring territory that they regarded as rightfully theirs at every opportunity. Five countries—Poland, Hungary, the Soviet Union, Bulgaria, and Romania—issued stamps honoring and justifying their territorial acquisitions. Hungary and Bulgaria each issued two sets, one for each of two separate territorial acquisitions.[5] These stamps are impressive miniature propaganda posters, and the purpose here is to explain their iconic content (to deconstruct the iconography) in order to show how they functioned as propaganda and to suggest the messages that they might have sent. The meaning and significance of the iconic content of these stamps would have been obvious and instantly recognizable to the citizens of the issuing countries, and probably to their foreign contemporaries. Over half a century later, however, they constitute *terra incognita* for populations far removed in time, space, and culture.

The iconic content of the seven stamps or sets of stamps issued by five different countries, each with its own unique history and culture, is surprisingly similar. A limited number of icons are used by all five countries to convey similar ideas. Such similarities suggest the existence of a visual vocabulary common to the region and to the period, as well as shared ideas and emotions. They also provide an analytical framework.

For these stamps or sets of stamps to function as propaganda posters, two types of icons must be present in the stamp design. First, an icon representing the occupying power (the country issuing the stamp) is necessary, something above and beyond simply the country's name on the stamp. A limited number of icons are used to serve this purpose. A picture of the head of state appears most frequently. Other icons include pictures of the army or individual soldiers (annexation, after all, usually involved a military operation), appropriate religious and allegorical figures, and the state flag. The second required icon is one representing the occupied territory. Another limited number of icons serve this purpose. They include pictures of ethnic co-nationals resident in the territory being occupied (since the justification for annexation was frequently based on ethnic claims), identifiable as such by their national costumes and broad smiles; a map of the occupied territory; or pictures of culturally significant landmarks located in the occupied territory. These two types of icons—occupying power and occupied territory—visually establish the fact of occupation/territorial acquisition.

The stamp designs also include optional iconic content that reinforces the message established by the required icons. One type is a depiction of the old border between the occupying power and the occupied territory which, due to annexation, has now been rendered null and void. A second type of iconic content justifies annexation by citing historical precedent through the portrayal of a historical figure or landmark dating from the period when the annexed territory belonged to the occupying power: "It was ours then, it is ours now." A third type is some reference to an alliance with the Axis, which made the "return" of the "lost" territories possible.

Poland is not usually regarded as an occupying power in connection with World War II; rather, it is remembered as the war's first victim. There was, however, the issue of Teschen. Located in Austrian Silesia (known as Eastern Silesia to some philatelists), it was claimed by both Poland and Czechoslovakia following World War I. As with so many of the disputed territories of this period, the issues were complex. Ethnically, it was predominantly Polish, but economic and strategic considerations made it attractive to Czechoslovakia. The territory contained coal mines, and the only rail line that connected the western provinces of the new state of Czechoslovakia with its eastern half ran through Teschen. The territory was split, north to south, by the River Olza. The victorious Entente Powers (who were redrawing the map of Europe) followed the line of the river and partitioned the territory. Poland received the city of Teschen, and Czechoslovakia received the suburbs, which contained the coal mines and the railroad line.

Twenty years later, when Hitler decided to detach the Sudetenland from Czechoslovakia, he wanted to make the annexation look like part of a multi-national movement undertaken to rectify the injustices (in his opinion) perpetrated by the peace treaties concluded at the end of World War I. Therefore, he suggested that other countries which had lost territory to Czechoslovakia press their claims. Poland, which had remained bitter over the partition of Teschen throughout the inter-war period and, as a result, had never established cordial relations with Czechoslovakia, did so with alacrity. The government reclaimed Czech Teschen and issued a stamp celebrating the "return" of the territory.[6] (Figure 1)

The icon representing Poland, the occupying power, is a personification of the Motherland (the woman in the white robe). Lest there be any doubt as to her identity, she is standing in front of a map of Poland (the Polish Corridor is visible in the upper left-hand corner of the stamp). The three figures in the foreground are icons representing the annexed territory: the left-hand figure is carrying a pick-ax, a reference to coal mining. They are stepping over a border post, the low striped wall in the lower foreground. Border posts stood upright and were painted with stripes of red and white, but this border post has been knocked down, rendered null and void by the Polish occupation of the territory.

FIGURE 1. A stamp celebrating the "return" of the Teschen territory to Poland. From the collection of Robin Gates Elliott.

The textual message on the stamp, "The Return of Trans-Olza to the Motherland," plus the date, tie everything together. "Return" implies that the territory had once been Polish. It is identified as Trans-Olza, the territory across the River Olza, not as Teschen (let alone *Czech* Teschen). Polish is a language of synonyms. The inscription on the stamp could have read "the return . . . to Poland," or "to the homeland," or "to the Fatherland." These various linguistic options suggest that the reference to Poland as "the Motherland" was deliberate.

And there she stands, the Lady in White. Here the icon representing the occupying power is a benign one, that of a mother welcoming her children home, not of an invading army or its soldiers. She holds a sword, but it is pointed down, not raised, and she is wrapping her robe around her children as they return home and walk into her embrace. This Polish stamp is a masterpiece. Just one stamp contains both required icons, one of the optional icons (the border), and a textual message that reinforces the message conveyed by the iconic content.

Hungary had also lost territory to Czechoslovakia. In fact, Hungary had lost territory to all of its neighbors following World War I. The Hungarian state was over a thousand years old (it had celebrated its millennium in 1896). As a result of the Treaty of Trianon, the peace treaty between the Entente Powers and Hungary, it had lost two-thirds of its territory and over one-half of its population.

Those population losses, furthermore, included more than three million ethnic Hungarians who, due to Hungary's new borders, suddenly became ethnic minorities in foreign countries. The Hungarians were inconsolable. In Hungary flags flew at half-mast the day the Treaty of Trianon was signed. The country's motto became "No, No, Never!"—never would Hungarians become reconciled to these losses. In Liberty Square, a park in Budapest behind the Parliament building, four statues were erected in memory of the lost territories: the territories to the north (lost to Czechoslovakia), the south (to Yugoslavia), the east (to Romania), and the west (to Austria).

These territorial losses were one of the reasons, if not the main reason, for Hungary's alliance with the Axis in the 1930s and during World War II. Hitler and Hungary, after all, shared a common goal: to destroy the peace settlements that had ended World War I by regaining the territorial losses. So when Hitler set his sights on Czechoslovakia in 1938, Hungary also participated with alacrity. Precisely how much territory Hungary would regain from Czechoslovakia was determined by German and Italian diplomats in Vienna; the resulting agreement is known as the First Vienna Award. Hungary received a strip of southeastern Czechoslovakia (territory from the eastern provinces, Slovakia, and Sub-Carpathian Ruthenia) which had a predominantly Hungarian population.[7] To celebrate the return of the territory Hungary issued a set of five semi-postal stamps,[8] which had the additional purpose of raising money to assist the ethnic brethren who had allegedly suffered financially under foreign rule. The inscription on all five stamps reads "Hungarians Help Hungarians."[9]

The first stamp in the series is of the Budapest statue memorializing the lost northern territory (the Hungarian word for north, *Eszak*, is inscribed on the base of the statue) plus the date of the Treaty of Trianon, 1920 (upper right-hand corner). The third depicts Admiral Horthy, Hungary's head of state, entering southern Slovakia on a white horse (significant in Hungarian folklore) at the head of the army, complete with flowers strewn in his path by the grateful Hungarian population. He is crossing into the occupied territory on a bridge over the River Danube at Komaron, where the river formed the (old) border between Hungary and Czechoslovakia. The iconic content is a reproduction of a photograph of his triumphal entry. The stamp design of the fifth stamp in the series contains icons representing both the occupying power and the occupied territory. (Figure 2) Hungarian soldiers are being welcomed by Hungarian girls in national costume. The date of the First Vienna Award, 1938, is in the upper right-hand corner, signifying the (partial) return of what had

FIGURE 2. The design of the fifth stamp in the "Hungarians Help Hungarians" series contains icons representing both the occupying power and the occupied territory. From the collection of Robin Gates Elliott.

been lost in 1920, and stands in contrast to the date on the first stamp in the series.

The designs of the remaining two stamps in the series are icons of culturally significant landmarks in the occupied territory: the medieval Cathedral of St. Elizabeth of Hungary in Kassa (Slovakia) and the fort at Munkacs (Sub-Carpathian Ruthenia), built during the reign of King Bela IV in the thirteenth century. Both date from the time when the territory was Hungarian, and, as such, can be read as a justification of the occupation by historical precedent. The selection of these two historic landmarks as icons to represent the occupied territory has an additional significance—and a certain irony—since they had appeared on stamps issued by Czechoslovakia, the fort in 1936 and the cathedral in June of 1938, just a few months before the Hungarian occupation.[10]

World War II began with the German invasion of Poland on September 1, 1939. The green light for the invasion was the Nazi-Soviet Pact, concluded in late August. Essentially, Stalin agreed to let Hitler do whatever he wanted militarily as long as the Soviet Union could annex territory on its western border, territory that either had been part of the old Russian empire or that the Bolsheviks had tried, but failed, to conquer in the aftermath of World War I. As a result, the Red Army invaded eastern Poland on September 17, 1939, and occupied the eastern half of the interwar Polish state. The territory was ethnically mixed and contained substantial numbers of Belorussians in the north and Ukrainians in the south.[11]

A set of five stamps present the Party line justifying the invasion, utilizing both iconic content and textual messages.[12] All five stamps portray the enthusiastic welcome of the Red Army (icon representing the occupying power) by the local inhabitants (icons representing the occupied territory), identified on two of the stamps as Ukrainians and Belorussians by the details of the women's clothing, specifically the embroidery. The first stamp in the series (Figure 3) shows a Red Army soldier holding a young boy who, in turn, is holding aloft a bouquet of flowers, presumably to give to the soldier. Adults stand in the background, and the embroidery on a woman's blouse suggests that the scene takes place in the Western Ukraine. (Figure 3) Additional stamps in the series portray villagers welcoming a tank crew (a soldier stands in front of his tank and shakes hands with villagers, while a little girl brings him a bouquet of flowers) and a soldier distributing newspapers (presumably announcing the "liberation") to eager villagers enthusiastically reaching for them. The final stamp shows villagers welcoming an approaching tank column (someone in the crowd is even waving a Soviet flag); the embroidery on the blouse of a woman in the foreground suggests that the scene is taking place in Western Belorussia. Everyone is all smiles.

The textual message on all five stamps reads "The liberation of the fraternal peoples of Western Ukraine and

FIGURE 3. The first stamp in a series of five that present the communist party line justifying the invasion of Poland by the Soviet Union. It shows a Red Army soldier holding a young boy who, in turn, is holding aloft a bouquet of flowers, presumably to give to the soldier. From the collection of Robin Gates Elliott.

Western Belorussia," along with the date, which explains and reinforces the iconic content of happiness, enthusiasm, and celebration created with smiles, flowers, and the Soviet flag. The message is that the fraternal Red Army has come to liberate the "fraternal peoples of Western Ukraine and Western Belorussia" from Polish rule. There is no mention of Poland, let alone the fact that it has been invaded. The territory will be annexed to the Soviet Socialist Republics of Ukraine and Belorussia, and the inhabitants will at long last join their ethnic brethren and, by definition, live happily ever after.

In June 1940 the Soviet Union occupied the Romanian province of Bessarabia. Bessarabia had been part of the old Russian empire since the nineteenth century but had been annexed by Romania following World War I. Now the Soviet Union, in accordance with the Nazi-Soviet Pact, wanted it back. No stamps were issued to mark the Soviet occupation of Bessarabia, but the Soviet move inspired other countries that had lost territory to Romania following the war, Hungary and Bulgaria, to press their claims.[13]

Hungary demanded the return of Transylvania, the lost territory to the east. Of all of the territorial losses that Hungary had sustained following World War I, the loss of Transylvania was the most traumatic to the Hungarian national psyche. Transylvania had been an integral part of the Hungarian state since the eleventh century, held considerable historical significance for Hungarians, and constituted about half of the territory of Historic Hungary. The fact that the Hungarian population of Transylvania was now being governed by *Romanians* simply added insult to injury. Precisely how much territory Hungary would gain was, once again, determined by German and Italian diplomats in Vienna; hence the decision was known as the Second Vienna Award. Hungary received northern Transylvania, an area with significant concentrations of non-Romanian ethnic minorities. They may not have all been Hungarian—they included Germans (known as the Saxons) and numerous Szeklars (a Bulgarian-Turkic tribe which had migrated to Transylvania in the eleventh century and, over time, had adopted the Hungarian language and customs)—but they were certainly *not* Romanians.[14]

To celebrate the return of northern Transylvania and its citizens, Hungary issued a set of three stamps, semi-postals to benefit the Pro-Transylvania Movement.[15] The first stamp in the series portrays Hungarian soldiers past (in the background, on a horse) and present (foreground) with the date of the return of the territory in the upper left-hand corner. (Figure 4) The mounted soldier in the background, with helmet and sword, is a reference to a Hungarian legend. Szeklars had settled in north-eastern Transylvania, a border

FIGURE 4. The first stamp in a series of three stamps that celebrate the return of northern Transylvania to Hungary portrays Hungarian soldiers past (in the background, on a horse) and present (foreground) with the date of the return of the territory in the upper left-hand corner. From the collection of Robin Gates Elliott.

FIGURE 5. The design of the second stamp in the Transylvania series is reminiscent of the Pieta. From the collection of Robin Gates Elliott.

region, as early as the thirteenth century and were entrusted with guarding the border. If ever they were threatened, so the legend went, Hungarian warriors from centuries past would arise from their graves and gallop to their rescue. The soldier in the background is doing precisely that. The stars in the middle of the stamp represent the Milky Way which, according to the same legend, was the "Road of the Armies," the path of the galloping warriors. The legendary figure serves two purposes. First, it is one of the optional elements, justification for annexation by citing historical precedent (Transylvania had been part of Historic Hungary for centuries). Second, it represents the theme of aid, appropriate for a stamp designed to raise funds.[16]

The design of the second stamp is reminiscent of the Pieta. (Figure 5) Hungary, the occupying power, is represented by the Virgin Mary, the Patroness of Hungary (lest there be any doubt, *Patrona Hungariae* is inscribed on her halo). The man, a Szeklar from north-eastern Transylvania, represents the occupied territory; his crown of thorns symbolizes the sufferings endured (according to Budapest) by ethnic minorities at the hands of the Romanians.[17] Szeklars are also portrayed on the third stamp in the series. A Szeklar mother is holding her child aloft, facing west (towards Budapest), and offering him to the Fatherland. The sun is rising in the background, suggestive of

the bright future that awaits the population now that it is once again part of Hungary. The iconic content of the second and third stamps in the series is highly emotional, more so than that of the Hungarian stamps issued to mark the return of territory from Czechoslovakia in 1938. The designs suggest the importance of Transylvania in the Hungarian national psyche—and the contempt in which Hungarians held the Romanians in general and those governing Transylvania in particular.

Bulgaria, not to be outdone, also demanded Romanian territory. Like Hungary, Bulgaria had been on the losing side in World War I, and, like Hungary, it had lost territory following the war. As a result of the Treaty of Neuilly, concluded between the Entente Powers and Bulgaria, Bulgaria had lost about ten percent of its territory to Romania, Greece, and Yugoslavia. When the terms of the treaty were publicized in Bulgaria, a national day of mourning was declared. By World War II, Bulgaria was allied with the Axis. With Axis support, it demanded the return from Romania of Southern Dobrudja, a highly developed and productive agricultural region bordering the Black Sea, in which Bulgarians were the predominant ethnic group.[18] This was accomplished in 1940 by the Treaty of Craiova, and Bulgaria issued a series of four stamps celebrating the territory's return.

All four stamps include pictures of Bulgaria's head of state, Tsar Boris, and the inscription "Dobrudja–1940."

Maps of Southern Dobrudja, the annexed territory, are on two of the stamps. An ethnic Bulgarian couple, residents of Southern Dobrudja (identifiable as such by their national costumes), are portrayed on a third. The woman holds a sheaf of wheat, a reference to the agricultural character and importance of the region. The reference to agriculture is repeated in the fourth stamp (Figure 6), which shows the Bulgarian flag (an additional icon of the occupying power) being carried through a wheat field; the wheat is so tall that the soldiers carrying the flag are barely visible. On this stamp, Tsar Boris is portrayed wearing a German helmet, possibly a reference to the alliance with the Axis which made the recovery of Southern Dobrudja possible.[19]

By 1941 Hitler was planning to invade the Soviet Union, the Nazi-Soviet Pact notwithstanding. In preparation, he invaded Greece and Yugoslavia in April to ensure that the entire Balkan Peninsula was firmly under Axis control. The philatelic paper trail generated by the dismemberment of Yugoslavia and the fate of its various component parts from 1941 to 1945 is a long and complicated one. Suffice it to say that Bulgaria, as an Axis ally, received coveted territory from both Yugoslavia (most of Macedonia

plus some of Serbia) and Greece (territory in Western Thrace, which included access to the Aegean Sea).[20] It publicized these acquisitions with a series of five stamps.[21]

Tsar Boris plus a map of the territory obtained from Yugoslavia are on one of the stamps. (Figure 7) The iconic content of the remaining four stamps depicts the territories acquired. Two signify the occupation of Macedonia. A Macedonian woman (identified as such by her national costume) plus the date of the occupation are on one, and the city of Ohrid, a culturally significant landmark in Macedonia dating from the ninth century (shown on the map of the territorial acquisitions from Yugoslavia), is on the second. Macedonia had been part of the medieval Bulgarian state, and modern Bulgaria's attempts to regain it had been a cause of Balkan instability since the Balkan Wars of 1912 and 1913. The city of Ohrid had been a center of learning in medieval Bulgaria and the seat of the Patriarch of the Bulgarian Orthodox Church. As a culturally significant landmark, the portrayal of Ohrid serves as a justification for annexation by citing historical precedent. The third stamp celebrates Bulgaria's acquisition of territory from Greece. For economic and strategic reasons modern Bulgaria had constantly sought an outlet on the Aegean Sea—and had been constantly frustrated in its attempts. Western Thrace, however, bordered the Aegean, thus fulfilling another of Bulgaria's territorial goals. Appropriately, the iconic content of the stamp of Western Thrace is a view of the Aegean Sea from the Thracian coastline, with the Island of Samos (another Bulgarian

FIGURE 6. In 1940, Bulgaria issued a series of four stamps celebrating the return of Dobrudja. The fourth stamp references agriculture by showing the Bulgarian flag being carried through a wheat field; the wheat is so tall that the soldiers carrying the flag are barely visible. On this stamp, Tsar Boris is portrayed wearing a German helmet, possibly a reference to the alliance with the Axis which made the recovery of Southern Dobrudja possible. From the collection of Robin Gates Elliott.

FIGURE 7. Bulgaria, as an Axis ally, received coveted territory from both Yugoslavia and Greece. It publicized these acquisitions with a series of five stamps. Tsar Boris plus a map of the territory obtained from Yugoslavia are on this stamp. From the collection of Robin Gates Elliott.

acquisition from Greece) in the distance and a rising sun blazing in the sky. The final stamp in the series is a view of the Poganovski Monastery.

Romania participated in Hitler's invasion of the Soviet Union in June of 1941 and sent troops into Bessarabia to reclaim the territory that Stalin had annexed the previous year.[22] On the first anniversary of its reconquest of Bessarabia, Romania issued a series of three semi-postal stamps.[23] All three portray General Antonescu, Romania's *de facto* head of state. Two of the three also portray the King of Romania, King Michael; King Michael's father, King Carol II, had been forced to abdicate in 1940 due to national outrage over the country's territorial losses. Due to Michael's youth, General Antonescu served as regent.

The first stamp in the series depicts the Romanian army crossing the Pruth River to retake Bessarabia; the Pruth was the western border of Bessarabia. The bridge is in the foreground, and the soldiers are viewed from the back as they march from Romania into Bessarabia. In addition to two icons representing the occupying power (General Antonescu plus the army), the iconic content includes one of the optional elements, the crossing of a border. Both King Michael and General Antonescu appear on the second stamp, along with a portrait of Stephen of Moldavia, a famous fifteenth-century Romanian ruler during whose reign Bessarabia was part of Moldavia (justification of occupation by citing historical precedent). The third stamp (Figure 8) is a map of Bessarabia; at the bottom of the stamp, beneath the map, are soldiers. Four portraits complete the stamp's iconic content. In addition to those of King Michael and General Antonescu, homage is paid to Hitler and Mussolini: a tip of the hat to the Axis, since Romania's alliance with the Axis made the return of Bessarabia possible.

The purpose here has been to explain the iconic content and textual messages of the stamps or sets of stamps issued by several eastern European countries to celebrate their territorial acquisitions obtained during the period from the Munich crisis in the fall of 1938 to Hitler's invasion of the Soviet Union in June 1941. The stamps have been described as propaganda posters, and the analysis of their iconic content and textual messages has shown how they functioned as such. In conclusion, the issue that remains to be addressed is the purpose of these miniature propaganda posters: specifically, what messages the five governments were seeking to convey with these stamps, and how they wished to influence public opinion. Philatelic literature, once again, is virtually silent on this topic, and a search for relevant government documents or memoir material is beyond the scope of this study. Any

FIGURE 8. On the first anniversary of its reconquest of Bessarabia, Romania issued a series of three stamps. The third stamp is a map of Bessarabia; at the bottom of the stamp, beneath the map, are soldiers. Four portraits complete the stamp's iconic content: King Michael, General Antonescu, Hitler, and Mussolini—a tip of the hat to the Axis, since Romania's alliance with the Axis made the return of Bessarabia possible. From the collection of Robin Gates Elliott.

conclusions, therefore, are purely speculative. Yet speculation is possible through seeking connections between the stamp designs and the historical background and circumstances that produced them.

First, all of these stamps convey a *positive* message: wrongs have been righted, integral parts of the homeland have been restored, and ethnic brethren have been rescued from foreign domination and returned safely home. Everyone is happy: soldiers are greeted with flowers, the ethnic brethren are smiling, flags are flying, and the sun is shining. Even the suffering Szeklar in the arms of the Madonna is at least still alive. The happiness portrayed stands in sharp contrast to the national mood caused by the loss of the territories. Hungary endured a year of political turmoil in 1919 due to its territorial losses, and the Treaty of Trianon the following year, which confirmed the losses, was an occasion for national mourning and defiance. Bulgaria marked the Treaty of Neuilly with a day of mourning. As a result of Romanian territorial losses in 1940, the king, Carol II, was forced to abdicate in favor of his young son, Michael. It also stands in contrast to the actual conditions that existed in eastern Europe when the stamps were issued: dictatorial regimes, political repression, economic hardship, and war.

Second, the various national governments (those same dictatorial regimes practicing political repression) are taking credit for these joyous events, the territorial acquisitions, by issuing stamps proclaiming and celebrating them. The iconic content of several of the stamps makes this connection obvious with portraits of the heads of state: Admiral Horthy of Hungary, King Boris of Bulgaria, and King Michael and General Antonescu of Romania. All of the other icons representing the occupying power also make the connection, if not as directly. None of the governments were parliamentary democracies, and none of the rulers portrayed on the stamps were governing with the consent of the governed, hence the importance of influencing public opinion in their favor (especially in the worst of times) through propaganda. Put very simply, the stamps do precisely that by associating the rulers and governments with something positive and popular (the returned territories) and giving them credit for it.

To skeptics at home and abroad, the stamps send a third message: the territorial acquisitions are justified, for all of the reasons listed above. They have saved the minorities of Transylvania from the Romanians, liberated Belorussians and Ukrainians from the Poles, and given Bulgaria its long-sought outlet to the Aegean Sea. Justification abroad through philately was probably most important—and most calculated—in the Soviet Union. The Soviet government made a point of selling its stamps to collectors overseas, and it is questionable whether the set of stamps celebrating and justifying its acquisition of eastern Poland even circulated domestically.[24]

A fourth message is support for the Axis. All of the territorial acquisitions discussed here were made possible by some type of agreement or alliance with either Nazi Germany or the Axis. The willingness to acknowledge the connection philatelically varied according to the country's degree of subservience.[25] Romania issued the clearest message of support (see Figure 8).[26] It is a reflection of Romanian foreign policy during the inter-war period.[27] Romania feared Soviet aggression, at least in part because it had annexed Bessarabia, and it had depended upon its relations with the Entente countries, particularly France, to guarantee its security. That guarantee evaporated with the fall of France to Nazi Germany in the summer of 1940. Eastern Europe had suddenly become a very dangerous neighborhood, with no effective Entente power to counter either Germany or the Soviet Union. Romania concluded an alliance with the Axis, which enabled it to retake Bessarabia when Hitler invaded the Soviet Union. Bulgaria and

Hungary also concluded alliances with the Axis. Bulgaria alludes to the Axis connection (see Figure 7); Hungary does not. The iconic content of the stamps issued by Poland and the Soviet Union contain no reference to their relations with Nazi Germany.

The stamps analyzed here are similar in their iconic content. The messages that these miniature propaganda posters are designed to send are also similar. Whether the iconic content employed and the messages sent are unique to these specific countries or are part of a visual vocabulary and a pattern common to all of Europe during the 1930s and World War II (and beyond, both in space and time) would be a subsequent topic to explore—but one beyond the scope of this study.

NOTES

1. Jack Child, *Miniature Messages: the Semiotics and Politics of Latin American Postage Stamps*, pp. 1–5, 15; Daniel A. Piazza, "Perforated Propaganda," (Lecture given at the Smithsonian National Postal Museum, Sept. 18, 2009); Donald M. Reid, "The Symbolism of Postage Stamps: a Source for the Historian," *Journal of Contemporary History*, vol. XIX, no. 2 (April 1984), p. 223; Carlos Stoetzer, *Postage Stamps as Propaganda*, pp. 1–3.

2. The description of the component parts of stamp design is based on David Scott, *European Stamp Design: a Semiotic Approach to Designing Messages*, in which he applies concepts from *The Second Trichotomy of Signs* by Charles Sanders Peirce to stamp design, and on Child, who applies Scott's resulting concepts of stamp design to his study of Latin American stamps.

3. Alf Harper, *Philately of the Third Reich: Postage and propaganda* (Raleigh, N.C.: Album, 1998); Albert L. Moore, *Postal Propaganda of the Third Reich* (Atglen, Pa.: Schiffer Military History, 2003); Montgomery Mulford, "Postage Stamps as Propaganda," *Mechanix Illustrated*, Oct. 1938, pp. 86, 135; Piazza; Scott; Stoetzer.

4. Richard and Ben Crampton, *Atlas of Eastern Europe in the Twentieth Century*, p. 37; Dennis P. Hupchick and Harold E. Cox, *The Palgrave Concise Historical Atlas of Eastern Europe*, maps 42, 44; Hugh Seton-Watson, *Eastern Europe Between The Wars: 1918–1941*, pp. 269–270.

5. In the United States the standard reference book for postage stamps is the *Scott Standard Postage Stamp Catalogue*, a multi-volume work issued annually. The Scott numbers for the stamps to be analyzed here are: Poland, Scott 334; Hungary, Scott B98–102 and B123–125; Russia, Scott 767–771; Bulgaria, Scott 360–363 and 392–396; and Romania, Scott B195–197.

6. Crampton and Crampton, pp. 41, 57, 67, 99, 101, 111; Hupchick and Cox, map 48; Margaret MacMillan, *Paris 1919: Six Months that Changed the World*, pp. 225, 238–240; *Scott 2004 Standard Postage Stamp Catalogue*, vol. 5, p. 272; Seton-Watson, pp. 364–365.

7. Crampton and Crampton, pp. 41, 77; Hupchick and Cox, maps 44, 48, 49; MacMillan, pp. 235–236, 238, 269–270; Kati Marton, *The Great Escape: Nine Jews Who Fled Hitler and Changed the World*, p. 39.

8. A semipostal stamp is a postage stamp that sells for more than the cost of postage. The difference between the postage rate and the price of the stamp is contributed to a charity. Therefore a semi-postal postage stamp has two functions: paying for postage and raising funds for a charitable cause.

9. *Scott 2004 Standard Postage Stamp Catalogue*, vol. 3, p. 698; Kent B. Stiles, "Of Topical Interest," *Scott's Monthly Journal*, vol. XX, no. 1 (March 1939), pp. 18–19, 24, 26; Frederick Wall, "The Designs of the Month," *Gibbons Stamp Monthly*, vol. XII, no. 6 (March 1939), pp. 105–107; Marian Carne Zinsmeister, *Hungarian Stamps and their Background, 1871–1940*, pp. 22–23.

10. The Czechoslovak stamps mentioned are Scott numbers 64 and 86.

11. Crampton and Crampton, pp. 111, 135; Hupchick and Cox, map 49.

12. *Scott 2004 Standard Postage Stamp Catalogue*, vol. 5, p. 520; Frederick Wall, "The Designs of the Month," *Gibbons Stamp Monthly*, vol. XIII, no. 11 (August 1940), p. 149.

13. Hupchick and Cox, map 45; Jacques Posell, "The War Issues of Romania," in *Sixteenth American Philatelic Congress Book*, pp. 157, 159; Seton-Watson, pp. 213–214, 400.

14. Crampton and Crampton, pp. 41, 77, 121; Hupchick and Cox, maps 44, 46, 49; Paul Lendvai, *The Hungarians: A Thousand Years of Victory in Defeat*, p. 25; MacMillan, pp. 260–261; Seton-Watson, pp. 270–271, 297–303, 343–344.

15. *Stanley Gibbons Simplified Catalogue: Stamps of the World*, 1997 ed., vol. I (London: Stanley Gibbons Ltd., 1996), p. 967; Lendvai, pp. 24–25; *Scott 2004 Standard Postage Stamp Catalogue*, vol. 3, p. 699; Frederick Wall, "The Designs of the Month," *Gibbons Stamp Monthly*, vol. XIV, no. 8 (April 1941), p. 57; Zinsmeister, pp. 25–26.

16. It appears on subsequent Hungarian semi-postal stamps issued to raise money for the Horthy National Aviation Fund (Hungary, Scott B141, B170). *Scott 2004 Standard Postage Stamp Catalogue*, vol. 3, pp. 699, 700.

17. In 1955 this stamp won third prize in an international contest for the best stamp portraying the Virgin Mary, sponsored by the St. Gabriel International Society for Collectors of Christian Motives [sic] on Postage Stamps. "Saar Stamp wins Gabriel Contest," *Linn's Weekly Stamp News*, vol. XXXIII, no. 6 (April 18, 1955), p. 10.

18. Crampton and Crampton, pp. 21, 41, 49, 121, 135; Hupchick and Cox, map 49; MacMillan, pp. 121, 123, 136–137, 140–142; Seton-Watson, pp. 270–271, 390.

19. *Scott 2004 Standard Postage Stamp Catalogue*, vol. 1, p. 962; Frederick Wall, "The Designs of the Month," *Gibbons Stamp Monthly*, vol. XIV, no. 6 (Feb. 1941), p. 47.

20. Crampton and Crampton, pp. 21, 41, 49, 133, 135; Hupchick and Cox, maps 47, 49; MacMillan, pp. 121, 123–124, 136–137, 142; Seton-Watson, pp. 271, 311, 313–316, 352, 355, 364.

21. R. J. Crampton, *A Concise History of Bulgaria*, pp. 12, 16; *Michel Europa-Katalog Ost, 1995/96*, p. 145; *Scott 2004 Standard Postage Stamp Catalogue*, vol. 1, pp. 962–963.

22. Hupchick and Cox, map 49; Posell, p. 159.

23. Paul Robert Magocsi, *Historical Atlas of Central Europe*, pp. 29–30; Posell; *Scott 2004 Standard Postage Stamp Catalogue*, vol. 5, p. 491; Seton-Watson, pp. 213–214.

24. Stoetzer, pp. 9–10.

25. On the varying degrees of subservience to Hitler and the Axis, see Seton-Watson, p. 197.

26. This was not the only Romanian stamp that reflected the country's pro-Axis, anti-Soviet foreign policy orientation. In August 1941 Romania issued a set of four semi-postal stamps to raise money for its Anti-Bolshevism crusade; one of them portrays a Romanian and a German soldier, side by side (Romania, Scott B 170–173). A second set of semi-postal stamps issued in 1943 marks the second anniversary of Romania's entry into World War II (Romania, Scott B207–209). Posell, pp. 157, 159; *Scott 2004 Standard Postage Stamp Catalogue*, vol. 5, pp. 491, 492; Stoetzer, p. 19.

27. MacMillan, p. 128; Posell; Seton-Watson, pp. 198, 213–216, 363, 385–386, 390–391, 400–401.

BIBLIOGRAPHY

Child, Jack. *Miniature Messages: The Semiotics and Politics of Latin American Postage Stamps*. Durham, N. C.: Duke University Press, 2008.

Crampton, R. J. *A Concise History of Bulgaria*. Cambridge, U. K.: Cambridge University Press, 1997.

Crampton, Richard, and Ben Crampton. *Atlas of Eastern Europe in the Twentieth Century*. New York: Routledge, 1997.

Harper, Alf. *Philately of the Third Reich: Postage and Propaganda*. Raleigh, N. C.: Album, 1998.

Hupchick, Dennis P., and Harold E. Cox. *The Palgrave Concise Historical Atlas of Eastern Europe*. New York: Palgrave, 2001.

Lendvai, Paul. *The Hungarians: A Thousand Years of Victory in Defeat*. Trans. Ann Major. Princeton, N. J.: Princeton University Press, 2003.

MacMillan, Margaret. *Paris 1919: Six Months that Changed the World*. New York: Random House, 2002.

Magocsi, Paul Robert. *Historical Atlas of Central Europe*, revised and expanded ed. Seattle: University of Washington Press, 2002.

Marton, Kati. *The Great Escape: Nine Jews Who Fled Hitler and Change the World*. New York: Simon and Schuster, 2006.

Michel Europa-Katalog Ost, 1995/96. Munich: Schwaneberger Verlag GmbH, 1995.

Moore, Albert L. *Postal Propaganda of the Third Reich*. Atglen, Pa.: Schiffer Military History, 2003.

Mulford, Montgomery. "Postage Stamps as Propaganda." *Mechanix Illustrated*, Oct. 1938, pp. 86, 135.

Piazza, Daniel A. "Perforated Propaganda." Lecture given at the Smithsonian National Postal Museum, September 18, 2009.

Posell, Jacques. "The War Issues of Romania." *Sixteenth American Philatelic Congress*, ed. W. R. McCoy. New York: W. R. McCoy, 1950.

Reid, Donald M. "The Symbolism of Postage Stamps: A Source for the Historian." *Journal of Contemporary History*, 19(2):223.

"Saar Stamp Wins Gabriel Contest." *Linn's Weekly Stamp News*, 33(6):10.

Scott, David. *European Stamp Design: a Semiotic Approach to Designing Messages*. London: Academy Editions, 1995.

Scott 2004 Standard Postage Stamp Catalogue, vols. 1–6. Sidney, OH: Scott Publishing Company, 2003.

Seton-Watson, Hugh. *Eastern Europe between the Wars: 1918–1941*. Boulder: Westview Press, 1986. [reprint of 1945 ed.]

Stanley Gibbons Simplified Catalogue: Stamps of the World. Vol. 1. 1997 ed. London: Stanly Gibbons, Ltd., 1996.

Stiles, Kent B. "Of Topical Interest." *Scott's Monthly Journal*, vol. XX, no. 1 (March 1939), pp. 18–19, 24, 26.

Stoetzer, Carlos. *Postage Stamps as Propaganda*. Washington, D. C.: Public Affairs Press, 1953.

Wall, Frederick. "The Designs of the Month." *Gibbons Stamp Monthly*, vol. XII, no. 6 (March 1939), pp. 105–107.

———. "The Designs of the Month." *Gibbons Stamp Monthly*, vol. XIII, no. 11 (August 1940), pp. 149–150.

———. "The Designs of the Month." *Gibbons Stamp Monthly*, vol. XIV, no. 6 (February 1941), p. 47.

———. "The Designs of the Month." *Gibbons Stamp Monthly*, vol. XIV, no. 8 (April 1941), p. 57.

Zinsmeister, Marian Carne. *Hungarian Stamps and their Background, 1871–1940*. Albany, Or.: The Western Stamp Collector, 1948.

Picking Up the Pieces: The Aftermath of Hiroshima

Janet Klug

INTRODUCTION

On May 7, 1945, Nazi Germany signed an unconditional surrender, and the Allied Powers declared victory in Europe. Two months later leaders from the Allied Powers met at Potsdam, where on July 26, they issued a joint declaration setting out their requirements for Japan's unconditional surrender or Japan would face the alternative, "a prompt and utter destruction."[1]

Japan did not surrender and what happened next changed the world forever. On August 6, 1945, the United States dropped a single atomic bomb on the Japanese city of Hiroshima, killing an estimated 80,000 to 140,000 people,[2] and destroying most of the city. Three days later another atomic weapon was dropped on Nagasaki with similar devastating effect.[3]

On the morning of August 15 (local Japan time), Japan's Emperor Hirohito made a radio broadcast that announced he had "ordered our Government to communicate to the Governments of the United States, Great Britain, China and the Soviet Union that our empire accepts the provisions of their joint declaration."[4]

On September 2, 1945, 200 Allied vessels assembled in Tokyo Bay to witness Japan's signing of the instrument of surrender on board the U.S. battleship *U.S.S. Missouri.*

OCCUPATION BEGINS

U.S. forces began the occupation of Japan immediately. The British Commonwealth, however, was delayed by internal affairs. One of the delays was deciding which of the Commonwealth countries would command the Commonwealth troops in Japan. Four nations within the Commonwealth would comprise the British Commonwealth Occupation Force, known by the acronym BCOF. The nations were Great Britain, Australia, India, and New Zealand. A total of 45,000 Commonwealth military served during the six years of BCOF occupation. During the peak of BCOF occupation in December 1946, 37,021 Commonwealth military personnel were serving in Japan, of which 11,918 were Australian (Figure 1).[5]

FIGURE 1. Envelope posted aboard the Australian light cruiser HMAS *Hobart* on September 2, 1945, the day the instrument of surrender was signed aboard USS *Missouri*. From the collection of Janet Klug.

Australia, whose war efforts against the Japanese had indeed been formidable, presented a winning case for Australian leadership in Japan, and BCOF came under the command of Royal Australian Army Lieutenant General John Northcott, who was recalled after four months to become governor of New South Wales. Northcott was replaced by Royal Australian Army Lieutenant General Horace "Red Robbie" Robertson, who remained BCOF commander through the end of 1951.

The internal BCOF negotiations delayed BCOF deployment. Months passed, and the Australian-dominated BCOF did not arrive in Japan until February 1946. It was the dead of winter, and most of the forces had been awaiting deployment in tropical holding areas in Northern Australia, Borneo, Malaya, and India.[6]

THE BLACK MARKET

BCOF forces arrived in Japan ill equipped for the cold weather. To make matters worse, BCOF was assigned the Hiroshima prefecture, where conditions were bleak. The military squarely addressed the occupation force needs with shiploads of supplies necessary for basic survival. Food, warm clothes and blankets, tents and shelters, water, vehicles . . . all of these things were required by the military. Coincidently, these necessities of life were also needed by the local Japanese survivors of the Hiroshima attack (Figure 2).

This created a perfect formula for trouble. Add a sudden influx of abundant military supplies, plus extreme local need, plus ingenious, underpaid soldiers, and all of that equals a thriving black market where "acquisitioned" military goods were sold to locals. Although both BCOF

FIGURE 2. Hiroshima in 1946. From the collection of Janet Klug.

and U.S. administrations attempted to control currency exchanges through the use of military scrip, the Australian BCOF contingent found a loophole (Figure 3).

It is at this point that postage stamps became an instrument to facilitate the black market.

IT'S ALL ABOUT POSTAGE STAMPS

There were nineteen Australian military post offices in Japan.[7] The bases served the Australian military's mailing needs by selling then-current Australian regular issue postage stamps. The face values of the stamps that were stocked by the military post offices were those most needed for both concessionary and non-concessionary rates and fees available to the military, that is, half penny, one penny, threepence, sixpence, one shilling, two shilling and five shilling values.

Australian military serving in Japan could send letters home to Australia by surface mail for free. This concessionary rate remained in effect for the duration of the occupation. Stamps were needed for airmail, registration, parcels, and non-concessionary overseas mail.[8]

Those members of the military who were engaged in black market activities discovered they could convert their illegal black market windfalls into currency by legally purchasing postage stamps from the base post office using military scrip, then sending the stamps home to friends or

family in Australia. Once the stamps arrived in Australia, the recipients could take them to their local post office and "cash them in" for face value, less 5%. This long-standing Australia Post policy accommodated individuals and corporations that had acquired unneeded surplus postage. Thus, Australian postage stamps became a key ingredient in maintaining the thriving black market.

By September 1946, BCOF command reviewed ways to eliminate the black market. Command's idea was to overprint all of the postage stamps sold by the Australian military post offices, making the stamps invalid for use outside Japan so they would have no exchange value within Australia.

In October 1, 1946, four proof sheets of overprints consisting of three lines of serif type and one proof sheet of san-serif type in three lines were made under military supervision at the Hiroshima Printing Company.[9]

SERIF TYPE OVERPRINTS

Two BCOF officers and the managing director of the Hiroshima Printing Company co-signed and dated the four serif-type proof sheets. Two of the four sheets were printed entirely in gray-black type. One of the sheets was printed in red type. The final sheet was printed with the left "pane" in a color called "gold" but actually brownish and the right "pane" in red (Figure 4).

a)

b)

FIGURE 3. a) One-shilling value British Military Authority payment certificate scrip note. Allied Occupation scrip notes produced by the U.S. government were also circulated by occupation personnel. b) Scrip tokens created by the Australian Canteen Services (ACS) were used by Australian BCOF troops to purchase refreshments in ACS canteens. From the collection of Janet Klug.

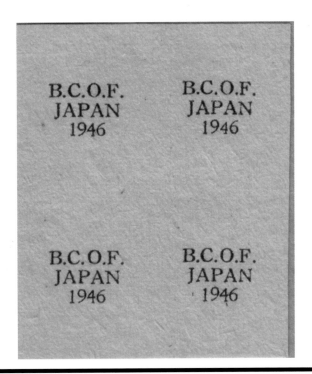

FIGURE 4. Proof of serif overprint in gray-black on plain paper. Thin numeral "4" at top left. From the collection of Janet Klug.

Trial printings of sheets of halfpenny, one penny and threepence stamps were thus overprinted with this type, using the same color formulations of gray-black, red and "gold" (Figure 5). Once seen on the stamps, it became apparent that the thin, spidery type was not suitable for the

FIGURE 5. Unadopted essay of serif overprint in red on half-penny stamp. From the collection of Janet Klug.

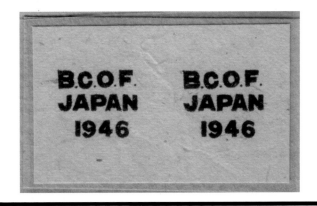

FIGURE 6. Proof of sans serif overprint in black on plain paper. From the collection of Janet Klug.

dark brown one penny and threepence stamps but could be used in black for the orange halfpenny stamp. The red and gold colors were not appropriate for any of the stamps.

SANS SERIF OVERPRINTS

In a similar fashion, the Hiroshima Printing Company made one sheet of heavy, black sans serif overprints. This, too, was co-signed by two military officers and the printing company's manager. The proof sheet indicates this was adopted for the one penny and threepence stamps (Figure 6).

HERE TODAY—GONE TOMORROW

An initial quantity of halfpenny, one penny and threepence stamps were overprinted and released without fanfare and without government authorization on October 12, 1946; only to be withdrawn two days later until the proper authorizations were acquired.[10]

That took seven months. On May 8, 1947, a set of seven stamps overprinted "B.C.O.F./ JAPAN/ 1946" was finally released.

STAMP COLLECTORS TAKE NOTICE

Contemporary reports in Australia's philatelic press confirm that stamp collectors quickly became aware of the BCOF overprints released in October 1946.

In its December 1946 issue *Australian Stamp Monthly* reported, "We mildly suggested in an editorial note in the

September, 1946, edition of the 'A.S.M.' that 'overprinted stamps would serve to remind Japan that it was an occupied country.'

"We confess, however that we had not expected such suggestions to bear fruit. Consequently we were profoundly surprised to learn at the beginning of November that Australian stamps had actually been overprinted.

"Information gathered from various sources—we acknowledge particularly our indebtedness to Mr. A.M. Leitch and Mr. H.D. McNess—indicate that a major reason prompting the issue was that large quantities of Australian stamps were being bought in Japan with black market money and sent to Australia.

"Australian postal regulations provide that unused stamps may be repurchased at a discount and this was apparently being done on a fairly large scale."[11]

Australian Stamp Monthly reported in early 1947, "We have been attempting to obtain reliable information concerning the issue of Australian stamps overprinted "B.C.O.F./JAPAN.1946" and to which we first made reference in our December, 1946, edition.

"Early in the previous month, just after we first gained knowledge of the stamps so overprinted, we wrote to the Postmaster-General's Department asking for full information of the issue. We also stressed the obvious danger of permitting but a few of the stamps (which had been pre-released) to be in philatelic circulation, and pointed out that it was most desirable that, in these circumstances, they should be placed on sale again.

"Actually, we think the Postmaster-General's Department to be blameless in the matter of issuing the stamps, but as Australian postal paper is involved the P.M.G.'s Department should, logically, make the proper explanations.

"Blackmarketing is still rife in occupied Japan. Indeed, the matter is so serious to warrant discussion by the Australian Cabinet, to whom a report on black market operations in the B.C.O.F. area was recently presented.

"The overprinting of Australian stamps was one of the means by which it was hoped to hamper black market operations, and, possibly, some Government explanation might now be forthcoming."[12]

MONEY IN STAMPS

Australian Stamp Monthly later reported, "Under the state of uncertainty that has existed, it is not surprising that many collectors have taken a chance and bought the stamps while the few available are on the market. We note that £7/10/- was paid for a mint block of the 3-pence at auction in Melbourne on February 27 (1948), while other reports indicate that high prices are being paid for the scarcer ½-penny and 1-penny stamps."

In the meantime, the entire set of seven stamps was being prepared for issue in May. The stamp collecting community in Australia and throughout the world wanted these stamps for their collections. The demand from collectors became acute. Collectors were offering occupation personnel more money for the overprinted stamps than they were making in the black market from exchanging unoverprinted stamps for cash.

Australian Stamp Monthly: "There is general local agreement that the stamps are very hard to secure in Japan, and if they are available persons are not allowed to purchase more than 10-shillings worth each day. Further, if a person does purchase this quantity each day a military order requires him to explain the reason therefore."

Australian government officials initiated an investigation about the stamps. (British) Royal Army Colonel E. Percy Dickson, acting Brigadier General Staff, and himself a philatelist, was requested to give evidence. In a letter dated April 29, 1948, Dickson writes, "I was on my way home [to Britain] when the original issue was made in October 1946 but I told some truths about prices these damned things were fetching. I advised unrestricted sale through the GPO in Australia and Australia House in London. I said the London Market would require about 50,000 sets, a figure that I think you gave me at one time. It remains to be seen if anyone takes any notice of the recommendation."[13]

No one did.

The 5-shilling stamp, the highest face value in the set, had the lowest printing quantity—32,508[14] (Figure 7).

BCOF overprinted stamps were withdrawn on February 12, 1949, ending a 20-month period of validity. The stamps intended purpose of eliminating the black market failed. The black market adjusted quickly and remained a threat to the occupation until the living conditions of the Japanese people improved significantly, and BCOF troops were withdrawn.

STAMP VARIETIES

There are three basic types of overprints—two types of serif overprints and the sans-serif overprints.

The halfpenny, sixpence and one shilling values in the set were serif printing overprints. The one penny and three-pence stamps were sans-serif overprints. The two high values, two and five shillings, respectively, were slightly larger

FIGURE 7. The highest value (five-shilling) stamp had the lowest printing quantity. From the collection of Janet Klug.

FIGURE 8. Doubled overprint of the three-pence value. Only one sheet of 160 was printed in error with a doubled overprint. From the collection of Janet Klug.

and the sheets were formatted differently. Thus the serif printing was spaced more widely apart but is otherwise similar to the other serif printings.

The serif printings have many varieties. Some of the more noticeable varieties, such as the wrong font "6" in "1946," are listed in some catalogs. *The Australian Commonwealth Specialists' Catalogue, King George VI* does the most extensive job of listing varieties of BCOF overprints. The serif BCOF overprints (including the high values) offer stamp collectors much challenge and resulting exultation when they have found something unusual.

The sans serif stamps have fewer varieties. The scarcest is a doubled overprint on the threepence stamp, of which only one sheet of 160 impressions was made by error (Figure 8).

POSTAL USAGE OF THE STAMPS

A large percentage of mail weighing four ounces or less sent by Australian BCOF military personnel to Australian addresses required no postage stamps, provided it was sent surface mail and inscribed "Free."

Airmail was preferred by many of the Australian military, at a concessionary rate of threepence per half ounce. This was the most common usage of BCOF stamps, mainly paid by a solo use of one threepence stamp (Figure 9).

Registered mail was used frequently, especially for sending cash equivalents such as uncancelled stamps and postal orders, as well as legally or illegally obtained currency. The basic registration rate that included no compensation for loss was threepence. Higher rates applied for articles requiring compensation for loss. Often another threepence stamp was used to pay for registration on airmail letters to Australia, but a sixpence stamp also covered basic registration and airmail.

Parcels to Australia were charged concessionary rates based upon weight. Australian military had to pay nonconcessionary standard postage on mail sent outside Australia and for other special services.

NON-AUSTRALIAN USE OF AUSTRALIAN MILITARY POST OFFICES IN JAPAN

British, Indian, and New Zealand forces used stamps from their respective countries of origin. However, when transiting through an Australian base, letters sent from non-Australian BCOF forces were readily accepted by the Australian military post offices and received corresponding cancels from the Australian field post office (FPO), unit postal station (AUPS), base post office (ABPO), Army post office (APO), or Royal Australian Air Force post office (RAAFPO).

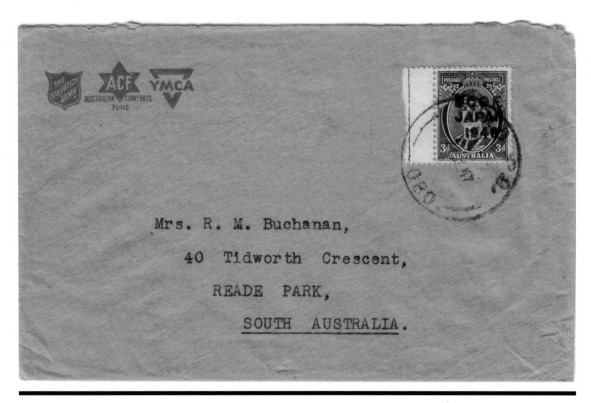

FIGURE 9. The most common use of BCOF stamps was to pay postage for airmail service from Japan to Australia. From the collection of Janet Klug.

THE END OF BCOF OCCUPATION

By 1950, most of BCOF had withdrawn from Japan. BCOF occupation formally ended on April 28, 1952, although BCOF air bases at Iwakuni and Kure continued to serve in "policing" activities in Korea and Malaya. Those former-BCOF who remained were nearly all Australians.

BCOF's duties and responsibilities during the occupation were to dispose of Japan's stocks of war material, including chemical agents and ordnance; repatriate returning Japanese soldiers; assist in the reconstruction of Hiroshima; honorably represent the British Commonwealth; safeguard all Allied installments within the BCOF area; and promote the democratic way of life.

To these ends, BCOF cleared BCOF area of stockpiled Japanese war material, including 100,000 tons of explosives and 500 tons of poison gas; repatriated 700,000 Japanese military personnel and civilians; patrolled BCOF area by land and sea to suppress smuggling and illegal immigration; built housing for dependants of Commonwealth military personnel eligible to bring their families to Japan (illustrating the "democratic way of life"); and provided humanitarian relief.[15]

COLLECTING THE BCOF STAMPS, POSTMARKS, AND ENVELOPES

Neither the stamps nor envelopes bearing stamps properly used from one of the Australian military base post offices in Japan are "common," but the lower face value denominations of halfpenny, one penny, threepence and sixpence are easy to find and inexpensive to purchase for collectors desiring representational examples for their collection. The higher denominations of one shilling, two shillings and five shillings are more difficult to find, especially properly used on an envelope or parcel.

A few of the Australian military post offices in Japan saw little use or were used for an abbreviated period of time. These are very difficult to find and collect, but only a limited number of collectors are actually seeking this material, so while much of this material is scarce or rare, the demand is not great.

AFTERWORD

In the course of their duty, some of the Australian BCOF personnel were exposed to residual radiation from the atomic bomb. One Australian soldier describes his experience: "We Aussies, our captain told us, had been given pride of place in BCOF by being stationed in the Hiroshima prefecture, historic target of the world's first atomic bomb and the launching site of a new age for mankind . . .

"Most of this dead inferno was fairly level and covered by brown talc-like dust several feet thick in places. The troops found it was a good soft surface on which to play football!

"And so time passed. Four months after reaching Hiroshima, I got sick. I began to pass blood in the urine and it burnt. . . . I was taken to 20th Field Ambulance and then sent by truck and barge to the island of Eta Jima in Hiroshima Bay.

"I was admitted [to the 130th Australian General Hospital] and put to bed and subjected to two days of tests. No organisms were found.

"On the third day I was prepared for theatre. There was to be a bladder inspection with something known to doctors as a cystoscope and the rest of the army as a hockey stick. A little blond nurse was fitting a white cap on my head.

'That's funny,' she said.

'What's funny?'

'Your hair—it's all coming out in handfuls.'

So it was. We laughed."[16]

The writer became a crusader for Australian BCOF veterans who had been exposed to radiation in Hiroshima, after having been denied a disability pension for radiation-related illnesses he claimed were a result of his BCOF service.[17]

NOTES

1. *Proclamation Defining Terms for Japanese Surrender,* Potsdam, July 26, 1945.

2. Data recorded by the Radiation Effects Research Foundation, Hiroshima, Japan.

3. Estimated number of deaths associated with the Nagasaki atomic attack is 60,000 to 80,000, according to the Radiation Effects Research Foundation.

4. Hirohito, *Accepting Potsdam Declaration Radio Broadcast,* as recorded by the U.S. Federal Communications Commission, August 14, 1945.

5. Australian Department of Defence, *The Forgotten Force,* "Chapter 7: BCOF: Time for Reappraisal," quotes statistics from Defence Committee assessment conducted April 22, 1948. By the end of 1947 the entire Indian contingent was gone as were most of the British and New Zealand forces.

6. Peter Bates, "The Long Wait." *Japan and the British Commonwealth Occupation Force 1946–52* (London: Brassey's, 1993), pp. 44–51.

7. P. Collas, *The Postal History of Australian Forces in Japan and Korea, 1945–1957* (Melbourne: Royal Philatelic Society of Victoria, 1994).

8. "Pre-Decimal Postal Rates, Forces Mail and Miscellaneous Services," *Australia Commonwealth Specialists' Catalogue.*

9. Marginal notes on proof sheets dated October 1, 1946 and attested by officers and manager on October 8, 1946. The proof sheets were photographed in black and white in the 1970s before being broken up and sold to collectors.

10. Yoshimi Ito, *B.C.O.F. Overprints and British Commonwealth and Indian Military Postal Services in Japan and Korea,* Japan Philatelist Club, undated. Quotes letter dated August 17, 1950 from F. R. Sinclair, Secretary of the Department of the Army, Commonwealth of Australia.

11. *Australian Stamp Monthly,* December 1946.

12. *Australian Stamp Monthly,* February 1947.

13. Letter sent from Kure, Japan by Col. E. Percy Dickson to Maj. A. Walker, London, April 28, 1948.

14. *The Australian Commonwealth Specialists' Catalogue, King George VI,* Brusden White, 2006.

15. Australian War Memorial, *As You Were, 1948,* Canberra, ACT: Halstead Press, 1948, Chapter 9; Occupation and *The Forgotten Force, The Australian Military Contribution to the Occupation of Japan, 1946–1952,* Australian Department of Defense, 2005.

16. J. G. Collins, *The War of the Veterans,* self-published, March 2001.

17. Muller, Brumfield, and Kennedy, "Administrative Appeals Tribunal, Repatriation Commission Tribunal and J. G. Collins," *VeRBosity,* Vol. 16, No. 1, March 21, 2000.

BIBLIOGRAPHY

Australian Department of Defense. "BCOF: Time for Reappraisal." In *The Forgotten Force: The Australian Military Contribution to the Occupation of Japan, 1945–1952.* St. Leonards, N. S. W.: Allen & Unwin, 1998.

Australian War Memorial. "Occupation." In *As You Were, 1948.* Canberra, A. C. T.: Halstead Press, 1948.

Bates, Peter. "The Long Wait." In *Japan and the British Commonwealth Occupation Force 1946–52.* London: Brassey's, 1993.

"B.C.O.F. Japan." *Australian Stamp Monthly*. July 1946.

Collas, P. *The Postal History of Australian Forces in Japan and Korea, 1945–1957*. Melbourne: Royal Philatelic Society of Victoria, 1994.

Collins, J. G. *The War of the Veterans*. Toowoomba, Qld.: Toowoomba Education Centre, 2001.

Dickson, E. Percy, Col. Letter to Maj. A. Walker, April 28, 1948. Personal Collection of Janet Klug.

"Frequently Asked Questions." Radiation Effects Research Foundation. http://www.rerf.or.jp/general/qa_e/qa1.html.

Hirohito. *Accepting Potsdam Declaration Radio Broadcast*. U. S. Federal Communications Commission: recorded, 14 August 1945.

Ito, Yoshimi. *B.C.O.F. Overprints and British Commonwealth and Indian Military Postal Services in Japan and Korea*. Tokyo: Japan Philatelist Club, 1979.

Kellow, Geoffrey, ed. "King Georg VI, Brusden White." *The Australian Commonwealth Specialists' Catalogue*. Section 7, pp. 7/1–7/10. 2006.

Kellow, Geoffrey and Richard Breckon, eds. "Pre-Decimal Postal Rates, Forces Mail and Miscellaneous Services." *The Australian Commonwealth Specialists' Catalogue*. pp. AA31–AA33, 1992.

Kennedy, Robert. "Administrative Appeals Tribunal: Re Repatriation Commission and J. G. Collins." *VeRBosity*, 16(1): 9–11. 2000.

United State Department of State. *Proclamation Defining Terms for Japanese Surrender*. Department of State Bulletin, Vol. XIII, No. 318. Potsdam: Germany. July 29, 1945.

Postal Censorship and Military Intelligence during World War II

Ann Elizabeth Pfau

In January 1943, Capt. Carney, a U.S. Army Air Corps officer stationed in North Africa, wrote a letter to a Miss Thomas in Tacoma, Washington. A passage from this letter caught the attention of military intelligence personnel assigned to postal censorship duties. It read:

> The Waacs [members of the U.S. Women's Army Auxiliary Corps] are here in force now. Had hoped . . . that our American girls would be spared that. After all, we want something decent to return to. Any country loses something more by placing their women in military servitude than by a military defeat. How can our leaders be so foolish as to destroy the very things we are supposedly at war to win? What man would want any woman after she had given herself to months of such an ordeal. I would rather go down the line and choose a common prostitute, at least, a person who gave herself for a reason and not just because some blabber-mouth fool glamorized it for her. We <u>dont</u> need our girls in the army. We <u>do</u> need them at home . . . as we left them so at least we can know there is something fine and honorable someplace awaiting our return.[1]

In the winter and spring of 1943, letters like this alerted Army officials to what would, by the summer, become a public relations nightmare—a wave of hostile rumors that hobbled WAAC recruitment and retention efforts. While WAAC administrators suspected that enemy operatives were responsible for the slander, intelligence officers correctly diagnosed the problem as homegrown.[2] Censorship revealed allegations of Waac impropriety (typically sexual in nature) to be common in male soldiers' letters home. Some men blamed Army life for the perceived problem; others accused the Army of actively recruiting former prostitutes for military service. Like Capt. Carney, they asserted that female soldiers were not only unnecessary but also detrimental to the nation's war effort. Many warned women away from the corps; some even threatened to divorce wives or to disown sisters who volunteered for service.[3]

In this case, forewarned was not forearmed. The force of the slander caught military officials off guard. But, in conjunction with attitude surveys, postal censorship provided the Army with a window into the anger and fear that gave rise to hostile rumors about purportedly promiscuous servicewomen.

FIGURE 1. Cover of letter condemned and held by U.S. Army postal censors. Courtesy National Archives, College Park, Md.

Although the primary purpose of postal censorship was to prevent strategic information from falling into enemy hands, censoring soldiers' letters was also a method of intelligence gathering (Figure 1). Reviewing soldiers' letters provided military officials with information about military morale and behavior. Censorship reports documented widespread attitudes, common complaints, and incidents of misconduct. These documents are, perhaps, even more valuable to historians than they were to the U. S. Army, for they provide scholars with access to thoughts and actions that are otherwise un- or underreported.

DOCUMENTING WARTIME ATTITUDES

In overseas theaters of operations, censorship responsibilities assigned to intelligence personnel included: training unit officers to censor the outgoing correspondence of enlisted men and women under their command; reviewing a percentage of already censored correspondence; censoring previously uncensored correspondence; inspecting packages and travelers' personal effects; reporting and analyzing censorship violations; and issuing monthly or bimonthly reports on troop morale[4] (Figure 2). Of particular interest to historians are morale reports and the comment sheets used to record censorship violations.

Censorship morale reports preserve soldiers' thoughts on such topics as Army food, mail service, military leaders, furlough and rotation policies, entertainment facilities, race relations, servicewomen, popular rumors, and enemy propaganda. The staff of the Office of the Theater Censor transcribed passages from soldiers' letters, identifying the correspondent not by name but by rank, military unit, and Army Post Office (APO). Comments and complaints reproduced in these reports were intended to reflect the soldiers' collective state of mind; they represent a range of opinion with an emphasis on the most commonly voiced ones. Censors classified comments as either favorable or unfavorable and noted changes in the volume of correspondence on a particular topic. Though crude, this method of analysis allowed military officials—and now allows scholars—to track shifts in soldiers' attitudes and concerns over the course of the war. Perhaps not surprising, censorship reports from the Pacific reveal that between November 1944 and war's end, servicemen's opinion of the Waacs who arrived in the theater in late summer 1944 steadily improved as the men became better acquainted with female soldiers. By contrast, soldiers' attitudes about "home affairs"—a broad category that included "political and economic situations, postwar plans, social and personal problems"—was harder to chart. Anger about strikes in defense factories, on the one hand,

FIGURE 2. Cover illustration from the U.S. Army's "Censorship Guide" for the Pacific Theater of Operations. Courtesy National Archives, College Park, Md.

and interest in the provisions of the GI Bill of Rights, on the other, produced fluctuations in soldiers' interest in and attitudes toward news from the home front.[6]

EVIDENCE OF MISCONDUCT

Censorship reports record not only popular opinion but also common violations of military law. Under the category "the enemy," for example, European theater morale reports examined "fraternization," or friendly relations between American servicemen and German civilians (typically young women) during combat and in the months between VE-Day and the Japanese surrender. Although some soldiers disapproved of such relationships, morale reports reveal that many other men were eager to explore new sexual opportunities. Despite the threat of imprisonment and steep fines, some even bragged about their conquests in letters home. One sergeant wrote, probably to a fellow soldier:

You should see my girl over here too, she sure is a honey. She is only 21 and she said she is sure she will like the U.S. when we are married and I take her back with me. As tho, after seeing these Nazis kill our boys off, I would be crazy enough to take her back with me even if I were not married. All the boys have German girls now and they sure are good. They will make good wives for the German boys after we leave them. They will be a lot smarter too.

The same morale report that reproduced the above passage also provides evidence of the mistreatment of German prisoners of war and of the looting and damaging of German homes by American soldiers. Both behaviors were violations of the Army's rules of land warfare.[7]

Pacific theater comment sheets and other censorship documents reveal that desecration of enemy dead was disturbingly widespread. In a letter to his mother, one young infantry lieutenant bragged:

```
                    C O N F I D E N T I A L

          ┌─────────────────────────────────────────────┬──────────────┐
          │        Mail Censorship                       │INDEX:        │
SUBJECT:  │  ATROCITIES   (CENSORSHIP) Mistreatment of   │Sect.   II    │
          │                           enemy personnel    │No.     8a    │
          └─────────────────────────────────────────────┴──────────────┘

       1. You are instructed to be on the alert for letters,
   packages or photographs that would show any evidence of
   atrocities or mistreatment by United States military person-
   nel toward enemy personnel.

       2. There have been instances where our personnel have at-
   tempted to send through the mails such items as enemy teeth,
   skulls, etc., as well as pictures of these items.

       3. No reference is to be made in letters or other commun-
   ications of such atrocities.

       4. No pictures must be allowed to pass that show United
   States personnel in familiar poses with native women.

       5. Pictures, the contents of which are obscene, should be
   confiscated.

       6. All types of material mentioned above should be for-
   warded to the Theater Censor.

       (k)  Reports of atrocities unless released by ap-
            propriate authority.
```

AUTHORITY:	TC 15 Par 9c3k 16 Feb 43	TC 66 Par 20k 12 May 43	WD	TC Ltr. 6 Oct 43	BC	USAFFE BIR 1-25 Par 3d

```
REFERENCES:  PHOTOS  V/8
             POW - reference to GENEVA CONVENTION I/29a
             RULES OF LAND WARFARE  I/29

                    C O N F I D E N T I A L
```

FIGURE 3. The U.S. Army's "Censorship Guide" for the Pacific Theater of Operations outlined the proper response to references to and photographs of atrocities in soldiers' letters home. It also advised censors to be on the lookout for body parts, such as gold teeth and polished skulls, in parcels. Courtesy National Archives, College Park, Md.

Say, next fight I get into I'll get enough gold teeth to make you a necklace. I had about 10 but lost them. The Japs have some good dental work. You see them lying around and just kick their teeth out. Some fellows have dozens. I think I'll get some and keep them and if I ever get married I'll have my old lady a ring made out of them."[8]

Another officer described the "souvenirs" collected by Marines on Guadalcanal, "A couple had Jap skulls they had boiled out. Others had small socks of gold tooth fillings. Bottles of pickled ears were reported and Jap occupation money was commoner than Aussie stuff."[9] Among items discovered by censors in soldiers' parcels was a polished skull with shells for eyes designed for use as an ashtray.[10] Such desecrations were so frequent that the "Censorship Guide" for the Pacific theater of operations included instructions for dealing with packages that contained skulls and similar trophies (Figure 3). Furthermore, in monthly operating reports, "Skulls"—later "Atrocities"—was one of thirteen categories of common violations enumerated. In January 1944, for example, censors found more mentions of such atrocities than of the results of enemy action.[11]

Circular Quay, Sydney.

BOTANIC GARDENS

BEER GARDEN — WHERE MIKE & I HAD A "BEER" BEFORE GOING TO THE ZOO!

THIS FERRY GOES TO THE ZOO

LUNA PARK FERRY

HARBOUR BRIDGE

FIGURE 4. This postcard was likely condemned by postal censors because it revealed the physical location of the soldier who sent it from Sydney, Australia to his family in the United States. Courtesy National Archives, College Park, Md.

PUZZLES AND CODES

The most common violation of censorship regulations was "intentional revealing of geographic location" (Figure 4). In June 1944, Pacific theater censors reported more than a thousand cases. At that time, no other category of censorship violation topped one hundred.[12] Rules preventing soldiers from disclosing their location were the most resented of all censorship regulations. Enforcing these restrictions was the postal censor's most difficult task, for many service personnel believed the prohibition to be both unfair and unnecessary.[13] Indeed even before heading overseas, many soldiers made preparations to flout this restriction by, for example, developing simple codes that would allow loved ones to follow troop movements (Figure 5). The word "apple" might represent Oro Bay in New Guinea, "banana" Port Moresby and so on. One problem with this strategy was that code keys were easy to misplace. For example, the wife of an Army Air Corps warrant officer lost the key to a code representing the months of the year and the numbers 1–30, presumably anticipating the date when her husband would complete his tour

of duty and return home on furlough. Censors discovered this scheme when the serviceman tried to send a copy of the key back to his wife with the information that "boomerang," or the month of July, would be significant.[14]

Censors were trained to identify simple codes—such as spelling out the name of a place with the first letter of each sentence in a paragraph. Though a more complex code might escape the censor's notice, it might also fail to communicate the sender's message to the intended recipient. For example, one infantry officer's effort to communicate through code seems to have produced domestic anxiety. In response to his wife's reply, the officer assured her that the "Zelma" mentioned in a previous letter "wasn't anyone. Just a name I used." He urged his wife to "get that letter out again and remember what we said we would do before I left. Study it close dear for it took a good many hours to write it." Another serviceman attempted to communicate his location through fictitious poker earnings and losses; this effort also backfired. The censor did not catch the coded message but neither did the soldier's wife, who worried about her husband's gambling. His follow-up letter attempted to clear up the

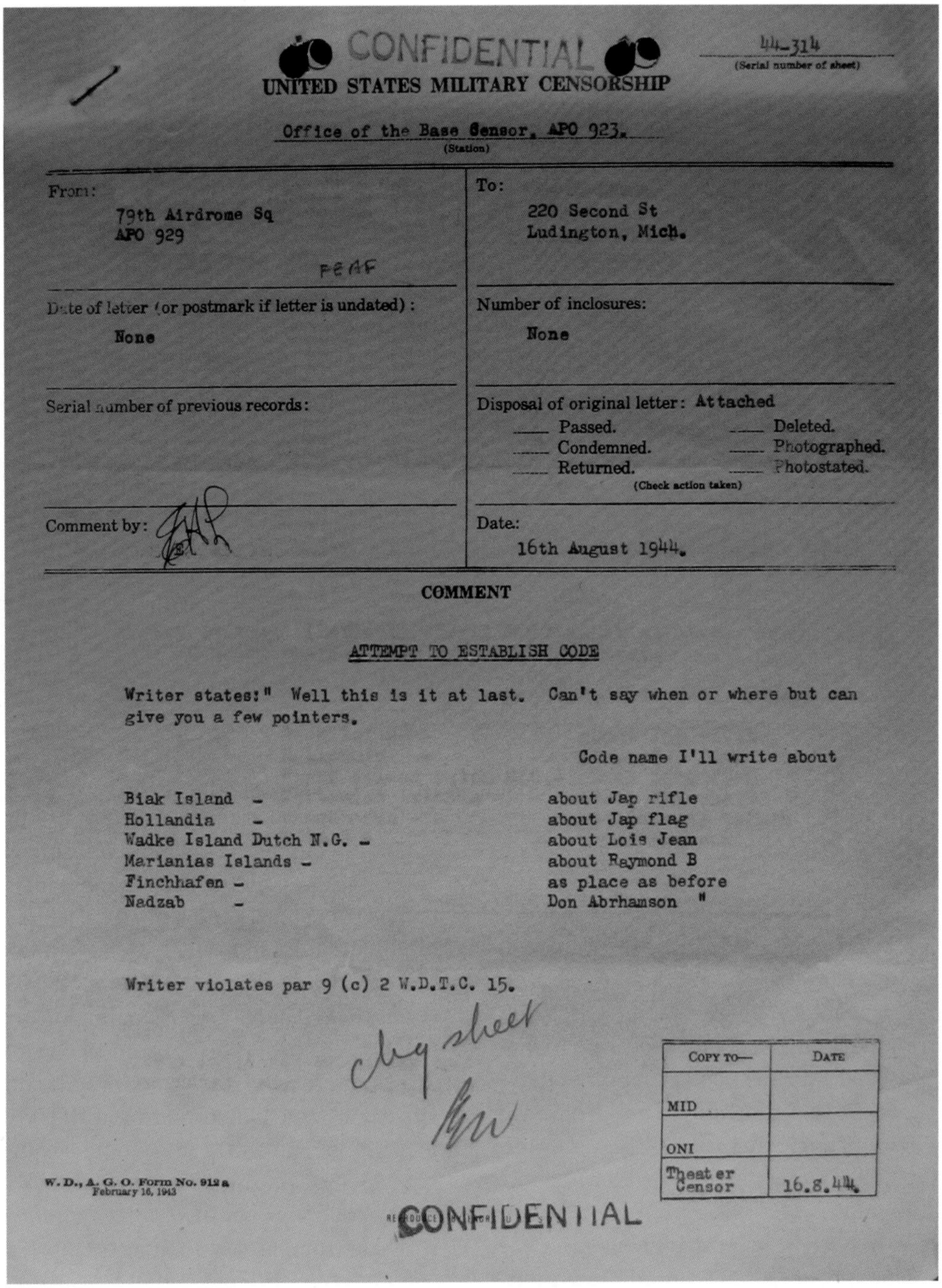

FIGURE 5. U.S. Army postal censors caught this soldier trying to establish a code that would let his loved ones know where he was stationed. Courtesy National Archives, College Park, Md.

misunderstanding by explaining that the numbers represented longitude and latitude; it also alerted censors to this violation of Army regulations.[15]

Service personnel were generally aware of the prohibition against disclosing their unit's geographical location and recognized the importance of preventing the enemy from learning about American troop movements. Many simply did not believe that security required them to keep friends and family in the dark. Indeed, a common complaint was that this restriction was nonsensical; American journalists and the Japanese military had already located the soldier's unit. Perhaps responding to this seeming irrationality, some soldiers regarded outsmarting the censor as something of a game. "I wish I could tell you where I am and just exactly what I am doing," one sergeant wrote, "but Censorship Regulations require strict abstinence from such remarks." As the censor noted, this sergeant then proceeded to do just what he knew he should not, which was to hint at where he was stationed.[16] Another soldier sent this "puzzel" to his mother: "[Y]ou know where Blanche lives. Well, take the first letter out of that and then . . . take the last letter out of where you live, and then take the third letter out of where Aunt used to live, then take the last six letters out of the place where we lived before we moved over by the park." The answer was Melbourne, Australia. Caught by the censor, this letter was returned to the sender for revision.[17]

CENSORSHIP AND THE SANCTITY OF MAIL

Even more than they resented restrictions on what they might write to their friends and loved ones, soldiers complained bitterly when censorship became an invasion of privacy. Although trained to respect the "sanctity of mail," many unit censors (unit officers assigned to censor the correspondence of enlisted personnel under their command) violated this precept.[18] Indeed some officers treated with derision personal concerns expressed in letters home. For example, in a gossipy letter to his wife, one Army Air Corps lieutenant wrote:

All of us dirty dogs get a kick out of censoring mail over here. We saw the one that broke the camels back today, though. Some guy wrote to his wife and just gave her hell because she was running around with some guy and wanting a divorce. Then he writes a letter to his girl friend and tells her how much he loves her. The only trouble was the damn fool put both letters in one envelope and addressed it to his wife. That ought to go over like a lead balloon.

In this case, one soldier's complicated love life and seeming hypocrisy was a source of amusement for the officers of the 90th Bombardment Group. Indeed, military intelligence caught another lieutenant recounting a slightly different version of this story in a letter of the same date.[19]

Although the hypocritical enlisted man might have merited scorn, in most cases, the object of a unit censor's ridicule was an earnest soldier seeking to maintain strained marital bonds by writing frequent love letters to his wife. For example, one lieutenant complained about an enlisted man named Nelson who wrote "at least one & sometimes 2 or 3 letters per day to his wife":

He goes on and on about my dearest beloved— How I would love to hold you in my arms and smell the sweet fragrance of your hair—Oh my loved one—how I miss you and so on for 30 pages. I would like to see Mrs. Nelson. I should think she would get awful tired of the same thing day in and day out. When we censor mail in the morning the guys always try to stack the deck so I'll get Nelson's letters to censor. Nelson always puts the following at the top of his letters No date or anything but:

'City of Love
Date of Wishes
9900 Hugs and
10,000 Kisses . . .'[20]

Another officer explained, "Most of our laughs come from censoring the mail." "However," he acknowledged, "we have to be very careful that the boys don't see us, as they wouldn't like the idea of our reading the mail and laughing about it."[21]

Censorship documents reveal that enlisted personnel were attuned to the problem of censors' failure to observe the "sanctity of mail": they overheard laughter; they recognized mocking references to personal affairs; they learned of comments improperly inserted by unit officers in enlisted men's letters; and they protested this intrusion. "Our most cherished thing we have is our mail," one corporal wrote. "With our own unit censors we cannot be too personal or write the things we wish to, but when peering into ones mails and gossiping about it is done, nobody can stand for that. At the [port of embarkation], we were told that we could write as we wished and nothing would be mentioned to anybody. This has definitely been breached." Sharing this corporal's distress, the non-commissioned officers of the 1059th Quartermaster Company produced a report on the problem, which they presented to their commanding officer. Although that officer dismissed the complaint, military intelligence officials took it seriously, for misconduct by unit censors might undermine morale and encourage evasions of censorship.[22]

Responding to real and perceived breaches of privacy, some soldiers censored not only strategic information but also private emotions. "If one or two of my letters have been cold and uninteresting," one sergeant wrote to a girl friend, "you can blame it on the censors. More than once I have heard cracks made about letters being written by the enlisted men that I didn't like. I feel that regardless of whom a GI writes to, that letter should not be 'cracked' about. That's my reason for the cold letter I mailed to you. I do hope you accept my reason." His seeming lack of ardor appears to have strained the relationship.[23] Other soldiers responded by curtailing their correspondence: "Darling, please forgive me for not writing for so long," one enlisted man wrote to explain his recent reticence, "but you see the officer who does the censoring in our battery talks quite a bit about what we write in our letters. I have seen him take a letter out and read the whole letter, out loud, to the other officers."[24]

Relationships between officers and enlisted men, the strains of war on marriage, the treatment of enemy soldiers and civilians, attitudes about censorship and mail service—all of these topics and more are illuminated by postal censorship documents. Indeed comment sheets and morale reports provide scholars with access to something lacking in most wartime correspondence—uncensored accounts of servicemen and -women's thoughts and experiences. These documents preserve what soldiers wanted to write and were prevented from communicating. They help us fill a gap in the historical record produced by military regulations and censors' excisions.

NOTES

1. Information Slip TFNY 1243, File: MID 322.12 W.A.A.C. 6–23–43 (6–11–43), Box 579, Army Intelligence Decimal Files, Entry 47B, Army Staff, RG 319, National Archives, College Park, Md. (hereafter NACP).

2. Mattie E. Treadwell, *The Women's Army Corps* (Washington, D. C.: Department of the Army, 1954), 201; Oveta Culp Hobby to Office of the Director of Administration, ASF (18 May 1943); J. M. Roamer to A. C. of S. G2 (22 May 1943); L. R. Forney to J. M. Roamer (3 June 1943; all in File: MID 322.12 W.A.A.C. thru 6–10–43, Box 579, Army Intelligence Decimal Files, Entry 47B, Army Staff, RG 319, NACP.

3. For more on the WAAC slander campaign, see Ann Pfau, *Miss Yourlovin: GIs, Gender, and Domesticity during World War II* (Columbia University Press, 2008), chap. 2, http://www .gutenberg-e.org/pfau/chapter2.html; Treadwell, *Women's Army Corps*, chap. 11; Leisa Meyer, *Creating GI Jane: Sexuality and Power in the Women's Army Corps during World War II* (New York: Columbia University Press, 1996), chap. 2.

4. Leo Taub, "History of Military Censorship in the European Theater of Operations, World War II, 1941–1945," Records of the Assistant Chief of Staff G-2, Histories, ETO, RG 498; "Censorship Guide, SWPA," Box 26, Entry 556, Theater Censor, USAFFE, RG 496; "History of Military Censorship in the SWPA," Box 40, Entry 558, Theater Censor, USAFFE, RG 496; all in NACP.

5. These documents have been preserved in Army administrative files at the National Archives in College Park, Maryland.

6. E. R. Thorpe, "The Censorship Survey of Morale, June 1943 to August 1945" (n.d.); "Censorship Survey of Morale," (November 1944–August 1945); both in Box T-1429, Theater Censor, G-2, SWPA, RG 496, NACP.

7. "Censorship Report on General Morale of Troops for Period 16–30 June 1945," File: 212 Morale, Box 41, Historical Division Administrative Files, 1942–June 1946, ETO, RG 498, NACP.

8. Comment Sheet TC-2155, File Comment Sheets, A–D, 1944, Box 21 (formerly T-1420), Summary of Censorship Violations, Theater Censor, G2, USAFFE, RG 496.

9. Comment Sheet 313, File: Comment Sheets, 1943, H–P, Box T-1419, Theater Censor, USAFFE, RG 496.

10. See Files 716 and 718, Box T-1410, General Records, 1944–1945, Theater Censor, G2, USAFFE, RG 496.

11. "Censorship Guide, SWPA," Box 26, Entry 556, Theater Censor, USAFFE; Office of the Base Censor, APO 923 to Theater Censor, Re: "Report for the month of January 1944" (7 February 1944), File: 319.1, Box T-1432, Theater Censor, AFPAC; both in RG 496, NACP.

12. "Statistical Report by Section, June 1944," File: 319.1, Box T-1432, Theater Censor, AFPAC, RG 496, NACP.

13. Supplement, "History of Military Censorship in the SWPA," Box 40, Entry 558, Theater Censor, USAFFE, RG 496; Research Unit, G-1, "Attitudes of a Cross Section of Enlisted Men in the South Pacific Area on Mail Service and Censorship," File: SPA-3, Box 1024, Research Division, Attitude Reports of Overseas Personnel 1942–1953, Entry 94, Office of the Secretary of Defense, RG 330; both in NACP.

14. Comment Sheet 44–100, File: Comment Sheets, 1944, R–Z, Box T-1420, Summaries of Censorship Violations ("Comment Sheets"), 1942–1944, Theater Censor, USAFFE, RG 496, NACP.

15. Comment Sheet TC-206, File: Comment Sheets TC-1 to TC-250, 1942, Box T-1418, Summaries of Censorship Violations ("Comment Sheets"), 1942–1944; Comment Sheet 44–278, File: 733, Box 1411, General Records, 1944–1945; both in Theater Censor, USAFFE, RG 496, NACP.

16. Comment Sheet TC-60, File: Comment Sheets TC-1 to TC-250 1942, Box T-1418, Summaries of Censorship Violations ("Comment Sheets"), 1942–1944, Theater Censor, USAFFE, RG 496, NACP.

17. Comment Sheet 692, File: Comment Sheets TC-651 to TC-840, 1942, Box T-1418, Summaries of Censorship Violation ("Comment Sheets"), 1942–1944, Theater Censor, USAFFE, RG 496, NACP.

18. Research Unit, G-1, "Attitudes of a Cross Section of Enlisted Men in the South Pacific Area on Mail Service and Censorship," File: SPA-3, Box 1024, Research Division, Attitude Reports of Overseas Personnel 1942–1953, Entry 94, Office of the Secretary of Defense, RG 330; "Censorship Guide, SWPA," Box 26, Entry 556, Theater Censor, USAFFE, RG 496; both in NACP.

19. Comment Sheets 45–91 and 45–89, File: 744, Box T-1412, General Records, 1944–1945, Theater Censor, USAFFE, RG 496, NACP.

20. Comment Sheet 375, File: Comment Sheets, 1944, R–Z, Box T-1420, Summaries of Censorship Violations ("Comment Sheets"), 1942–1944, Theater Censor, USAFFE, RG 496, NACP.

21. Comment Sheet 46, File: Comment Sheets 1943 HP, Box Box T-1419, Summaries of Censorship Violation ("Comment Sheets"), 1942–1944, Theater Censor, USAFFE, RG 496, NACP.

22. Comment Sheet 45, File: Comment Sheets 1943 H–P, Box T-1419, Summaries of Censorship Violation ("Comment Sheets"), 1942–1944, Theater Censor, USAFFE, RG 496, NACP.

23. Information Sheet 3173, File: Consolidated Morale Reports, X Army, Box G-1489, Censor Weekly Reports 1945, G2, AFPAC, RG 496, NACP.

24. Information Sheet 1360, File: XXIV Corps, 1 May–13 August 1945, Box G-1489, Censor Weekly Reports 1945, G2, AFPAC, RG 496, NACP.

BIBLIOGRAPHY

Meyer, Leisa. *Creating GI Jane: Sexuality and Power in the Women's Army Corps during World War II*. New York: Columbia University Press, 1996.

National Archives and Records Administration, Archival Collections: RG 319, Records of the Army Staff; RG 330, Records of the Office of the Secretary of Defense; RG 496, Records of the Southwest Pacific Area and U.S. Army Forces, Pacific; RG 498, Records of the European Theater of Operations, U.S. Army. College Park, Md.

Pfau, Ann. *Miss Yourlovin: GIs, Gender, and Domesticity during World War II*. New York: Columbia University Press, 2008.

Treadwell, Mattie E. *The Women's Army Corps*. Washington, D. C.: Department of the Army, 1954.

Introduction to the Fourth Symposium

The fourth annual postal history symposium, sponsored by the Smithsonian National Postal Museum, the American Philatelic Society, and the American Philatelic Research Library, was held in Bellefonte, Pennsylvania, at the American Philatelic Center on October 30 and November 1, 2009. The theme was "Post Office Reform," bringing together collectors of classic stamps with scholars, academicians, and public historians to examine these highly collectable cultural objects through the lens of the post office reforms that gave rise to them. The introduction of postage stamps in 1840 represented a complete overhaul in the organization and operating principles of the British Post Office. The subsequent rapid introduction of stamps to nearly every country in the world before the end of the nineteenth century is tangible evidence of the worldwide adoption of similar post office reforms.

The keynote address, "The Political Economy of Postal Reform in the Victorian Age," was delivered by Richard John, Ph.D., professor of history and adjunct professor of communication at the University of Illinois, Chicago, and can be read starting on page 3. There were twelve papers, seven of which are included here.

The first panel was on "Early Reform," and Larry Lyons presented his paper "America's First Carrier Service the U.S. City Despatch Post Government Carrier Service in New York August 16, 1842–November 28, 1846." Harvey Mirsky also discusses in his paper "The U.S. 1847 Issue: Stamps That Changed the System."

The second panel highlighted "Post Office Reformers," and three papers were presented. Diane DeBlois and Richard Dalton Harris, presented "The Sunday Mail Controversy Paves the Way of Postal Reform." David L. Straight, Washington University (St. Louis), presented his paper "Cheap Postage, A Tool for Social Reform." Rachel A. Moore, Clemson University, presented "From the Pulpit to the Post: Anti-clericalism and Communication in Orizaba, 1857–1867."

The third panel was on "Reform Icons and Collectibles," and Catherine J. Golden, Skidmore College, presented her paper "Why Is a Raven Like a Writing Desk?—Post Office Reform, Collectible Commodities, and Victorian Culture."

The fourth panel continued the discussion on "Postal Reform." Harry K. Charles, Jr., The Johns Hopkins University, presented "The 1895 Provisional and Bisect Postage Due Stamps: A Result of the Transfer of the Stamp Production to BEP."

The 1895 Provisional and Bisect Postage Due Stamps: A Result of the Transfer of Stamp Production to the BEP?

Harry K. Charles, Jr.

INTRODUCTION

There was a marked increase in the use of provisional and bisected postage due stamps on mail beginning in 1895. As is well documented in the case of the Jefferson, Iowa bisects,[1] the bisects were created due to a shortage of one-cent postage-due stamps. In other instances, both the one-cent and two-cent stamps seemed to be in short supply. Could these shortages have resulted from the 1893–94 transfer of postage stamp production from the American Bank Note Company (ABNCo) to the Bureau of Engraving and Printing?

In an article by Noll,[2] the controversy surrounding the awarding of the stamp production contract to the BEP rather than a Bank Note Company was well described. In his article Noll states, "And instead of accepting the offer of the established bank note printers, the Post Office Department accepted a bid from a printing establishment with almost no experience in postage stamp production and none of the rare but requisite gumming machines: the United States Bureau of Engraving and Printing . . ." This leads one to the belief that the BEP might have had trouble getting into full production (nominally three billion stamps were needed annually at the time), thus leading to stamp shortages. Even if the BEP could have generated sufficient supplies in Washington, DC, it did not mean that they were delivered efficiently and when needed to postmasters throughout the country.

Prior to the awarding of the stamp production contract to the BEP, the ABNCo was responsible for maintaining the requisite inventory necessary to fill the demands for stamps presented by the stamp agent of the Post Office Department. This stamp agent and his staff took care of filling orders from the various post offices, but keeping stamps available was the responsibility of the ABNCo. Thus, the BEP not only had to learn how to make stamps, but also how to build and maintain sufficient inventory to meet the Post Office demand. It should also be mentioned that the U.S. postal stamp agent (USPSA) and his staff originally resided at the ABNCo in New York. When the BEP took over the stamp printing, he was moved to Washington and his staff reduced. Thus, it is reasonable

FIGURE 1. An approved large die proof (J32P1) of the first two-cent bureau postage due stamp, dated August 11, 1894. This proof is signed by Kerr Craige, the Third Assistant Postmaster General. From the collection of Harry K. Charles, Jr.

to believe that the distribution of the newly printed BEP stamps might not have been as efficient as it was at the banknote company, especially in the beginning years.

The following sections trace the early postage due stamp production at the BEP, determine the remaining inventories of ABNCo dues, project the demand for postage due stamps in the 1894–1895 period, and examine the postmasters' response to shortages—the use of provisional and bisected postage due stamps.

BEP PRODUCES POSTAGE DUE STAMPS

The BEP began creating a new design for postage due stamps soon after its contract began on July 1, 1894. A die proof for the new two-cent postage-due stamp (Scott No. J32)[3] is shown in Figure 1. The two-cent value was engraved first because the two-cent banknote dues were in short supply as will be shown below. The BEP assigned the two-cent die, the number 50. The die was used to lay down Plate No. 34. A plate proof (on card) of Scott No. J32P4 is shown in Figure 2 illustrating the marginal markings and the plate number. It should be mentioned that while the card proof in Figure 2 appears claret in color, it fluoresces under long wavelength ultraviolet light, thus placing it amongst the vermilion shades (e.g. Scott No. J30), that also fluoresce under UV light.[4] A plate proof in deep claret was approved on July 14, 1894. The BEP sent the two-cent to press immediately, and it was issued on July 20, 1894. Note the die proof shown in Figure 1 was approved on August 11, 1894, by Third Assistant Postmaster General Kerr Craige. The approval date was almost a month after the plate proof was approved and three weeks after the stamps were issued.

The one-cent die was the next postage-due design prepared. It was assigned die number 56, and it was used to lay down Plate No. 57. A plate proof from Plate No. 57 was pulled and approved on August 11, 1894. The color of this plate proof sheet was deep carmine.

The ten-cent bureau due was issued on September 24, 1894. The plate for the ten-cent due was prepared from die number 55. A large die proof for the ten-cent value was approved on August 30, 1894, by Wesley R. Davis, the United States postage stamp agent. Kerr Craige also approved another copy of the ten-cent die proof on August 30th. Although the dies and plates for the three-cent, five-cent, thirty-cent, and fifty-cent values were prepared at about the same time, they were not issued until April 27, 1895, when supplies of these other values in postmasters' hands ran low. Die numbers and large die approval dates for the first bureau dues are given in Table 1. Many issues plagued the early production of the new bureau postage dues including the three-cent cracked die which necessitated the creation of a new die prior to plate production[5] (See Table 1). Bureaucratic delays and other administrative

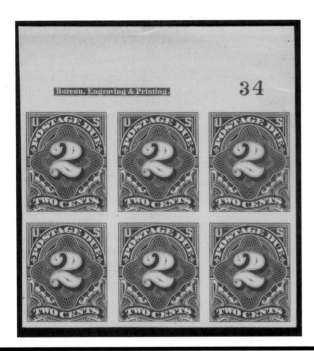

FIGURE 2. A plate proof on card (J32P4) of the two-cent small numeral postage due illustrating the original plate number (no. 34) and the marginal marking. From the collection of Harry K. Charles, Jr.

TABLE 1. Die Numbers and Approval, Hardening, and Issue Dates for the First Postage Dues Produced by the BEP

Scott No.	Value	Die No.	Die Approval	Die Hardening	Plate No.	Plate Certification	Issue Date
J31	1¢	56	8/11/1894[a]	8/10/1894[b]	57	8/11/1894	8/14/1894
J32	2¢	50	8/11/1894[a]	7/13/1894[b]	34	7/14/1894	7/20/1894
J32	3¢	54	[c]	8/18/1894[d]			
	3¢	64	8/23/1894[a]	8/28/1894	70	[f]	4/27/1895
J34	5¢	57	8/30/1894[a,e]	8/29/1894[b]	71	[f]	4/27/1895
J35	10¢	55	8/30/1894[a,e]	8/29/1894[b]	72	[f]	9/24/1894
J36	30¢	53	8/23/1894[a]	8/30/1894	73	[f]	4/27/1895
J37	50¢	61	9/1/1894[a,e]	9/4/1894	74	10/4/1894	4/27/1895

[a] Approved by 3rd Assistant Postmaster General, Kerr Craige

[b] Apparently hardened before official approval.

[c] Die Approval Information Unavailable.

[d] Die Cracked upon hardening. It was put in a clamp and used to make a transfer roll. The transfer roll had the raised crack line removed and then was used to lay down a new die—die 64. The complete story of the die crack is given by McIntire.

[e] Approved by Wesley R. Davis (U.S.P.S.A.).

[f] The exact dates are unavailable to this author, but they are likely to be within a few days of die hardening.

problems allowed stamps to go into production prior to their approval by the third assistant postmaster general and/or the U.S. postage stamp agent (See approval dates in Table 1 and the approval date on the signed proof in Figure 1).

INVENTORY AND DEMAND PROJECTIONS

In an article by Dickey,[6] a letter from the chief of the Bureau of Engraving and Printing, Claude M. Johnson, was quoted in which Johnson provided a forecast by denomination for the number of postage due stamps needed to be supplied by the BEP for fiscal year 1895 (beginning July 1, 1894). This forecast is shown in Column 2 of Table 2. For comparison, the actual shipment of postage due stamps by the ABNCo in fiscal year 1893 (July 1, 1892, to June 30, 1893) is given in Column 3 of Table 2.[7] This was the last full year's worth of data available to Johnson when he made his prediction in early 1894. It can be seen that the forecast by Johnson is essentially the 1893 fiscal year data with two notable exceptions, the estimates for the thirty-cent and fifty-cent postage-dues. These estimates were approximately six times higher for the thirty-cent dues and thirteen times higher for the fifty-cent dues. This was extremely optimistic since the thirty-cent and fifty-cent dues had averaged only about 6,800 and 2,100 respectively in the previous six years.[8]

Table 2 also contains the ABNCo large numeral postage-due shipment data for fiscal year 1894 (July 1, 1893, to June 30, 1894). It can be seen that although Johnson's forecast for total number of postage-due stamps is slightly greater than the actual totals in both FY 1893 and FY 1894, his estimate was over one-half million under the actual shipment of two-cent postage-dues in FY 1894. The ten-cent value estimate was almost 90,000 below the FY 1894 shipments, while the three-cent was slightly over 40,000 below the actual data for FY 1894.

Near the end of its contract, the ABNCo supplied the remaining stock of large numeral dues to the BEP so that it would have a supply of postage dues to begin the 1895 fiscal year (Table 3). The quantity supplied was 2,796,543 postage due stamps. This quantity, broken down by denomination, is shown in Column 2. The shipments of large-numeral postage-due stamps by the BEP to postmasters in fiscal year 1895 is given in Column 3. Column 4 indicates the difference or the remaining large-numeral postage-dues in the hands of the BEP. The BEP indicated that these remainders were scrapped in early calendar year 1895 to avoid "elaborate" daily inventory reports.

By comparing the data in Tables 2 and 3, it is quite clear that the ABNCo dues were insufficient to meet the demand. In fact, the 50,164 two-cent postage-dues represented only 0.76 percent of the estimated needed supply. This percentage equates to about 2.8 days, assuming a linear usage rate throughout the year. The one-cent supply was about fifteen percent of the estimated needed supply or fifty-five days worth, and the ten-cent large-numeral dues on hand could satisfy the demand for about sixty-seven days. Even the five-cent supply was only good for 306 days or about ten months. Only the thirty cent and fifty cent dues were in sufficient numbers to last multiple

TABLE 2. BEP Forecast of Postage Due Stamp Requirements for fiscal year 1895 and Shipment Records of Large Numeral Postage Dues for fiscal years 1893 and 1894

Value	Johnson's Forecast for Fiscal Year 1895	ABNCo Shipment in Fiscal Year 1893	ABNCo Shipment in Fiscal Year 1894
1¢	9,000,000	8,967,456	8,441,900
2¢	6,600,000	6,598,500	7,131,700
3¢	200,000	198,955	242,900
5¢	800,000	808,510	603,780
10¢	1,520,000	1,525,550	1,608,470
30¢	40,000	6,650	6,290
50¢	40,000	2,350	3,106
Total	18,200,000	18,101,950	18,038,146

TABLE 3. ABNCo Large Numeral Postage Dues Transferred to the BEP and Subsequently Distributed by the BEP during Fiscal Year 1895

Value	ABNCo Shipment[a]	BEP Distribution[b]	Difference
1¢	1,350,369	1,350,369	0
2¢	50,164	50,164	0
3¢	294,783	190,300	104,483
5¢	670,148	604,320	65,823
10¢	277,794	277,780	14
30¢	96,502	23,430	73,072
50¢	56,783	15,030	41,753
Total	2,796,543	2,511,393	285,150[c]

[a] Post Office Bill Book, June 30, 1879–March 30, 1895
[b] John N. Luff, *The Postage Stamps of the United States 1902 Edition*, Scott Stamp and Coin Company Limited, pp 245–352.
[c] Excess scraped.

years (14.5 years and 24.2 years respectively, based on actual usage in Fiscal Year 1893. See Table 2).

If the distribution of the new one-cent and two-cent bureau dues were delayed by even a few days, there would have certainly been shortages of both values, especially the two-cent dues. Shortages of the one-cent and two-cent values were more likely to have occurred in the western states and in the rural areas of the east, but occasionally even large cities were without these values of postage dues. Also, it is believed that both the five-cent and ten-cent values experienced localized shortages.

POSTMASTERS' SOLUTION

With any shortage of a particular denomination stamp, the postmaster or postal clerk would simply make up the required value using other denomination stamps. For example, a two-cent shortage could be made up with two ones, a five-cent shortage with one two- and one three-cent stamp, and so forth. In the 1895 period, however, a shortage of one-cent postage-due stamps would be problematic (no half-cent postage dues existed), unless the postmaster could substitute a regular issue one-cent stamp in its place. Although common practice later on, postmasters of the 1890s were reluctant to just use a regular-issue stamp unless it was suitably marked "Postage Due" or "Due 1" or some other variant of "due" to indicate its intended function. Examples of this approach will be described below in the section on provisionals.

Another and perhaps more common approach was to bisect a higher value stamp to achieve the desired value. For example, a two-cent postage-due stamp could be bisected to make two one-cent stamps. Since these bisected stamps (vertical, horizontal, or diagonals) were still postage-dues, most postmasters did not feel the need to add a "due" marking to the bisected stamp. The notable exception to this was the Jefferson, Iowa, bisects of October 1895, where each half of a vertically bisected two-cent postage due stamp was overprinted with "Due 1 cent." Clinton, Iowa, also used diagonal bisects hand stamped with "Due 1" in early 1896. These and other bisects will be described below in the section on bisects.

It should be noted that both provisional use of regular-issue stamps as postage-dues and postage-due bisects have been used to address more than a shortage of one-cent stamps. Provisionals have been used for local two-cent postage-due shortages and ten-cent bisects have addressed a shortage of five-cent postage-due stamps. Much later in the 1920s and 1930s when half-cent postage rates were

in effect, both provisional due markings on half-cent regular-issue stamps and bisected one-cent postage-due stamps exist. A detailed discussion of these usages is beyond the scope of this article. Similarly, some postmasters printed (stamped) "**Due __ cents**" diagonally on regular issue stamps. The blank was filled in with a manuscript number—thus, any value postage-due stamp shortage could be addressed.

DETROIT PROVISIONALS

As mentioned above, provisionals (or locals) typically resulted when a postmaster had a shortage of a commonly used stamp. In such instances, the postmaster would overprint the required value (and intended function) on another stamp, and use these overprinted stamps until his replacement stamps (stamps in shortage) arrived. The most famous provisionals of the 1895 era were those created by the postmaster of Detroit. In the early summer of 1895, the Detroit postmaster found himself short of both one-cent and two-cent postage-due stamps. Thus, he stamped in black "DUE 1" on Scott No. 246, one-cent ultramarine regular-issue stamps and "DUE 2" on Scott No. 250, two-cent carmine regular-issue stamps, both issued in 1894.

A cover illustrating a pair of "Due 1" overprints used to address a two-cent deficiency is shown in Figure 3. It has a Detroit circular date stamp (CDS) with the date June 23, 1895. A similar cover with the two-cent carmine "Due 2" is illustrated in Figure 4. Again, this cover has a Detroit CDS, dated June 23, 1895, at 11:30 am. June 23, 1895, is supposed to be the first day of provisional use according to an accompanying note dated 1947 by Fred R. Schmalzreidt, a noted Detroit philatelic dealer of the time who claimed they were used from June 23 to June 26, 1895. Brower[9] states that they were used from June 21 to June 27, 1895. Brower's dates were taken from Luff's book published in 1902. If the note from Schmalzreidt is correct, then both of these covers were postmarked on the first day of provisional use in Detroit. Both covers have identical envelopes with crossed out return addresses. The cover with the pair of one-cent dues is addressed to Hubel and Company Electricians, City, while the cover with the two-cent due is addressed to Ernst Stolze, Buhl Block, City. Figure 5 illustrates another Detroit provisional pair used to pay two-cents postage due. The stamps are Scott No. 264 and were issued in April 1895. They are blue in color rather than the ultramarine of the stamps (Scott No. 246) on the cover shown in Figure 3. This cover was addressed to Geo. N. Rice, 186 East High Dr., City, and

FIGURE 3. Detroit Provisional. "Due 1" overprinted on a pair of regular one-cent ultramarine stamps (Scott No. 246). The pair satisfied the need for a two-cent postage due stamp. Cover is dated June 23, 1895. From the collection of Harry K. Charles, Jr.

FIGURE 4. Detroit Provisional. "Due 2" overprinted on a regular issue two-cent carmine stamp (Scott No. 250). The stamp satisfied the need for a two-cent postage due. Cover is dated June 23, 1895. From the collection of Harry K. Charles, Jr.

was dated on June 26, 1895. Special thanks are given to Dr. Clark Yarbrough for allowing the author to scan and illustrate this cover.

A fourth Detroit provisional usage is also known. It is an oversize envelope containing four two-cent carmine "DUE 2" stamps to pay the eight-cent postage-due

assessment. Unlike the "2¢ due" above this "DUE 2" was overprinted on Scott No. 267, two-cent carmine regular issue of 1895. The "Due 8¢" cover in question was also mailed with two-cents postage paid by a Scott No. 267. Thus, this oversize cover has five Scott No 267 stamps, four with the "DUE 2" overprint and one plain. The plain

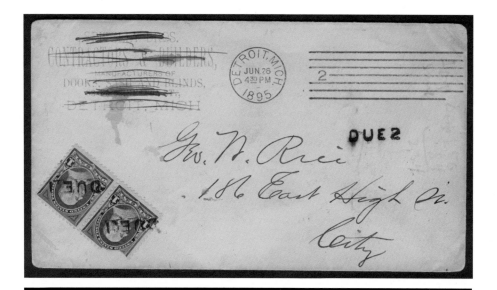

FIGURE 5. Detroit Provisional. "Due 1" overprinted on a pair of regular one-cent blue stamps (Scott No., 264). Cover is dated June 26, 1895. From the collection of Clarke Yarbrough. Reprinted with permission.

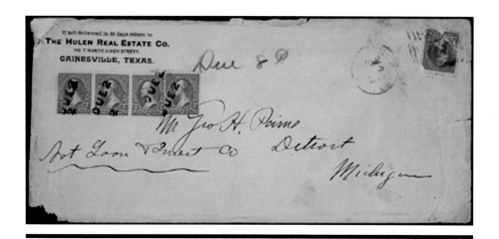

FIGURE 6. Detroit Provisional. "DUE 2" overprinted on four two-cent carmine regular issue stamps (Scott No. 267). The legal size envelope was also mailed in 1895 with the same two-cent carmine stamp. The four "Due 2" stamps made up the eight-cent-due penalty. Image supplied courtesy of HR Harmer Nutmeg.

Scott No. 267 is tied with an 1895 Gainesville TX duplex cancel, while the "postage dues" are not tied. "Due 8¢" is written in blue crayon on the envelope. This cover is illustrated in Figure 6. The image of this cover was kindly provided by the auction house HR Harmer Nutmeg. It appeared in the Nutmeg Mail auction 184 of June 9, 2009 (Lot No. 3172).[10] Additional details of this and other provisional usages are given in Table 4.

J23 BISECTS

As described above, bisects or bisected stamps typically resulted when a postmaster had a shortage of a particular stamp value and the value was small enough that he could not make the needed value up from lower value stamps. The classic case is, of course, a shortage in one-cent stamps which comprise the lowest value in the stamp

TABLE 4. Postage Due Provisionals of the 1895 Period

Stamp (Value)	Town/City	State	Number Known	Date	Provisional Type
— (1-cent)	Winside	NE	2	July 20, 1895 August 6, 1895	"Due 1" surcharged on 1¢ regular issue newspaper wrappers
246 (1-cent)	Detroit	MI	1	June 23, 1895	"Due 1" hand stamped on 1¢ ultramarine regular issue stamp. Pair on cover to make up 2¢ deficiency
250 (2-cent)	Detroit	MI	1	June 23, 1895	"Due 2" hand stamped on 2¢ carmine regular issue stamp. Single on cover
267 (2-cent)	Detroit	MI	1	1895	"DUE 2" hand stamped on 2¢ carmine regular issue stamp. Four overprints for "Due 8¢"
264 (1-cent)	Detroit	MI	1	June 26, 1895	"Due 1" hand stamped on 1¢ blue regular issue stamp. Pair on cover to make up 2¢ deficiency

series. A shortage of one-cent postage-due stamps is apparently exactly what happened in Thompson, New York, in October 1895; Jefferson, Iowa, in October 1895; and Clinton, Iowa, in early 1896.

The Thompson, New York, one-cent postage-due shortage led to covers with J23 bisects, and the Iowa shortages led to covers with J39 bisects. There are four known J23 bisect covers from Thompson, New York, fourteen covers[11,12] with the J39 bisect from Jefferson, Iowa, and three covers containing a J39 bisect from Clinton, Iowa.

The four Thompson, New York, J23 bisects are all addressed to Mr. H.W. Tilford, Thompson Mills, Wash. Co., N. Y., and bear the date Oct. 3, 1895. The J23 bisects are right side diagonals on two covers and one vertical (left half) and one horizontal (bottom half) bisect on the other two covers. The diagonal bisects are cut from the upper left to the lower right, probably indicating that the postmaster or clerk who did the bisecting was right-handed (the left hand was used to hold the stamp and the straight edge while the right hand wielded the knife or razor). The author has not seen a J23 bisect cut from the upper right to the lower left. Since the known J23 bisects include two diagonals (right sides), the lower part of a horizontal bisect, and the left side of a vertical bisect, thus, it is conceivable that at least four more covers exist with J23 bisects from Thompson, NY. Table 5 lists these and other bisect postage-due uses during the 1895 period.

J39 BISECT

The bisect covers of Jefferson, Iowa (Scott No. J39), are a legend and a source of philatelic controversy. J39

TABLE 5. Postage Due Bisects of the 1895 Period

Stamp (Value)	Town/City	State	Number Known	Date	Bisect Type
J23 (2-cent)	Thompson	NY	4	Oct. 2, 1898	Diagonal (2), Vertical and Horizontal
J39 (2-cent)	Jefferson	IA	14	Oct. 11–13, 1895	Vertical, "Due I cent" overprint
J39 (2-cent)	Clinton	IA	3	Feb. 14, 1896	Diagonal, "Due 1" Hand stamp
J39 (2-cent)	Riverside	MA	1	unknown[a]	Unknown
— (2¢ and 10¢)	Brooklyn	NY	1	Dec 1895	2¢ and 10¢ each bisected to make 6¢ Postage Due
— (2-cent)	North Branch	NJ	1	June 1895	Diagonal
— (2-cent)	Warwick	RI	8	August 7, 1897 Sept 11, 1897	Vertical

[a] Assumed to be during the 1895 Period

FIGURE 7. J39 bisect cover by the postmaster of Jefferson. This cover is Pauley No. 5.[11] From the collection of Harry K. Charles, Jr.

bisected postage-due stamps were created by Postmaster Fred R. McCarthy of Jefferson, Iowa. He told the story of the bisects in an affidavit dated February 12, 1898. McCarty's two-page affidavit is currently mounted on two large album pages in the Miller Collection (owned by the New York Public Library) with a Scott No. W301 wrapper (Pauley No. 1 See below) mounted on the bottom of the second page. A full-color copy of the McCarthy affidavit is shown in Trepel's excellent publication documenting the Miller Collection.

There are several key points in the McCarthy affidavit:

1. His supply of one-cent postage-dues was exhausted and his previously requisitioned one-cent postage-dues were in transit.
2. He had a local printer print "Due 1 cent" in black on a few vertically bisected two-cent postage-due stamps.
3. He had 30 of these vertically bisected two-cent postage-due stamps overprinted, and he used, according to his recollection, somewhere between eighteen and twenty.
4. Once the replacement one-cent stamps arrived from Washington, no additional bisects were used.

Both Trepel and the Scott Catalogue (in a footnote following the J39 listing) agree that a total of twenty bisects were used. There is some controversy over the sequence of printing and bisecting between Trepel and Scott and the McCarthy affidavit. Both Trepel and the Scott Catalogue say the stamps were overprinted first and then bisected (which seems more logical for ease of handling and printing) while McCarthy's statement implies that they were bisected first and then overprinted ("... had a local printer print 'Postage Due 1 cent' on a few half two-cent postage due stamps ..."). A more detailed discussion of this and other factors surrounding the J39 bisect has been given by Charles and Swed.

A typical example of the J39 bisect is shown in Figure 7. This cover is one of the thirteen examples known to Pauley and reported by him in his excellent series of articles on the J39 bisect. Pauley's articles spanned almost eighteen years from January 1973 to November 1990, during which time he tried to discover and report details of all the known J39 bisects on cover. In fact, the cover shown in Figure 7, addressed to George Herring, is No. 5 in Pauley's arbitrary numbering scheme. This cover is franked with a copy of Scott No. 265, one-cent blue Franklin, which was machine cancelled (Oct 11, 1895 at 2 PM in Chicago). At the left side of the cover the words "POSTAGE DUE" were stamped in purple ink followed by a manuscript "1¢" in red ink. The word "FORWARDED" was stamped in purple ink followed by a manuscript "to Jefferson" in red ink. Also, a line in red ink is drawn through Waucoma. The left half bisect is tied by a Jefferson, Iowa circular date stamp (CDS) dated Oct 13, 1895 at 11 AM.

The cover is back stamped with a partially legible Waucoma, Iowa CDS dated OCT 12, 1895 in purple ink. A purple star in a circle appears next to the Waucoma CDS. Also, the cover is back stamped with a small portion

FIGURE 8. J39 bisect cover by the postmaster of Jefferson. This cover is now cover No. 14 in Pauley's arbitrary numbering scheme. From the collection of Harry K. Charles, Jr.

of the Jefferson, Iowa CDS and a circular bars cork cancel in black ink. Further details of this cover and the other twelve covers reported by Pauley are given in notes 11 and 12, as well as in the other articles by Pauley.

There is a fourteenth cover which was unknown to Pauley, at least through November 1990, the date of his last article. This cover is shown in Figure 8. As can be seen from Figure 8, the cover is very similar to the one in Figure 7 except it is addressed to J. M. Alexander, rather than George Herring. Only Pauley covers Nos. 1, 2, and 13 were distinctly different. Cover No. 1 is on a wrapper in the Miller Collection; cover No. 2 is addressed to a different town and resides in the Pauley Collection; and cover No. 13 is again a wrapper addressed to Benjamin Jacques, the same addressee as on Pauley No. 1. It is believed that all the Jefferson, Iowa, bisect covers except Pauley's No. 1, No. 2, and No. 13 were prepared by E. B. Stillman and sent to himself, his family, and co-workers, employees, or friends. Apparently, Stillman recognized the importance of the locally prepared bisect and prepared covers which would require McCarthy to use one of his newly created "rarities." In fact, it is likely that the newspaper print shop run by Stillman's sons did the printing. The back stamps on cover "No. 14" (maintaining Pauley's numbering scheme) are almost identical to the markings on the back of the cover shown in Figure 7 (Pauley No. 5). The back stamps on the cover in Figure 7 are described in the text above.

There are five Stillmans, four Herrings, two Jacques, and, now, two Alexanders among the Jefferson, Iowa, covers. There are also eight left-side bisects and only six rights. As can be easily seen in Figures 7 and 8 , the commonly referred to "Due 1 cent" was actually "Due I cent" apparently due to the typesetter's error in selecting an upper case "I" instead of a "1" in the type face used.[13] The black surcharge is approximately 2.5 mm high by 17 mm long.

A Clinton, Iowa, bisect is shown in Figure 9, again through the courtesy of Dr. Clarke Yarbrough. The diagonal bisect is hand-stamped "Due 1" in black ink and was cancelled on February 14, 1896, Valentine's Day.

SUMMARY

United States stamp production was unexpectedly transferred from the American Bank Note Company to the Bureau of Engraving and Printing in 1894. The BEP had little experience with stamp production and lacked critical machinery necessary to produce postage stamps. Up to 1894, it was strictly focused on producing currency. Although the BEP mounted Herculean efforts, there were many start-up problems including maintaining inventory, lack of distribution infrastructure, and general issues associated with the learning curve of a new business. Such problems led to spot stamp shortages especially in small towns and rural areas. In certain instances, postmasters

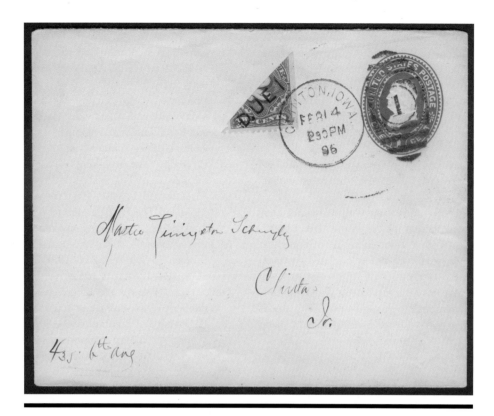

FIGURE 9. J39 Clinton, Iowa, diagonal postage due bisect. "Due 1" is hand stamped in black ink. This is one of the three known examples. From the collection of Clarke Yarbrough. Reprinted with permission.

responded to these shortages by creating bisects and provisionals. The postage-due bisects and provisionals of the 1895 period were created in direct response to the lack of certain postage-due values. Being few in number,[14] these postage-due varieties represent some of the scarcest and least-known United States stamp usages and are worthy of further study.

NOTES

1. R. Trepel with K. Lawrence, *Rarity Revealed: The Benjamin K. Miller Collection*. Published by the Smithsonian and the New York Public Library, 2006, p.162.

2. Frank Noll, "Postage and Progressivism: Political Ideology and the Start of Postage Stamp Production at the Bureau of Engraving in Printing 1893–1894" Winton M. Blount Symposium on Postal History, November 3–4, 2006, pp 1–26. http://www.postalmuseum.si.edu/symposium2006/papers.html PDF.

3. Scott Numbers can be found in the *Scott Specialized Catalogue* by the Scott Publishing Company, PO Box 828, Sidney, Ohio 45365-0828.

4. Plate No. 34 was only used to make Scott No. J30 stamps according to Durland. J30 is the vermilion shade and it fluoresces under long wavelength UV light. The plate proof in Figure 2 fluoresces although it is clearly claret in color. Much controversy still remains over the colors of the first issue Bureau dues, but the current thinking is that most values of the early Bureau dues were printed using both fluorescent and nonfluorescent inks.

5. Walter A. McIntire, "United States Postage Due Stamps, The Broken 3¢ Die-Series of 1894," *The Bureau Specialist*, Volume XXXVI, No. 4 April 1965, pp 124–126.

6. Budd Dickey, "The Beginning of Postage Stamp Production by the Bureau of Engraving and Printing," *The United States Specialist*, Vol. 55, No. 11, November 1984, pp 487–493.

7. John N. Luff, *The Postage Stamps of the United States*, Scott Stamp and Coin Company, New York, New York, 1902, pp 245–252.

8. Warren R. Bower, "Puzzles in (the) 1894 ABN Transfer of its Postage Dues to (the) BEP" *The United States Specialist*, Vol. 56 No. 4, April 1985, pp 153–156.

9. Warren R. Bower, "The 1895 Bisected J23 Dues of Thomson, New York," *The United States Specialist*, Vol. 54, No. 2, February 1983, pp 88–89.

10. Nutmeg Stamp Sales, "Comprehensive Mail Auction 184, United States, British Commonwealth and Worldwide Selected Stamps, Postal History and Premium Graded Stamps", Tuesday, June 9, 2009 Bethel, Connecticut, Lot No. 3172 page 34.

11. Harry K. Charles, Jr. and Robert C. Swed "Thirteen and Counting: Reflections on the Scott J39 Bisect Covers of 1895," *The United States Specialist*, Volume 80, No. 9, September 2009, pp 410–419.

12. James A. Pauley, Jr., "The J39 Bisect-Example Number 13," *The United States Specialist*, Volume 61, No. 11, November 1990, pp 617–622.

13. A recent private communication with William Sihler (September 14, 2009) suggests that the "I" in the "Due I cent" overprint was indeed a "1" from a non-lining set of numerals in the Oldstyle No. 7 (Monotype) or a closely related typeface which was in use during the 1890s.

14. It is estimated that less than fifty covers containing bisects and provisionals as described in this study exist. This study lists a total of thirty-eight uses with the bisect stamped covers totaling thirty-one.

BIBLIOGRAPHY

Bower, Warrant R. "The 1895 Bisected J23 Dues of Thomson, New York." *The United States Specialist*, 54(2):88–89. February 1983.

———. "Puzzles in 1894 ABN Transfer of its Postage Dues to BEP." *The United States Specialist*, 56(4):153–156. April, 1985.

Charles, Harry K. Jr., and Robert C. Swed. "Thirteen and Counting: Reflections on the Scott J39 Bisect Covers of 1895." *The United States Specialist*, 80(9):410–419. September 2009.

"Comprehensive Mail Auction 184: United States British Commonwealth and Worldwide Selected Stamps, Postal History and Premium Graded Stamps." Lot No. 3172, p 34. Bethel, Conn: Nutmeg Stamp Sales, June 9, 2009.

Dickey, Budd. "The Beginning of Postage Stamp Production by the Bureau of Engraving and Printing." *The United States Specialist*, 55(11):487–493. November 1984.

Luff, John N. *The Postage Stamps of the United States.* New York: Scott Stamp and Coin Company, 1902.

McIntire, Walter A. "United States Postage Due Stamps: The Broken 3¢ Die-Series of 1894." *The Bureau Specialist*, 36(4):124–126. April 1965.

Noll, Frank. "Postage and Progressivism: Political Ideology and the Start of the Postage Stamp Production at the Bureau of Engraving and Printing 1893–1894." Paper presented at the Winton M. Blount Symposium on Postal History, November 3–4, 2006. http://www.postalmuseum.si.edu/symposium 2006/abstracts.html#Noll.

Pauley, James A. Jr. "The J39 Bisect-Example Number 13." *The United States Specialist*, 61(11):617–622. November 1990.

Scott 2010 Specialized Catalogue of United States Stamps. 88th ed. Sidney, Oh.: Scott Publishing Co., 2009.

Trepel, Scott R. *Rarity Revealed: The Benjamin K. Miller Collection.* Washington, D. C.: Smithsonian National Postal Museum, 2006.

Sunday Mail Controversy, Postal Reform, and Mail Transportation

Diane DeBlois and Robert Dalton Harris

INTRODUCTION

The Sunday Mail controversies of 1810–1817 and 1828–1831 were the first broad-based initiatives of the American public to influence federal policy for what was perceived as moral good.[1] The forms of protest used—hundreds of petitions and scores of memorials to Congress—introduced tools of advocacy that proponents of postal reform would use to good advantage in the 1840s. In these political terms, the Sunday Mail conflict presaged the 1845 postal reform.

But the rejection by Congress of the anti-Sabbatarian protest in favor of Sunday Mails reveals confidence in some 'first principles' of the United States postal system—the primacy of a 'line of posts' that should not be interrupted, and the aim of transporting the mail along with passengers wherever possible. The Postal Reform Act of 1845 confirmed that celerity, certainty, and security were the fundamental aims of the Post Office Department and signaled a change from stage coach to railroad—both for personal mobility and for the transportation of the mail.

JOHNSON'S REPORTS ON SUNDAY MAILS

The postal service was the one arm of the federal government with intimate connections to all Americans—so it had enormous political potential.[2]

Consider Richard Mentor Johnson of Kentucky's extraordinarily active campaign for the vice presidency. He first angled for Andrew Jackson's ticket in the 1832 election but withdrew when it was clear Martin Van Buren was the favorite. For the 1836 election, Van Buren was the clear Democratic choice for president, but several others were jockeying for the second position. The Democratic national convention was held in Baltimore, May 20–22 1835, and Johnson followers had at least three campaign bandanas to wave in his favor—each reprinting one of his Sunday Mail reports.[3] One Boston and two Baltimore publishers exactly reproduced the texts on silk—Henry Bowen for Jared Austin, Boston: *Johnson's Report on Sunday Mails. In Congress, March 4, 1830*; James Lovegrove, Baltimore: *Report of the committee of the Senate of the United States to whom was referred the several memorials on the subject of the transportation of the mails on the Sabbath, or the First Day of the Week: Made January 20, 1829*; William Wooddy, Baltimore: *Report of the Committee of the Senate of the United States, With which the Senate concurred, January 20, 1829*. American political bandanas had been introduced during Andrew Jackson's 1824 campaign, and versions of Johnson's reports printed on muslin appeared during the 1832 campaign.[4]

Johnson had defended the transportation and distribution of mail on Sunday as chairman of the Senate Committee on Post Office and Post Roads in 1829 and then as chairman of the House Committee on the Post Office and Post Roads in 1830. For his political campaigning these reports were also reprinted on paper,[5] even in a handy pocket-size 1834 edition to reach a broader readership.[6] The two reports were also reprinted as part of an 1833 campaign biography.[7]

Ely Moore, the 'friend of labor,'[8] publicly endorsed Johnson in 1833, claiming that, in protecting the mails from being stopped on Sundays, "He has proved himself the friend of pure religion, by guarding it against a contaminating alliance with politics." He predicted that the Johnson reports would continue to be read and admired, "when the edicts of kings and emperors, and the creeds of councils, shall have been swept from the memory of man."[9]

Clearly, a great deal of political capital was invested in Sunday Mails. But what did this controversy have to do with the postal reform of 1845?

Johnson had two strong arguments FOR Sunday Mails: the separation of church and state; and expediency. To religionists he said, in effect, you do not want the federal government telling you when or how to observe the Sabbath.[10] Look to the state governments for any protection of religious observance (where also resides, although he did not say, the power of incorporation for transportation contractors).

For Johnson, transporting the mails, "should be regarded simply as a question of expediency," and government should leave decisions over the post office to, "the legal discretions of the postmaster general." Underlying this argument was a postal understanding that mail transportation was a matter of design optimized by fixed schedules and smooth flow.

MAILS ON STAGE COACHES AND POSTAL REFORM

The structure of the postal network that Johnson's reports protected owed much to Abraham Bradley's long tenure as first assistant postmaster general (1793–1829) but was formalized under his replacement, Selah R. Hobbie (1829–1851, 1853, 1854).

The four-horse post coach—big enough for passengers and mail and newspapers—had been the vehicle of choice for mail on the major post routes (Figure 1). The

FIGURE 1. A 'Troy' stage coach, illustration from a version of Johnson's 1830 report printed on silk by William Wooddy of Baltimore, presumably for the 1835 Democratic Convention. From the collection of the authors.

advent of railroads signaled changes in the design of the system (Figure 2) which were reflected in portions of the Reform Law of March 3, 1845 that are often overlooked. The introduction of the Star Route system of contract lettings,[11] and the statutory provision for railroads as mail's ultimate vehicle, were part of postal reform.

Section 18: And be it further enacted, That it shall be the duty of the Postmaster General in all future lettings of contracts for the transportation of the mail, to let the same, in every case, to the lowest bidder, tendering sufficient guaranties for faithful performance, without other reference to the mode of such transportation than may be necessary to provide for the due celerity, certainty, and security of such transportation; nor shall any new contractor hereafter be required to purchase out, or take at a valuation, the stock of vehicles of any previous contractor for the same route.

This relieved the post office from securing the capitalization of private stage contractors and freed up the possibility of dropping stage coach contracts where they weren't needed.

Section 19: And be it further enacted, That to insure, as far as may be practicable, an equal and just rate of compensation, according to the service performed, among the several railroad companies in the United States, for the transportation of the mail, it shall be the duty of the Postmaster General to arrange and divide the railroad routes, including those in which the service is partly by railroad and partly by steamboats, into three classes according to the size of the mails, the speed with which they are conveyed, and the importance of the service; and it shall be lawful for him to contract for conveying the mail with any such railroad company, either with or without advertising for such contract.

On a stage coach, mail was equated with baggage; on a railway train or steamboat it became freight. Mail traveling as freight increased the margin between price and cost, which permitted reduction of postage rates.

In 1845, the postmaster general pointed out that the star route contract provisions had already saved the department $250,000. "The most expensive as well as the

Comparative table of mail service for the last eight years, exhibiting the aggregate extent and cost for each year.

Years ending	Length of routes.	On horse.		In coaches.		By railroad and steamboat.		Total annual transportation.	Total annual cost.	Remarks.
		Transportation.	Cost.	Transportation.	Cost.	Transportation.	Cost.			
	Miles.	Miles.		Miles.		Miles.		Miles.		
June 30, 1837	141,242	11,999,282	*$861,578	18,804,700	*$1,726,600	1,793,024	*$307,444	32,597,006	*$2,895,622	
June 30, 1838	134,818	11,573,918	831,028	20,651,432	1,896,157	2,356,852	404,123	34,582,202	3,131,308	
June 30, 1839	133,999	11,447,147	864,569	19,653,676	1,900,451	3,396,055	520,602	34,496,878	3,285,622	
June 30, 1840	155,739	12,182,445	789,668	20,299,278	1,911,855	3,889,053	595,353	36,370,776	3,296,876	
June 30, 1841	155,026	12,088,862	781,897	18,961,213	1,791,635	3,946,450	585,843	34,996,525	3,159,375	
June 30, 1842	149,732	11,644,693	737,605	18,767,036	1,700,510	4,424,262	649,681	34,835,991	3,087,796	Add expenses of mail agencies incident to the railroad and steamboat service, and payable under the head of transportation, $22,987.
June 30, 1843	142,295	11,146,229	602,064	18,414,174	1,611,568	5,692,402	733,687	35,252,805	2,947,319	Add agenc's as above $28,965.
June 30, 1844	144,687	11,373,952	577,703	18,288,317	1,558,842	5,747,355	802,006	35,409,624	2,938,551	Add agenc's as above $29,744.

* These amounts are estimated; they do not appear in any report.

S. R. HOBBIE,
First Assistant Postmaster General.

FIGURE 2. Tabulation by mode of scheduled transportation facilities used by the Post Office 1837 to 1844. Comparison of mail transportation by miles and cost for horse, coach and railroad/steamboat, prepared by Selah R. Hobbie, First Assistant Postmaster General, from the 1844 annual report. From the collection of the authors.

most important branch of business under control of [the post office] department is the transportation of the mails." And he stressed the paramount importance of maintaining connections between routes.[12] However, a contract should go, not to the lowest bid in dollars and cents, but to the lowest bid that gave a mode of conveyance adequate for the mails in respect to the certainty, security, and celerity of their transportation—without regard for passenger accommodation. The cheapest was often not robust enough to embrace changes in the flow of mail.

These arguments had first been made by Abraham Bradley in 1831 in defense of more expensive stage coach contracts where necessary. The amount of money critics claimed was squandered was the same quarter of a million dollars saved in 1845.

> An offer to carry in stages, on the same terms, is always considered as a better bid than one to carry in sulkies or on horseback; on the ground that such vehicles are a public convenience and deserve encouragement; also, that on great mail routes, in case of a double or triple mail, they can carry the whole of it on, and in the hope that passengers will increase; and in the end, by joining the two objects, it can be conveyed at less expense. And in many cases it has been judged good policy to accept a stage bid, if one-third higher than the demand for a horse-mail. This preference ought not to be extended to routes where the mail is small, for the establishment of stages is not a constitutional or legitimate object of the General Government.[13]

LINES OF POST AND SUNDAY MAIL CONTROVERSY 1810–1817

Celerity, certainty, and security (abbreviated within the Post Office Department to three asterisks, or stars, hence Star Routes) were by the postal reform law an explicit guarantee of uninterrupted 'lines' of posts.

The colonial line of posts ran on Sundays—the explanatory paragraph on Herman Moll's *New and Exact Map of the Dominions of the King of Great Britain on the Continent of North America* of 1715 has the Western Post setting out from Philadelphia on a Friday and arriving in New York on Sunday night, to continue eastward on Monday morning to meet the Boston post at Saybrook on Thursday (the Boston post having begun at the northern end of the line of posts which extended, at that time,

to Charleston in the south from Piscataway, Maine, in the north).

Moreover, the line of posts of the new republic ran on Sundays. The Abraham Bradley map of 1796 (Figure 3) shows the line of mails across a full weekly schedule, with Sunday as day one. This line connected all the major centers, and such laws that existed with penalties for travel on Sundays were local and scattershot and did not affect the cities.[14]

In 1802, the Post Office Department reported on its 1799 experiment with capitalizing a government line of stages between Philadelphia and Baltimore—revealing a new appreciation of the expense involved and a wish to continue to rely on private enterprise.[15] Where a stage line was in place, it made sense to give it a mail contract—if only to discourage carriage of letters out of the mails. Giving a mail contract to a start-up stage line helped promote the country's expansion, though such a line had to count on passenger fares not mail contract fees for profit.[16] In 1800, Distributing Post Offices were introduced.[17] Lines of posts, which had been established between the principal centers of population, were modified to provide for lines of posts among the distribution post offices (which were not necessarily centers of population, see Figure 4)—and the postal system became a network. Inasmuch as the principal mails traveled with the celerity of four-horse stage coaches, upon regular schedules and safeguarded by accompanying passengers, the arrival of the mail was a dramatic event on any day of the week.

The postmaster at the Distributing Office of Washington, Pennsylvania, was in 1808 excommunicated by his Presbyterian synod for receiving and dispatching the mail on a Sunday and, as a courtesy to his patrons which was strongly recommended by the postmaster general, opening his office on that day. In response to the furor over this particular and other comparable situations, a new postal law of 1810 required the receiving of mail AND the opening of the post office on every day of the week that the mail arrived.

> . . . every postmaster shall keep an office, in which one or more persons shall attend on every day on which a mail, or bag, or other packet or parcel of letters, shall arrive, by land or water, as well as on other days, at such hours as the postmaster general shall direct for performing the duties thereof; and it shall be the duty of the postmaster, at all reasonable hours, on every day of the week, to deliver, on demand, any letter, paper, or packet,

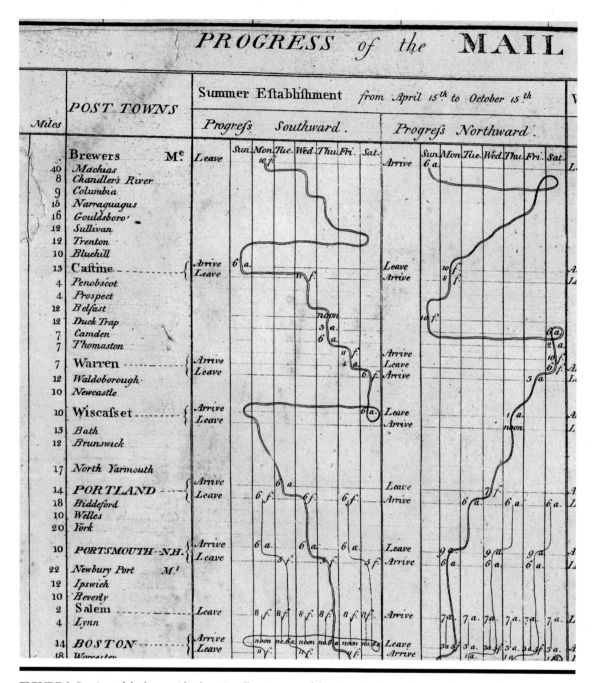

FIGURE 3. Portion of the key to Abraham Bradley, *A Map of the United States. Exhibiting Post Roads and Distances*, 1796, showing the summer routing across seven days of the week for mail between the northernmost point in Maine and Boston. Courtesy Smithsonian National Postal Museum (Accession 0.293996.1).

to the person entitled to or authorized to receive the same.[18]

The Post Office Department had been mindful—from the beginning—that handling the mails on a Sunday might be a hardship and had mitigated the law with a regulation that the post office be kept open for just an hour after the mail arrived and was sorted on a Sunday and that such an hour could be after the local religious services.[19]

Policy was to avoid mails arriving in places on a Sunday "except where the omission to transport on that day would break chains of communications."[20]

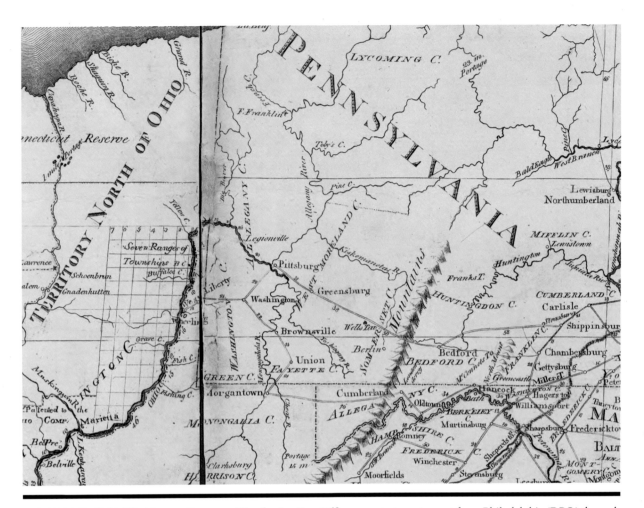

FIGURE 4. In 1804, Washington, Pa. was a Distributing Post Office on a stage route west from Philadelphia (DPO) through Chambersburg (DPO), Bedford, Greensburg, and Pittsburgh (DPO 1820) en route to Morgantown, Va. (DPO). Another state route west from Baltimore (DPO) passed through Hagerstown, Md. (DPO) and Cumberland, Md. (DPO 1817). Mail from Washington, Pa. was batched to other Distributing Post Offices, particularly at Marietta on the Ohio River. Portion of Bradley map of 1796. Courtesy Smithsonian National Postal Museum (Accession 0.293996.1).

Still, Congress was bombarded with memorials asking that the new law be changed to prevent the mails from traveling and from being distributed on Sundays. But the Senate, in 1815, cited the mitigating instructions and voted to keep things as they were.[21] Congressional arguments centered on the need to keep major communication lines unbroken—during war but also for the continuity and expansion of the postal system.[22]

For an appreciation of the expanded system, a retrospective of the post office establishment as of 1811 displays, at six different times, the development of the measures of the department since its beginnings in 1792 (Figure 5). Not only are the numbers of post offices and the lengths of post roads shown but also a differentiation in terms of modes according to the miles of weekly transportation.[23]

In the beginning, the miles of weekly transportation of the mails carried in sulkies and on horseback were ten percent less than that carried on stages but, by 1811, had grown to exceed stage mail by about thirty percent. This signifies the penetration of mail into the hinterland—ahead of roads and passenger traffic suitable for coaching. The total transportation of the mails divided by the length of the post roads at each interval indicates a systematic frequency of about 1.4 mails a week—a constant of the system—an integration of modes and frequency which

A View of the Progress of the Post-Office Department.

The Several Periods referred to.	Number of Post-Offices.	Length of the Post Roads.	Weekly transportation of the mail in Stages.	Weekly transportation of the mail in Sulkies and on Horse-back.	Weekly transportation of the mails.	Yearly transportation of the mails.
		Miles.	Miles.	Miles.	Miles.	Miles,
March 3, 1793.	195	5,642	8,567	7,662	16,229	845,468
March 3, 1797.	539	14,226	14,902	19,708	34,610	1,799,720
March 3, 1801.	957	21,840	24,490	34,380	58,870	3,057,964
January 24, 1803.	1,283	24,458	30,172	37,228	67,400	3,504,800
January 1807.	1,848	31,616	41,528	45,000	86,528	4,499,456
February 10, 1811.	2,403	37,035	46,380	61,171	107,551	5,592,652
Increase of the last ten years.	1,446	15,195	21,890	26,791	48,681	2,534,688

The yearly transportation of the mail in Stages, amounts to . . . . 2,411,760 miles.

ditto in Sulkies and on Horse-back, ... 3,180,892 do.

Total . . . . 5,592,652 do.

Averaging one Office to 15 1-2 miles of Post-Road.

FIGURE 5. Over ten years, the postal system grew 12-fold in number of offices, and 7-fold in miles of post road and mail transportation. Table from the Postal Guide of 1811. From the collection of the authors.

persisted throughout Bradley's tenure in managing the mail transportation contracts.

POSTAL ROUTE REORGANIZATION AND SUNDAY MAIL CONTROVERSY 1828–1831

In 1825, Abraham Bradley was asked to reorganize postal transportation because of duplication of facilities and parallel routes.[24] The result was reallocation and an extension of stage routes, with a fresh spate of their dramatic presence in remote places. Opposition to travel on Sundays had intensified in western New York after the Erie Canal insinuated a potent arm of secular commercialism.[25] An opposition Pioneer Line of stages was formed in 1828 to operate between Albany and Niagara Falls through Buffalo six days a week and to observe Sunday rest. The "Old Line"—which had the mail contract—not only operated seven days a week, it also ran at night, employed experienced drivers, gave their horses the best care, and maintained a faster service.[26] Apparently to remain solvent this "Pioneer Line" of stages broke their own protocols,[27]

failing completely by 1831: a line of stages had to run continually to serve a commercial market.[28] Stopping on Sunday, for capitalist ventures like transportation lines, meant 'idle money.'

Yet a second wave of anti-Sunday Mail protest flooded Congress with memorials.[29] Most argued from religious conviction, but many men who signed even these petitions were involved in business.

An 1829 petition circulated to all members of Congress by a group of New Yorkers, which included a former mayor and John Jay's son (Figure 6), argued from a commercial rather than a religious viewpoint—and proposed that closing the postal system for a day would "save no inconsiderable part of the expenses of the Post-Office Department".[30]

On the contrary, the 1829 annual report (Bradley's last, before Hobbie)[31] showed that running post coaches six days a week instead of seven would not save any money. In his experience, if a failure of a day's mail occurred, and its bulk was added to the next day's mail, the total was enough to fill a mail coach so that passengers were excluded. Indeed, if Sunday mails were stopped,

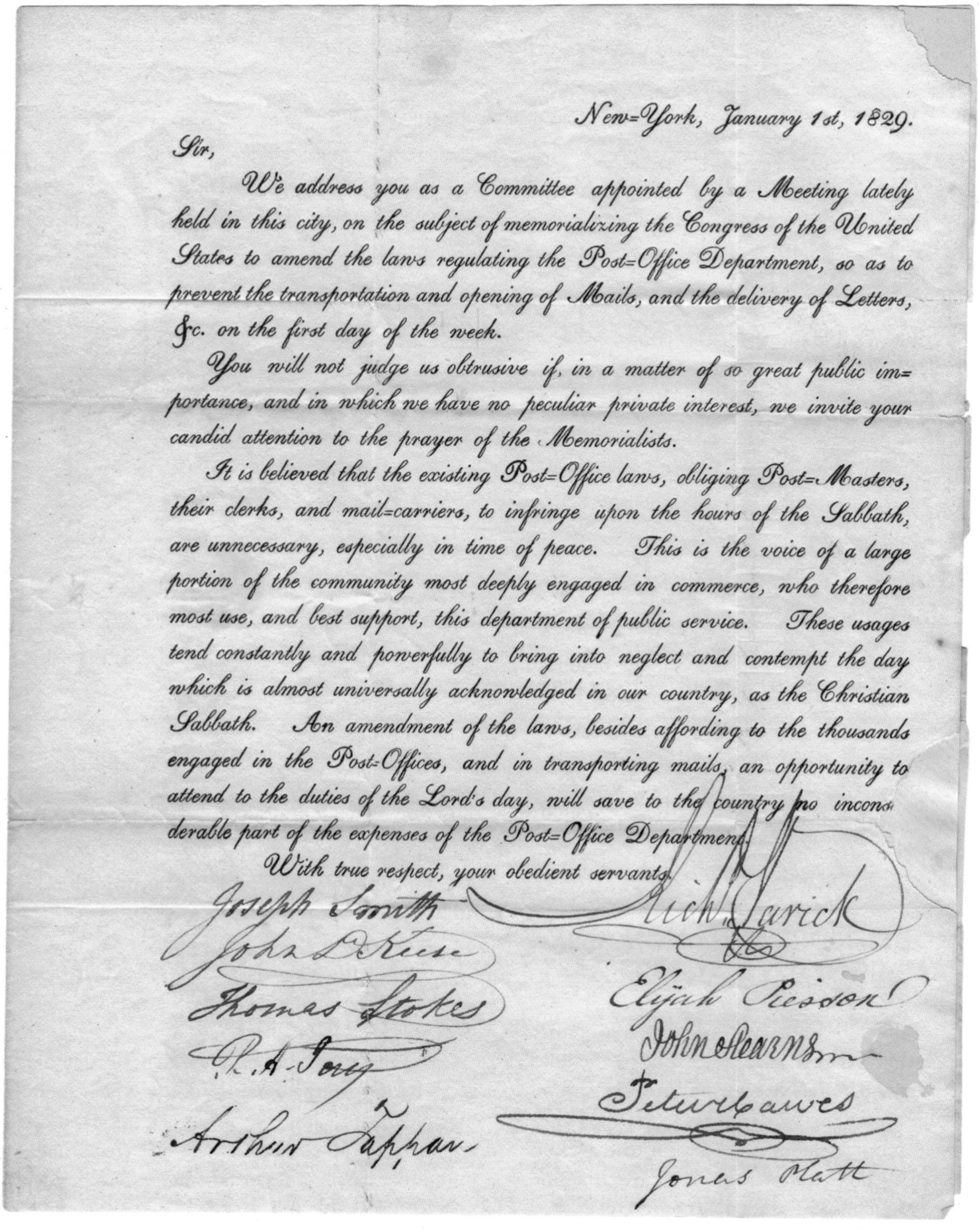

New=York, January 1st, 1829.

Sir,

We address you as a Committee appointed by a Meeting lately held in this city, on the subject of memorializing the Congress of the United States to amend the laws regulating the Post=Office Department, so as to prevent the transportation and opening of Mails, and the delivery of Letters, &c. on the first day of the week.

You will not judge us obtrusive if, in a matter of so great public importance, and in which we have no peculiar private interest, we invite your candid attention to the prayer of the Memorialists.

It is believed that the existing Post=Office laws, obliging Post=Masters, their clerks, and mail=carriers, to infringe upon the hours of the Sabbath, are unnecessary, especially in time of peace. This is the voice of a large portion of the community most deeply engaged in commerce, who therefore most use, and best support, this department of public service. These usages tend constantly and powerfully to bring into neglect and contempt the day which is almost universally acknowledged in our country, as the Christian Sabbath. An amendment of the laws, besides affording to the thousands engaged in the Post=Offices, and in transporting mails, an opportunity to attend to the duties of the Lord's day, will save to the country no incon-siderable part of the expenses of the Post=Office Department.

With true respect, your obedient servants,

Joseph Smith
John D Keese
Thomas Stokes
P. A. Jay
Arthur Tappan
Rich.d Varick
Elijah Pierson
John Stearns
Peter Hawes
Jonas Platt

FIGURE 6. Printed circular petition January 1, 1829, signed by ten men and mailed to members of Congress. John D. Keese was a merchant; Thomas Stokes was a trustee of Columbian College; Peter Augustus Jay, son of John Jay, was president of New York Hospital; Arthur Tappan was a silk importer who helped found the *New York Journal of Commerce*; Richard Varick was formerly mayor of New York; Elijah Pierson was a merchant turned religious reformer; Peter Hawes was secretary of the Washington Fire Insurance Company; Jonas Platt was formerly a judge of the Supreme Court. From the collection of the authors.

while purely passenger stage lines continued, and private expresses could be used, the Department could lose between 50,000 and 100,000 dollars annually.

Outlined also were all the specific delays that would occur if the transportation of the mail were interrupted on Sundays, and the possible consequences of that—primarily the possibility of private expresses delivering sensitive market information ahead of the mails so that there could be an uneven speculative advantage.

Although he did not use the terms, Bradley showed that a regular interruption of the mails would cause a systematic breakdown, and expediency would be compromised.

An 1832 compilation represents the post office immediately after a fifty percent increase in mail transportation, inaugurated not only upon a manifold of new post roads but also in terms of facilities (mode and frequency) on post roads already in operation. This report was made in anticipation of lettings in New England and New York for the next year which would, altogether, practically double the postal establishment in miles of mail transportation since Hobbie took over from Bradley. (The implication is that Hobbie completed the system reforms begun by Bradley; certainly he was, by 1832, in command of more ways to measure the system.[32])

With respect to Bradley's compilation in 1811, not only is there a new mode of transportation—steamboats—but also a geographic distribution state by state. In the southern section the stage and horse mails serve equally, while in the northeastern section the stage mails range between three and ten times the horse mails. This inequality is paralleled by an average weekly frequency in the southern section of 1.4 mails per week to 2.6 mails per week in the northeastern section. The picture in the south in 1832 looks very much like the system as a whole in 1811. Systematic progress in terms of frequency and mode favored the northeast.

Moreover, in respect to the steamboats, a high proportion serve in the south and southeast although New York has the largest steamboat service over all, even considering that such contracts were made in conjunction with stage mails because of seasonal navigation.

The rapid expansion of the system was expensive in the short term but eventually demonstrated that postal revenues are an elastic function of transportation expenditures.

POSTAL REFORM AND BEYOND

The above picture of the system in 1832 (Figure 7) was the climax of a postal design serviced by stage coaches as the principal vehicle. Railroads immediately thereafter dominated contract negotiations. They were larger corporations whose refuge was within the states and whose local capital and clientele resisted blandishments to serve postal schedules. Nonetheless, they had been brought to serve postal design (Figure 8). Postal reform regularized railroad contract protocol.

What did the system look like in the period after postal reform? In 1860, in addition to the statistics by state, the modes are now designated: "not specified"—which are the Star Routes; "in coach;" "in steamboat;" and "by railroad."[33] Beginning in 1852, not only are statistics given for the length of postal routes but also their allocation to the various modes of transportation, by state—modal frequencies that provide a nuanced view of postal design.

In 1860 the south and west show a 'primitive' organization of the posts, represented by a frequency of about 1.5 mails per week, dominated by the Star Routes which serve most of their post route miles. In New York and New England, the average weekly transportation frequency is 6.1, almost double the modal frequency of coaching system-wide.

Railroads now constitute the majority of transportation dollars and miles of transportation by mode, averaging almost ten trips per week, but operate only the trunk lines on not a very high proportion of miles of routes served. In some cases, as in Ohio and Illinois where there are practically no miles of transportation by rail or steamboat, the coach miles are high with respect to the unspecified modes. In Massachusetts, however, the majority of the post route miles are by railroad.

Fifteen years after postal reform, thirty years after Johnson's report, and after sixty years of networking, the postal system is still fitted to the exigent means of transportation.

CONCLUSION

What happened to Johnson at that 1835 Democratic convention in Baltimore? Well, he was nominated to the Jacksonian ticket of Martin Van Buren. He faced competition from three other candidates in the 1836 election and did not receive a majority of the electoral college votes—so that he was our nation's first, and only, vice president to have been elected by the senate. He was also the first vice-presidential candidate to use broad-based and inventive canvassing—elevating 'pamphleteering' to a new level. He was wise to capitalize on the national exposure of his role in defending Sunday Mails.

The length of post roads in the United States was, on the 1st of July last, exclusive of those established by the law of the last session of Congress, 104,467 miles, viz:

States.	Miles.	States.	Miles.
In Maine	3,170	In North Carolina	6,465
New Hampshire	2,270	South Carolina	3,948
Vermont	2,337	Georgia	4,171
Massachusetts	4,657	Florida	731
Rhode Island	448	Louisiana	1,076
Connecticut	2,500	Mississippi	2,074
New York	12,306	Alabama	3,430
New Jersey	1,883	Tennessee	5,478
Pennsylvania	9,783	Arkansas	1,939
Delaware	424	Missouri	1,522
Maryland	1,953	Illinois	3,276
Michigan	940	Indiana	4,445
Ohio	8,060		
Kentucky	5,629	Making together, as above,	104,467
Virginia	9,542		

Over these roads, the annual transportation of the mail was, on the 1st of July, 1832:

States.	In stages. Miles.	In steamboats. Miles.	On horseback and in sulkeys. Miles.	Total. Miles.
In Maine	527,017	3,328	211,068	741,413
New Hampshire	524,352	-	96,774	621,126
Vermont	596,538	-	82,160	678,698
Massachusetts	1,387,780	23,712	137,953	1,549,445
Rhode Island	108,212	-	13,572	121,784
Connecticut	507,075	-	154,416	661,491
New York	2,889,124	96,735	681,495	3,667,354
New Jersey	494,482	-	96,368	590,850
Pennsylvania	2,351,184	-	600,891	2,952,075
Delaware	92,674	-	11,024	103,698
Maryland	579,448	58,380	151,588	789,416
Michigan	108,136	-	43,912	152,048
Ohio	1,181,909	47,150	510,926	1,739,985
Kentucky	575,604	45,000	510,496	1,131,100
Virginia	1,136,250	88,500	706,782	1,931,532
North Carolina	786,775	15,288	386,308	1,188,371
South Carolina	613,882	-	246,064	859,946
Georgia	282,598	-	374,236	656,834
Florida	14,560	-	48,808	63,368
Louisiana	48,516	3,848	121,212	173,576
Mississippi	78,002	-	211,496	289,498
Alabama	412,090	96,360	255,580	764,030
Tennessee	440,445	-	365,144	805,589
Arkansas	-	-	193,076	193,076
Missouri	79,508	-	116,792	196,300
Illinois	210,314	-	183,170	393,484
Indiana	196,268	21,000	391,666	608,934
Total	16,222,743	499,301	6,902,977	23,625,021

FIGURE 7. Geographic distribution of postal transportation facilities in 1832. Assistant Postmaster General Hobbie's statistics for the 1832 annual report. From the collection of the authors.

A.

Table of mail service for the year ended June 30, 1860, as exhibited by the state of the arrangements at the close of the year.

[The entire service and pay are set down to the State under which it is numbered, though extending into other States, instead of being divided among the States in which each portion of it lies.]

States and Territories.	Length of routes.	ANNUAL TRANSPORTATION AND COST.								Total annual transportation by mode not specified.	Total annual transportation by coach.	Total annual transportation by steamboat.	Total annual transportation by railroad.	Total annual transportation.	Total annual cost.
		Mode not specified.		In coach.		In steamboat.		By railroad.							
	Miles.	*Miles.*	*Dollars.*	*Miles.*	*Dollars.*	*Miles.*	*Dollars.*	*Miles.*	*Dollars.*	*Miles.*	*Miles.*	*Miles.*	*Miles.*	*Miles.*	*Dollars.*
Maine	4,416	1,923	19,218	1,999	38,668	....	....	494	48,693	458,068	699,660	....	415,740	1,573,468	106,579
New Hampshire	1,780	714	6,861	577	6,570	60	829	429	36,750	183,300	167,128	18,720	371,904	741,052	51,010
Vermont	2,221	385	4,236	1,347	14,697	....	....	489	56,956	98,514	433,420	....	320,268	852,202	75,889
Massachusetts	2,722	561	9,432	624	12,539	240	7,250	1,297	153,835	223,262	259,974	140,400	1,396,590	2,020,226	183,056
Rhode Island	363	138	2,199	88	1,152	28	800	109	14,255	52,208	35,152	17,472	126,984	231,816	18,406
Connecticut	1,063	475	10,619	483	9,136	260	10,000	745	84,248	203,164	230,620	162,240	737,100	1,333,124	114,003
New York	10,265	2,858	33,308	4,358	78,896	168	6,963	2,881	334,025	697,946	1,687,244	98,652	3,948,578	6,432,420	453,122
New Jersey	2,137	379	4,442	1,270	16,298	33	3,138	455	62,206	85,228	434,616	28,080	536,376	1,084,300	86,084
Pennsylvania	13,010	6,759	74,683	4,448	77,920	85	4,636	1,718	166,830	1,289,600	1,550,310	53,040	1,646,969	4,539,919	324,069
Delaware	536	160	2,231	263	6,581	....	....	113	13,683	38,372	94,068	....	127,296	259,636	22,495
Maryland	2,942	1,660	30,364	439	12,718	....	....	843	*189,058	241,986	165,360	....	1,232,276	1,639,622	232,140
Ohio	12,855	7,235	70,263	2,032	48,096	187	6,500	3,401	414,346	1,094,440	718,548	78,312	3,140,676	5,031,976	539,205
Virginia	13,745	10,802	121,056	946	28,453	637	46,905	1,360	199,014	2,121,472	338,894	371,658	1,032,896	3,864,920	395,488
North Carolina	9,081	7,549	73,316	752	20,953	132	3,468	648	89,100	1,239,406	355,919	48,984	550,066	2,194,375	186,837
South Carolina	5,498	4,087	42,134	182	4,630	175	2,612	1,054	162,368	615,995	53,170	27,590	1,172,734	1,869,489	211,744
Georgia	6,741	4,595	62,137	530	14,317	332	15,000	1,284	183,933	886,106	200,409	69,056	1,113,653	2,269,224	275,387
Florida	4,330	1,853	30,421	475	33,239	1,860	121,800	142	13,187	292,026	213,114	270,248	101,902	877,290	198,647
Michigan	6,840	4,129	41,207	1,049	18,342	725	10,478	937	111,245	584,688	396,916	102,500	1,070,028	2,154,132	181,272
Indiana	7,969	5,811	57,167	640	11,114	....	....	1,509	186,437	884,702	199,576	....	1,491,938	2,576,216	254,718
Illinois	10,297	5,416	65,270	2,190	55,062	100	3,419	2,591	254,975	925,444	713,882	31,200	3,112,824	4,783,350	378,726
Wisconsin	6,434	4,665	59,415	802	9,704	60	600	907	74,887	862,831	155,584	21,840	934,596	1,974,851	189,907
Iowa	8,232	4,775	57,911	2,938	104,108	140	7,020	379	20,868	777,998	1,208,172	242,892	394,715	3,228,693	558,716
Missouri	14,484	8,757	93,812	4,628	353,939	659	59,750	440	51,215	469,334	328,510	232,752	....	1,030,596	117,255
Minnesota	5,358	3,407	53,093	1,578	41,162	373	23,000	....	....	792,090	1,034,950	318,852	....	325,832	258,899
Kentucky	8,282	4,892	44,990	2,120	198,912	952	†55,705	318	29,292					2,471,724	

* The Baltimore, Wilmington, and Philadelphia Railroad, is under a Maryland number.
† This includes steamboat service from Louisville to Cincinnati.

FIGURE 8. 1860 Postal transportation facilities—the national system before the rupture of war. Chart from 1860 annual report. From the collection of the authors.

Sunday post office hours, of course, did disappear, beginning in 1910.[34] The Distributing Post Office system disappeared, beginning in 1859 (replaced, during the Civil War, by Railway Post Office distribution). But the 'expediency' argument—that a postal system needed to grow according to its own internal laws of transportation arrangements—held, and accommodated many postal reforms.

NOTES

1. See Richard R. John, "The Invasion of the Sacred", a chapter in *Spreading the News: The American Postal System from Franklin to Morse*, Harvard University Press 1995; and Wayne E. Fuller, *Morality and the Mail in Nineteenth-Century America*, University of Illinois Press 2003, chapters 1, 2, 3.

2. When President Andrew Jackson elevated the position of postmaster general to a cabinet post after his 1828 election, political clout increased—see Dorothy Ganfield Fowler, *The Cabinet Politician*, Columbia University 1943.

3. Few contemporaries believed Johnson actually wrote his reports. Since they show such a nuanced appreciation of the postal system, Johnson's friend Amos Kendall was suspected, although Leland Winfield Meyer's biography *The Life and Times of Col. Richard Mentor Johnson of Kentucky* (Columbia University 1932) gamely claimed Johnson was clever enough to have been the sole author. William Stickney's 1872 *Autobiography of Amos Kendall* (New York 1872), however, had revealed that Kendall believed the writing "doubtless attributable" to the Baptist preacher and postal clerk Obadiah Brown with whom Johnson boarded in Washington.

4. We have recorded six different versions of Johnson's Sunday Mails report printed on either muslin or silk—to be used as neckscarves, handkerchiefs, or attached to walking sticks, buggy whips, etc. Given the address changes of Henry Bowen (see the compilation in Patricia Fenn and Alfred P. Malpa, *Rewards of Merit*, Ephemera Society 1994), the printer of the four versions of the 1830 report, it is likely that two different layouts on muslin were produced in 1830 at the very beginning of Johnson's campaign to run in the election of 1832, and then a second muslin version with the same typesetting as one of the above but

with a different heading and a note that it would be "sold by David Kimball" was produced for the 1836 election campaign. It is our belief that all three silk versions, one by Bowen with the cut of a mail coach, and two by Baltimore printers (one with the same cut), were produced specifically for the 1835 convention in Baltimore.

5. Joel H. Silbey in *The American Party Battle: Election Campaign Pamphlets 1826–1876* (Harvard 1999) explained: "Pamphlets were a major part of a panoply of campaign documents, from single-page broadsheets and handbills to elaborately compiled textbooks and campaign biographies, that the parties put out each year, and were at the center of the parties' mobilizing efforts." Page xii.

6. *Sunday Mails. Mr. Johnson's Report on the Transportation of the Mail on Sunday.* Stereotype Edition. Boston: published by J. Q. Adams, Investigator Office. *1834.* 12 pages 3.25 × 5.5 inches, sewn. The *Investigator* was a weekly periodical edited by Abner Kneeland dedicated to the "development and promotion of universal mental liberty." Representative and former President John Quincy Adams was occasionally plagued with the mistaken identification with the Boston printer.

7. William Emmons, *Authentic Biography of Col. Richard M. Johnson*, N. Y. 1833

8. "In 1833 he was elected the first president of the newly formed federation of craft unions of the city of New York, the General Trades' Union . . . , and he edited a paper, the *National Trades' Union*, which became its official organ." *Dictionary of American Biography.*

9. Ely Moore "Tribute to Col. Richard M. Johnson. Author of the Sunday Mail Reports adopted by Congress in 1829 and 1830", from a speech at Masonic Hall, New York, March 13, 1833, published in Emmons biography.

10. The editor of the *Evangelical Magazine and Gospel Advocate*, Utica, January 2, 1830 (who continued support for Johnson's view throughout the year), reported that Johnson's report had the backing of the Baptists in Kentucky specifically because "an association of civil and ecclesiastical power or an union of Church and State, [is] one of the greatest calamities which could befall our country . . ." Another popular weekly from New York City, *The Cabinet of Instruction, Literature and Amusement*, wished to remain neutral on the topic, but clearly leaned towards Johnson's views, giving in its March 27, 1830, issue front page coverage to a synopsis of the report. Editor H. R. Piercy saw Sunday Mails as "the preservation of what may justly be esteemed one of the withes composing the bond of our national union; and a guarantee for the quickest possible conveyance of messages and information, often important to religion and the church, as well as to secular concerns."

11. "Report of the Postmaster General December 1, 1845" Doc. 2, pp 850–893. Appendix 6. In responding to questions about route 1025: "The lowest class of routes, the horseback routes, are advertised without any designation of the mode of conveyance, and the bids are usually made in the same way. There are specific bids in four-horse coaches, and in two-horse coaches; also in one-horse vehicles. But the novel species of bids, peculiar to the present lettings and the new law, are those which specify no mode of service, but seem to imply more than horse bids, by engaging to convey the mail with certainty, celerity, and security. They are designated on the books in a particular way, and are hence called, for brevity's sake, *star bids.*" The concept of Star Routes has been erroneously attributed to an earlier period, as in Hugh V. Feldman *U.S. Contract Mail Routes by Water (Star Routes 1824–1875),* understandable because the National Archives gave an anachronistic retroactive classification to the ledgers: "Registers for Star Route Contracts 1814–1960" (Vol. 021 of 326, Entry 125.)

12. The PMG was responsible for adjusting "the degree and mode of service—to regulate the connections between routes, so as to effect a speedy intercommunication between the several parts of the country—to secure contracts for the faithful and punctual performance of the service—to settle questions which constantly arise, involving public and private interests to the amount of some millions of dollars each year—to meet the urgent demands of the public for mail accommodations, which the growth of the country and its rapidly increasing population require." The PMG report for 1846 reiterated the savings already incurred using the new protocols for the next round of four-year contract lettings. Cave Johnson emphasized the freeing up of competition now that contractors no longer had to purchase their predecessor's equipment. Report of the Postmaster General, December 7, 1846, Doc. 1, pp 679–704.

13. Abraham Bradley was first assistant postmaster general from 1793 until ousted by Jackson after the 1828 election. His letter defending the apparent excesses of the contracts entered into by Postmaster General William T. Barry (but critical of other aspects, such as failure to implement service that was contracted for on certain routes) was published in the *Independent Chronicle and Boston Patriot*, 31 August 1831, page 2.

14. See William Addison Blakely, *American State Papers Bearing on Sunday Legislation*, D. C. 1911.

15. *Report of the Committee of The Senate of the United States, appointed March 12, 1802, on the subject of Transporting the Mail of the United States.* March 30, 1802. 35 pp. This report outlines the cost of the government stage line between Philadelphia and Baltimore that started in 1799 and projects the cost of extending such. Stage lines were particularly lacking in the southern states.

16. See Oliver W. Holmes, "Shall stagecoaches Carry the Mail?" Originally published 1963, reprinted in *A Tribute to Oliver Wendell Holmes*, Washington D. C. 1972. Holmes quotes Charles Pinckney's 1786 remarks on establishing a line of stages in the South: "the intention of Congress in having the mails transported by stage carriages, was not only to render their conveyance more certain and secure, but by encouraging the establishment of stages to make the intercourse between the different parts of the Union less difficult and expensive than formerly." Holmes adds: "Here was the first mention of a new and powerful motive impelling Congress to the support of the mail stages,

a motive that in later periods was to operate in the subsidizing through the post office of other modes of transportation notably the merchant marine and commercial air lines." p. 14.

17. John, page 74. See, also, Daniel Y. Meschter "The Postmasters General of the United States IIIa. Joseph Habersham and the Mail Distributing System," *La Posta*, January 2004, pp 31–38. Washington Pa. was one of the original thirty-one distributing offices. The PMG report for 1859, in explaining why the distribution offices were being disbanded, reviewed their history: "Offices of this description were formerly a very valuable, and, in fact, indispensable element in the postal system of the country, owing to its vast extent, and the rapidity with which population spread into new districts, causing cities, towns, and villages to struggle for existence with the forest and prairie, and rendering it impossible to keep pace with the names and locations of the numberless new offices demanded by the habits of a people accustomed to the constant interchange of thought and intelligence. Some offices therefore, had to be designated as the receptacles of correspondence from a section of contiguous country, and for re-mailing and sending it in packages to others of similar functions, more or less distant, thence to be distributed to its destination. In this manner these offices situated in the east and west, the north and south, mutually acted upon each other, and performed useful service. This was when the mails were carried in stages and other vehicles, and when pauses were necessarily made for the refreshment of passengers and the change of animals, allowing at the same time of 'distribution' at the post office."

18. "An Act, Regulating the Post-Office Establishment" section 9, passed April 30, 1810.

19. The Post Office Law, with Instructions and Forms, published for The Regulation of the Post-Office. "At post offices where the mail arrives on Sunday, the office is to be kept open for the delivery of letters, &c. for one hour after the arrival and assorting of the mail; but in case that would interfere with the hours of public worship, then the office is to be kept open for one hour after the usual time of dissolving the meetings for that purpose."

20. *Report Of the Select Committee, to which was referred sundry petitions, remonstrating against the practice of transporting and opening the mails on the Sabbath, and praying a discontinuance thereof.* March 1, 1817. Rep. 3, 9 pp. ". . . in forming arrangements, and fixing times for the arrivals and departures of the mails on the lesser and cross routes, care is taken to avoid the transport of the mail on the Sabbath, except where the omission to transport on that day would break chains of communications, producing great delays to public and private intercourse; and it is the mutual desire of the contractor and the department to avoid running the mail on the Sabbath."

21. *Report of the Committee to whom was referred the petitions of Numerous citizens of the states of New Hampshire, Massachusetts, Connecticut, North Carolina, and Ohio, praying the Congress to prohibit the transportation and opening of the mail on the Sabbath. January 27, 1815.* Washington City: printed by Roger C. Weightman, 1815. 4pp. The Committee on

Post Offices and Post Roads noted the practice of carrying mails daily on the great roads while trying to avoid Sunday on the lesser routes. Postmasters, however, were only required to open their offices and distribute the mail received, not to accept money or perform other functions. Letter datelined New York 20 April 1817: "I owe you an apology for writing on Sunday, which is the reason I cannot pay the postage." J. Warren Brackett to William Meredith in Philadelphia [authors' collection].

22. *Report of the committee on the Post-Office and Post-Roads, to whom was referred the memorial of the "American Bible Society."* January 25, 1817. In denying a request for a free frank: "It has hitherto been (except during the late war,) and the committee believe will continue to be, the policy of the government to apply all the revenue accruing from postages to the extension of post-routes . . ." p. 2.

23. *Table of Post Offices in the United States, with the distances from Washington City, and the names of the postmasters.* (Washington 1811) page 69. Two earlier compilations of similar material are included in *American State Papers*, No. 10 at page 28 includes the data to 1803, and No. 21 at page 40 to 1807.

24. *American State Papers*, Class VII. Post Office Department. (Washington 1834), No. 56, pp 120–136, Postmaster General McLean January 14, 1825: "A complete revision of all the mail routes in the Union is believed to be indispensable; and, though a work of great labor, will be accomplished, it is hoped, before the next session of Congress."

25. See the chapter "Yorker Benevolence" in Whitney R. Cross *The Burned-Over District: The Social and Intellectual History of Enthusiastic Religion in Western New York, 1800–1850,* Cornell 1950.

26. Their fastest run between Buffalo and Albany was reported September 10, 1828—45 hours and 14 minutes including stops. See a full description of these stage line wars, Richard F. Palmer, *The "Old Line Mail": Stagecoach Days in Upstate New York,* 1977.

27. A letter to the editor of the *Evangelical Magazine and Gospel Advocate,* Utica, Saturday, April 10, 1830, page 119, reported the shocking discovery that the Pioneer "Pious Line" was operating in Albany and Greenbush on successive Sundays. The editor in the September 25th issue, page 309, noted the discontinuance of the Pioneer line of boats and the selling out to the Old Line of the Western route for lack of profitability.

28. Henry O'Reilly, *Sketches of Rochester; with incidental notices of Western New-York,* Rochester 1838, admits that the backers of the Pioneer Line were financially ruined by the enterprise but believed that, in moral terms, it had positively affected religious observance and had led directly to the outpouring of memorials to Congress against Sunday Mails. He refers to Lyman Beecher's Review of Senator Johnson's Report on Sabbath Mails having been republished in Rochester and "sent gratuitously to all parts of the land." Pages 303–304. Isaac Kramnick and Robert Laurence Moore, *The Godless Constitution,* New York, 1996, page 135 claim 100,000 copies were distributed by the organization formed in Rochester by Beecher and Josiah Bissel

of the Pioneer Line, the General Union for the Promotion of the Christian Sabbath. Our suspicion is that these numbers refer to a republication in O'Reilly's newspaper which he could freely distribute.

29. For a digest of geographic distribution of these memorials, a sampling of their content, and a list of selected signatories with their occupations, see *An Account of Memorials Presented to Congress During its Last Session, by Numerous Friends of Their Country and its Institutions; praying that the mails may not be transported, nor post-offices kept open, on the Sabbath*, New York May, 1829. Authors' copy includes on the wraps announcement of its availability at the bookstores of Jonathan Leavitt, 182 Broadway, and John P. Haven, 142 Nassau Street. 32 pp.

30. Printed circular datelined New-York January 1st, 1829. Signed by ten men, mailed "free" to Hon. Jonathan Harvey, Representative from New Hampshire.

31. Reprinted in *Niles' Weekly Register*. Third series. No. 25-Vol. XL, Baltimore, Feb. 14, 1829, page 405.

32. From the Annual Report of the Postmaster General, compiled in *American State Papers. Class VII. Post Office Department*. (Washington 1834), No. 121, page 351.

33. Report of the Postmaster General, December 1, 1860. Table A, pages 489–490.

34. Robert Dalton Harris "Sunday Post Offices", *P.S. A Quarterly Journal of Postal History*, No. 1, February 1977.

BIBLIOGRAPHY

American Council of Learned Societies. *Concise Dictionary of American Biography*. New York: Scribner, 1997.

An Account of Memorials Presented to Congress During its Last Session, by Numerous Friends of Their Country and its Institutions; Praying that the Mails May Not be Transported, nor Post-Offices Kept Open, on the Sabbath. New York: May 1829.

Blakely, William Addison. *American State Papers Bearing on Sunday Legislation*. Washington. D. C.: Religious Liberty Association, 1911.

Bradley, Abraham. "Letter." *Independent Chronicle and Boston Patriot*, 31 August 1831, p. 2.

Cross, Whitney R. *The Burned-Over District: The Social and Intellectual History of Enthusiastic Religion in Western New York, 1800–1850*. Ithaca, N. Y.: Cornell University, 1950.

Emmons, William B. *Authentic Biography of Colonel Richard M. Johnson, of Kentucky*. New York: H. Mason, 1833.

Feldman, Hugh V. U.S. *Contract Mail Routes by Water (Star Routes 1824–1875): A History of the U.S. Post Office Department's Contracts Made with Independent Contractors for the Carriage of the Mails by Water within the United States of America from the Inception of Such Contracts in 1824 to 1875*. Chicago: Collectors Club of Chicago, 2008.

Fenn, Patricia, and Alfred P. Malpa. *Rewards of Merit: Tokens of a Child's Progress and a Teacher's Esteem As an Enduring Aspect of American Religious and Secular Education*. Schoharie, N. Y.: Ephemera Society of America, 1994.

Fowler, Dorothy Ganfield. *The Cabinet Politician: The Postmasters General, 1829–1909*. New York: Columbia University Press, 1943.

Fuller, Wayne E. *Morality and the Mail in Nineteenth Century America*. Champaign, Ill.: University of Illinois Press, 2003.

Harris, Robert Dalton. "Sunday Post Offices." *P. S. A Quarterly Journal of Postal History*, 1(February 1977).

Holmes, Oliver W. *Shall Stagecoaches Carry the Mail?* Washington, 1972.

John, Richard R. "The Invasion of the Sacred." In *Spreading the News: The American Postal System from Franklin to Morse*. Cambridge: Harvard University Press, 1995.

Kendall, Amos. *Autobiography of Amos Kendall*, ed. William Stickney. Boston: Lee and Shepard, 1872.

Kramnick, Isaac, and R. Laurence Moore. *The Godless Constitution: The Case against Religious Correctness*. New York: W. W. Norton. 1996.

McLean, John. *American State Papers, Class VII. Post Office Department*. No. 56. Washington D. C.: 1834.

Meschter, Daniel Y. "The Postmasters General of the United States Illa. Joseph Habersham and the Mail Distributing System." *La Posta*, January 2004:31–38.

Meyer, Leland Winfield. *The Life and Times of Colonel Richard Mentor Johnson of Kentucky*. New York: Columbia University, 1932.

O'Reilly, Henry. *Sketches of Rochester: With Incidental Notices of Western New-York*. Rochester, N. Y.: William Alling, 1838.

Palmer, Richard F. *The "Old Line Mail": Stagecoach Days in Upstate New York*. Lakemont, N. Y.: North Country Books, 1977.

"Registers for Star Route Contracts 1814–1960." Volume 021 of 326, Entry 125. College Park, Md.: National Archives and Records Administration.

Silbey, Joel H. *The American Party Battle: Election Campaign Pamphlets 1826–1876*. Cambridge: Harvard University Press, 1999.

Sunday Mails. Mr. Johnson's Report on the Transportation of the Mail on Sunday. Stereotype Edition. Boston: J.Q. Adams, Investigator Office. 1834.

U.S. Congress. *An Act, Regulating the Post-Office Establishment*. 11th Congress, 2nd Session. Enacted 30 April 1810.

U.S. Congress. House. *Report of the Select Committee to which was Referred Sundry Petitions Remonstrating against the Practice of Transporting and Opening the Mails on the Sabbath, and Praying a Discontinuance Thereof*. Report 3. 1 March 1817.

U.S. Congress. House. Committee on Post Offices and Post Roads. *Report of the Committee on the Post-Office and Post-Roads to whom Was Referred the Memorial of the American Bible Society.* 25 January 1817.

U.S. Congress. Senate. *Report of the Committee of The Senate of the United States, appointed March 12, 1802, on the sub-*

ject of Transporting the Mail of the United States. 30 March 1802.

———. Report of The Committee to whom Was Referred the Petitions of Numerous Citizens of the States of New Hampshire, Massachusetts, Connecticut, North Carolina, and Ohio, Praying the Congress to Prohibit the Transportation and Opening of the Mail on the Sabbath. January 27, 1815. Washington D. C.: Roger C. Weightman, 1815.

United States Post Office Department. The Post Office Law, with Instructions and Forms, Published for the Regulation of the Post-Office. Washington D. C.: General Post-Office, 1817.

———. Report of the Postmaster General, December 1, 1845. Washington, D. C.: Government Printing Office, 1845.

———. Report of the Postmaster General, December 1, 1846. Washington, D. C.: Government Printing Office, 1846.

———. Table of Post Offices in the United States, with the Distances from Washington City, and the Names of the Postmasters. Washington D. C.: Post-Master General, 1811.

"Why Is a Raven Like a Writing Desk?" Post Office Reform, Collectible Commodities, and Victorian Culture

Catherine J. Golden

A lthough we know Lewis Carroll as the creator of *Alice's Adventures in Wonderland* (1865), Carroll (née Charles Lutwidge Dodgson) immersed himself in the world of letter writing and postal ephemera. An avid letter writer,[1] Carroll is also author of a letter-writing manual, *Eight or Nine Wise Words About Letter-Writing* (1890), and inventor of a postage stamp case marketed with it. His fascination with letter-writing culture allowed his Mad Hatter in *Alice in Wonderland* to stump an already befuddled Alice with the riddle, "'Why is a raven like a writing-desk?'"[2] Although ravens were denizens of the Tower of London long before the creation of the Penny Black, we can trace the upsurge of writing desks, letter-writing manuals, illustrated envelopes, ink wells, pens, and a whole variety of postal products to the historical moment in Victorian Britain when the Penny Post and the prepaid, adhesive postage stamp were born (1839–1840). On January 10, 1840, affordable mail extended across England; a letter weighing up to one-half ounce could travel anywhere in the UK for only a penny. With this revolutionary change in communications came postal products, a new field of industry. Cheap postage and the introduction of postage stamps led to new jobs, hobbies—timbromania, now called philately—and innovative postal practices as well as a proliferation of telling material objects. Writing desks, pictorial envelopes, and valentines—the focus of this essay—grew in variety and popularity; when viewed as cultural objects, these collectible commodities help us to reconstruct aspects of the Victorian British way of life.

THE RISE OF THE PENNY POST

We can trace the increase in postal ephemera to the years witnessing the rise of the Penny Post, 1837–1840. Prior to postal reform, letter writing, the only way to communicate with a distant audience, was a luxury mostly afforded by the rich. Two landmarks frame postal reform in nineteenth-century Britain. In 1837, Rowland Hill published multiple editions of a landmark postal reform pamphlet called *Post Office Reform: Its Importance and Practicability,* arguing why the British needed postal reform.[3] That same year, Queen Victoria

FIGURE 1. Penny Black, posted May 6, 1840. From the collection of James Grimwood-Taylor, M.A., F.R.P.S.L.

came to the throne. One of the first things she did as queen was to appoint a Select Committee on Postage, chaired by postal reformer Robert Wallace, MP, and charged to look into the condition of the post with a view towards postal rate reduction. Victoria, on August 17, 1839, gave royal assent to the Postage Duties Bill and, in 1840, ushered in Uniform Penny Postage. Instrumental to this legislation were widely publicized, arguably exaggerated tales about economic hardship and depravities resulting from high postage, which appeared in Hill's pamphlet as well as *The Post Circular*, a newspaper which today we would call a postal reform "propaganda sheet."[4] The Victorians also rallied for and welcomed Uniform Penny Postage as a means to improve economics, morality, science, employment, and education. Visions of young women saved from becoming fallen women, sober and literate soldiers, contented mill workers no longer interested in striking, and home control—these imagined situations became aligned with affordable postage and moved the early Victorians, still shaken by the example of the French Revolution, to

support a reform that had widespread social, political, and economic implications.

Although we now humorously refer to posted letters as "snail mail," when the postage stamp first appeared, it was as revolutionary as e-mail, text messages, tweets, and blogs are to us today. By 1860, Victorians of all social classes rushed to their post offices to make the last daily posting, as George Elgar Hicks captures in his monumental narrative painting of St. Martin's-le-Grand, London entitled *The General Post Office, One Minute to Six* (1860). The Penny Post transformed the mail from an expensive tax for revenue to a civic service for "the peer to the peasant."[5] The abolition of franks—postmarks granting free carriage of mail—for Members of Parliament and the Queen chipped away at England's rigid class system. In turn, the Penny Post led to an unprecedented boom in letter writing and became a vehicle for education, kinship, friendship, and commerce (Figure 1).

Prepayment came via two inventions attributed to Rowland Hill: a postage stamp called the Penny Black, and prepaid postal stationery (Mulready letter sheets and envelopes), which Hill believed would be more popular for personal letters than stamps—although the Victorian public proved him wrong. As Douglas Muir aptly notes, "Derision was the common response to the Mulready design. It was caricatured in words and imitative drawings."[6] Some Victorians objected to the allegorical-pictorial-historical design of Britannia overseeing a glorious postal outreach extending to all four corners of the globe while others, for example, opposed it for practical reasons—the design left little space for an address. Moreover, as soon as the Mulready design appeared, caricaturists lampooned it. The Victorian public, which refused to purchase the officially commissioned design, bought in droves caricature envelopes ridiculing the Irish (a dig at the Irish-born academy-trained artist and designer William Mulready) as well as the monarchy, the Opium Wars, social practices, and major politicians of the day.[7] The Penny Black, in contrast, won instant success. Demand for stamps far exceeded the number of available postage stamps when they first appeared in May 1840.[8] The stamp and the scheme of prepaid, affordable, uniform postage quickly became a model for other nations; the United States, for example, issued its first postage stamps in 1847, featuring George Washington on the ten-cent stamp and Benjamin Franklin on the five-cent stamp.[9]

In Hill's heyday, *Punch*, the Victorian Londoner's *New Yorker*, dubbed the hallowed postal reformer "Sir Rowland Le Grand," and Queen Victoria knighted him in 1860.[10] Today Rowland Hill is no longer a household name, even in Britain. On a January 2008 visit to the National Portrait Gallery in London, I sadly discovered that Hill's portrait has been relegated to storage.[11] Nonetheless, Hill's legacy resonates today. The system he designed brought the Victorians postal blessings—it facilitated family ties, promoted business, and spread information to an ever-widening postal "network" that anticipates computer-mediated communication—but it also became a tool for blackmail, unsolicited mass mailings, and junk mail, problems that remain with us today.[12]

VICTORIAN COMMODITY CULTURE

The Victorians manufactured and imported a range of materials for consumption, including fiction, food, drink, clothing, and—of importance to this essay—postal ephemera. In fact, modern day consumerism has its roots in the Victorian age of production and consumption. Britain was the undisputed leader of the Industrial Revolution, which led to an increase in speed of work and production, granting opportunities for leisure, choice, shopping, and collecting a host of Victorian things, such as postage stamps. The Great Exhibition of 1851, the first ever world's fair, held at the Crystal Palace in London, showcased technological, economic, and military achievements and, in turn, created a greater demand for consumer products. Once connected with sin and indulgence, consumerism became a form of self-expression—identity intertwined with books readers chose for their libraries, foods people ate, fashions they wore, and, post-1840, goods they bought for daily life, including correspondence. Traveling inkwells, decorative stamp boxes, steel-nibbed pens, colorful stationery, envelopes with innovative gummed flaps, an envelope-folding machine, envelope cases, and writing desks of various styles appear in the *Official Descriptive and Illustrated Catalogue* of the Great Exhibition of 1851 among exhibitions of art and architecture, handicrafts, geological displays, steel-making equipment, and then innovative appliances. Did the Victorians anticipate that in passing Uniform Penny Postage, they would foster a new field of industry? (Figure 2)

Over two decades ago, Asa Briggs established the importance of commodities as "emissaries"[13] of nineteenth-century culture in a now seminal work entitled *Victorian Things*. Setting a precedent for critical inquiry of household goods, song lyrics, museum artifacts, and postage stamps, Briggs calls attention to things Victorians "designed, named, made, advertised, bought and sold, listed, counted, collected, gave to others, threw away or bequeathed."[14] Writing desks, pictorial envelopes, and valentines quintessentially are, to recall Briggs's terms, "emissaries" of culture and civilization, transmitting information about aesthetics, gender, social class, and Empire. These collectible commodities tell us what the Victorians treasured and commemorated and carry opinions on current events, customs, humor, prejudices, and preferences.

WRITING DESKS FROM THE INSIDE OUT

Lewis Carroll's writing-desk riddle, which appears in one of literature's most famous tea party scenes, directs our attention to the growing popularity of an item demanded by and created for women and men of the middle and upper classes. Carroll's own postal products piggybacked on the popularity of his enduring *Alice's Adventures in Wonderland*. Different from other manuals on the market, *Eight or Nine Wise Words About Letter-Writing* seems, in the words of Carroll's biographer Morton

FIGURE 2. Postal ephemera. From the collection of Catherine J. Golden.

Cohen, "practical, sensible, and tongue-in-cheek."[15] Carroll advises the writer to reread a letter before answering it; to affix the stamp and address the envelope before writing the letter to avoid the "wildly-scrawled signature—the hastily-fastened envelope, which comes open in the post—the address, a mere hieroglyphic"; to write legibly; to avoid extensive apologies for not writing sooner; to use a second sheet of paper rather than to "cross"—"Remember the old proverb '*Cross-writing makes cross reading*'"; and so on. Carroll even suggests where to store the postage stamp case: "*this* is meant to haunt your envelope-case, or wherever you keep your writing-materials."[16] "Curiouser and curiouser," why didn't Carroll designate "writing desk" as the logical depository for his postage stamp case given his riddle and the writing desk's popularity among the Victorians?

Beginning in the 1830s, writing desks came within economic reach of members of an increasingly literate middle class. Moreover, the grand display of writing products at the Great Exhibition of 1851 increased middle-class demand for affordable desks. The Victorians found their writing desks indispensable for storing writing materials; valuables, including money and jewelry; vital documents, such as passports and wills; and private correspondence, such as *billets-doux*. The writing desk—also called a writing box, lap desk, writing slope, dispatch box or case, portable or traveling writing desk, or simply a box or a desk—likely grew out of the medieval lectern[17] and paved the way for subsequent innovations in writing that have replaced it: the brief case, the laptop, the Palm Pilot, the BlackBerry, and the iPhone.

There were four types of writing desks—the most basic being a box with a sloping lid, hinged at either top or bottom.[18] The desk has a writing slope; a place for stationery, blotting paper, envelopes, sealing wax, and small writing manuals; a pen rest for quill pens or steel nib pens (as the century progressed); a stamp compartment (used for wafers before the invention of stamps); one or two ink bottles (one likely for pounce, a chalky substance to blot ink, commonly used before the invention of blotting paper); and a key lock. Elaborate desks contain multiple storage compartments,[19] and some fancy boxes are combination desks—writing desk/work boxes and writing desk/dressing cases.

Writing desks—which we might aptly call Victorian laptops—tell us about privacy, security, and portability at

FIGURE 3. Victorian writing desk and laptop. From the collection of Catherine J. Golden.

a time when heating was inefficient, houses were not routinely electrified, and people made long visits to friends and family lasting weeks and months. Desks typically fit into one's luggage, making them popular for travel. The portability and size of the writing desk facilitated comfortable writing conditions and confidentiality since a writer could move it to be close to a good light source and a warm fire or into a private study to write undisturbed (Figure 3).

We can determine the gender and social class of a desk's owner by looking at its size, raw materials, and degree of decoration. A man's writing desk is large enough to be useful (typical dimensions are fourteen inches by ten inches by six inches). Manufacturers and designers made gentlemen's desks of mahogany, walnut, ash, or rosewood, with superior veneers of good grain, color, and patina, leather-lined slopes, and brass bindings on the corners and edges. In contrast, affordable commercial desks are more commonly of oak or pine. The Victorian gentleman favored clean lines, quality materials, simple but tasteful decoration, and, in writing desks that were not industrial, understated elegance. In contrast, ladies' desks appear smaller and daintier than gentlemen's desks (e.g. ten inches by eight inches by three inches) and carry knowledge of the growing Victorian fancy goods trade. Slopes have silk or velvet linings; lids contain mosaic and marquetry inlays, engraving, embossing, painting, and piercing. Expensive desks feature elaborate designs of fruits, flowers, birds,

hearts, and topographical views and are exquisitely ornamented with pearls, gold, silver, precious gems, seashells, tortoiseshell, and china. The lady's desk still had to be useful for teaching, household accounts, correspondence, and, in some cases, novel writing: Jane Austen's father gave her a writing desk filled with stationery to encourage her talent;[20] the Brontë sisters composed their memorable novels on writing slopes on display in the Brontë Parsonage Museum in the Yorkshire town of Haworth (Figure 4).

Some desks contain hidden chambers, called secret drawers. These were places to safeguard bank notes, *billets-doux*, and jewels that a wife might not wish her husband to know about—William Thackeray's infamous Becky Sharp in *Vanity Fair* (1848) uses her writing desk for that very purpose. While the outside of a desk teaches us about aesthetics, gender, and social class, the inside, including the key lock and hidden drawers, reveals how the writing desk functioned as a transportable, private space to safeguard among other things the clandestine life of its Victorian owner.

POPULAR PICTORIAL ENVELOPES

With the rise of the postage stamp came a surge in envelope production. Victorians, who rushed in record numbers to attend the Great Exhibition of 1851, marveled

FIGURE 4. Victorian gentleman's mahogany writing desk and woman's papier-mâché writing desk. From the collection of Catherine J. Golden.

over Edwin Hill's and Warren De La Rue's envelope-folding machine, invented in 1845 by Edwin Hill, Rowland Hill's brother; fans of this "cutting-edge" Victorian technological wonder include Queen Victoria. With the rise of envelope production came an increase in pictorial envelopes. Briggs suggests in *Victorian Things* that "the failure of the Mulready envelopes may have given an impetus to the popularity of other envelopes bearing views of places and sketches of people and things."[21] The "failure" of the Mulready gave rise to Mulready caricatures, which, as satires of Victorian politics and culture, in turn, sparked the popularity of a whole range of pictorial envelopes that record pressing social and political reforms as well as activities from daily Victorian life. Today a Victorian time traveler might be surprised to find people standing on street corners, holding protest signs and conducting rallies; this same Victorian, over 150 years ago, might have expressed his or her views by purchasing and posting pictorial envelopes. Popular pictorial envelopes, a ready means of advertising or what we would now refer to as "propaganda," advocated, for example, affordable transatlantic postage, peace, abolition, brotherhood, vegetarianism, and temperance.

One mid-century temperance envelope shows scenes of inebriation in the home, pub, and street and includes the caption in capital letters: "INTOXICATING DRINKS—ARE THE BANE & CURSE OF SOCIETY." Still others preach the positive side of abstinence by flanking the Goddess of Temperance with flag-bearing delegates from Europe, Asia, Africa, and America, all paying her homage.[22] Pictorial envelopes also promoted Overseas Penny Postage, a movement aligned with peace and brotherhood and spearheaded by Elihu Burritt, United States consular agent in Birmingham. One such 1849 envelope designed, engraved, and produced by J. Valentine of Dundee includes Mercury in a winged cap positioned above an overseas vessel and contains the words "Ocean Postage." Clasped hands of individuals of different races join with a dove holding an olive branch and transportation symbols: a railway train, a canal boat, and mail packets. Scrolls unfurling along the top and bottom of the design display boldly in capital letters, "BRITAIN! FROM THEE THE WORLD EXPECTS AN OCEAN PENNY POSTAGE—TO MAKE HER CHILDREN ONE FRATERNITY."[23] (Figure 5)

While such didactic pictorial envelopes sermonize, others simply entertain. Scenic or tourist envelopes showcase picturesque Victorian locales—the rural landscape, Oxford, Windsor Castle, and Stirling Castle, for instance. Beginning in 1840, Richard and James Doyle created

FIGURE 5. Ocean Penny Postage envelope, 1849. © Royal Mail Group Ltd 2009, courtesy of The British Postal Museum & Archive.

Fores's Comic Envelopes, offering a comical view of daily Victorian activities—musical soirées, dancing, hunting, horse racing, shooting, courting, and Christmas celebrations.[24] Envelope designs also marked important celebrations, such as the marriage of Victoria and Albert (1840), the Great Exhibition of 1851, and much later, in 1890, the jubilee of uniform inland penny postage. Looking at pictorial envelopes today, we glean what picturesque sites fascinated the Victorians, the causes they supported, the social activities in which they participated, the milestones they celebrated, and what they found humorous.

THE ICONOGRAPHY OF VICTORIAN VALENTINES

Legend has it that valentines as we know them today date to the fifteenth century in England—Charles, the duke of Orleans, allegedly sent a valentine to his wife in 1415 while held prisoner in the Tower of London—but valentines greatly increased after the coming of Uniform Penny Postage. In 1841, just one year after postal reform, Victorians sent more than 400,000 valentines throughout England; by 1871, three times that number passed through the London post alone.[25] Today we typically purchase a ready-made valentine in a store, but in the Victorian era,

stationer's shops sold an array of materials for creating original valentines: colored and gilt papers and cards; paper cupids and hearts; bows and ribbons; printed verses and mottoes; appliqués of lace, feather, shell, and gold and silver foil. The many types of valentines offer insight into Victorian conceptions of humor, love, and national identity.

Very popular were mechanical valentines that open to reveal a hidden message or can be manipulated: a man nods his head, a woman beckons with her hand, and in bawdy valentines, a female figure shows her ankle or petticoat. Novelty valentines sometimes took the form of telegrams from "Loveland" or notes from the "Bank of True Love." Some cards offer gentle humor, for example, urging a bachelor to marry; others are insulting. Dean & Son of Ludgate Hill, London, produced a pair of valentines circa 1860 that deride a dandy and a lady of fashion. The valentine poem for the dandy, inscribed "À Monsieur Chandelle," reads:

> In your dandified hat,
> From your boot to your glove,
> I think I've quite pat,
> Drawn your portrait above;
> Pray don't take offence,
> Nor to anger incline,

In dress show more sense,
You queer Valentine.[26]

The picture accompanying this verse shows a dandy sporting a red cravat, yellow gloves, a yellow checked vest, a black felt jacket and pants, stylish black leather boots, and an exceedingly tall top hat. The dandy puffs on a cigar, carries a walking stick, swells his chest, and wears an expression of self-satisfaction that augments his "dandified" air.

My survey of over two hundred period valentines in two major collections in Bath, UK[27] reveals that romantic valentines teach us about Victorian aesthetics and the new moral attitude of love that burgeoned in the 1830s, accompanying the coronation of Victoria and marking an end to the rakish ways of Victoria's "wicked" uncles, George IV and William IV. From romantic valentines, we discern stories of ardent passion, shy or secret love, warm affection, imagined happiness, and feared rejection. Flowers, churches, angels, birds and nests, cupids, flaming torches, bows, butterflies, hearts and darts, arrows, musical instruments, and wedding rings are all common Victorian icons of romantic love. Romantic valentines feature clichéd messages, such as "Constant and True," "Be for ever mine," "Thine forever," and "Ever Affectionate," aligning romantic love with constancy and lasting affection as well as monogamy.

The two most ever-present icons on romantic valentines are flowers and churches or church spires.[28] The Victorians were well-versed in what they called the "language of flowers," the sentiments and values that different types of flowers represent. Today, we still associate roses with love, but we might not link a foxglove with insincerity or realize that the color of a flower, such as a rose, could change its meaning. To the Victorians, a red rose meant "passionate love," but a yellow rose signified "jealousy."[29] Placing specific flowers on a romantic missive offered a way to express love without words. Thomas Hardy in *Far from the Madding Crowd* (1874), for example, includes three flowers on the larky valentine that Bathsheba Everdene wantonly posts to Farmer Boldwood—red rose, blue violet, and carnation—which mean, respectively, "love," "faithfulness," and "Alas! for my poor heart" (for a red carnation).[30] No wonder Boldwood is entranced, even though Bathsheba intends the valentine as a practical joke. Other flowers that commonly appear on period valentines include lilies of the valley for "return of happiness," bluebells meaning "constancy," forget-me-nots for "true love," daisies meaning "innocence," and white lilies for "purity and sweetness."[31] (Figure 6)

FIGURE. 6. "Love & Duty." Undated Victorian valentine from the Frank Staff Collection. Reproduced by kind permission of Bath Postal Museum, UK.

The church and its steeple signified fidelity in love and honorable intentions as well as marriage plans. This was an age when engagements often lasted for years. A couple could not marry until a man was financially secure, so a fiancé, by sending a card with a church spire, could assure his betrothed of his unfailing love. For those not yet engaged, the church icon offered a way for a suitor to inform his sweetheart of his honorable intentions. Popular nautical-themed valentines, which pair fidelity in love with duty, tell us that the Victorian soldier or sailor, occupied in Empire building, promised to remain faithful to his true love as he dutifully served his country. In one such undated period valentine called "Love and Duty,"[32] the heart on the side of the valentine is presumably the soldier's heart, and the church spire (in the background) stands as an assurance that marriage will reward a virtuous heart.

A FINAL NOTE: WHY IS A RAVEN LIKE A WRITING DESK?

These three popular postal products—writing desks, pictorial envelopes, and valentines—provide a window on the habits of Victorian consumers post-1840. Real and fictional Victorian letter writers used writing desks for correspondence and safekeeping as well as to store pictorial envelopes, valentines, and other writing materials, including quill pens—conceivably even those made from a raven's feathers. To return to Carroll's riddle: "Why is a raven like a writing-desk?" When Alice demands to know the answer, the Mad Hatter tells Alice, "'I haven't the slightest idea.'"[33] In a preface to an 1896 edition of *Alice in Wonderland*, Carroll—who was hounded for the answer to his riddle for over thirty years—declares:

> Enquiries have been so often addressed to me, as to whether any answer to the Hatter's Riddle can be imagined, that I may as well put on record here what seems to me to be a fairly appropriate answer, viz: "Because it can produce a few notes, tho they are *very* flat; and it is nevar put with the wrong end in front!" This, however, is merely an afterthought; the Riddle, as originally invented, had no answer at all.[34]

Carroll could "nevar" resist a play on words, much as Carroll enthusiasts are "nevar" satisfied with Carroll's answers. Fans have come up with other clever responses, including: "Edgar Allan Poe wrote on both," and "Both have quills dipped in ink."[35] How "curious" that Carroll's riddle has outlasted the Victorian writing desk.

NOTES

1. Carroll kept an accurate register of all the letters he wrote and received throughout his lifetime.

2. Lewis Carroll, *The Annotated Alice: Alice's Adventures in Wonderland & Through the Looking Glass* (New York: Norton, 2000).

3. The first "private" version printed by William Clowes and Sons came out in January 1837. A second edition for the general public published by Charles Knight appeared on February 22, 1837; two more editions followed, one later in 1837 and a fourth in 1838. Hill, who analyzed the costly, unwieldy British postal system from the vantage point of an enlightened outsider, went on to become Secretary to the Postmaster General of the Post Office in 1846, and, by 1854, Secretary of the Post Office.

4. *The Post Circular* had a run of 16 issues (March 14, 1838, until November 20, 1839).

5. This appears in an article in *The Post Circular* 11 (Wednesday, April 17, 1839), 54.

6. Douglas Muir, *Postal Reform and the Penny Black: A New Appreciation* (London: National Postal Museum, 1990), 176.

7. Printers of caricature envelopes include J. W. Southgate, Ackermann & Co., and Messrs. Fores of Picadilly. For a full discussion of the reception of the Mulready envelope, I recommend my book *Posting it: The Victorian Revolution in Letter Writing*, particularly two sections in the second chapter, "A Tale of Ridicule" and "Mulready Caricatures: A National Lampoon," 95–101.

8. Asa Briggs, *Victorian Things* (Chicago: University of Chicago Press, 1989), 331.

9. Zurich issued the 6 Rappen and 4 Rappen on March 1, 1843; Geneva released the Double Geneva on October 1, 1843. The Canton of Basel issued the Basel Dove on July 1, 1845. Brazil produced the Bull's Eye stamp on August 1, 1843, and on July 1, 1847, the United States issued five- and ten-cent stamps featuring, respectively, Benjamin Franklin on a red-brown stamp and George Washington on a black stamp.

10. "Sir Rowland Le Grand" is a John Tenniel cartoon appearing in *Punch* on the occasion of Hill's retirement as Secretary of the Post Office in 1864.

11. In a November 20, 2009, correspondence with Corinne Harrison, print cataloguer at the National Portrait Gallery, I learned that the Hill portrait (NPG 838) remains in storage; the portrait and the gallery's holding of photographs and prints of Hill can be viewed privately by appointment.

12. For more on this subject, I recommend the concluding chapter of my book entitled *Posting It: The Victorian Revolution in Letter Writing* (University Press of Florida, 2009).

13. Briggs, p. 11.

14. Briggs, p. 12.

15. Morton N. Cohen, *Lewis Carroll: A Biography* (New York: Alfred A. Knopf, 1995), 493.

16. Lewis Carroll, *Eight or Nine Wise Words About Letter-Writing* (Oxford: Emberlin, 1890), pp. 2–3, 16–17, and 37.

17. References to writing desks appear in Shakespeare's *A Comedy of Errors* in order to safeguard a purse of ducats. See Harris, *Portable Writing Desks*, pp. 10–11 for a complete history. Some Victorians like Carroll hyphenate the word "writing-desk."

18. The top of the box serves as a writing slope if the box is hinged at the top, but the open lid acts as the writing surface if the box is hinged at the bottom.

19. For descriptions and pictures of a range of Victorian writing desks, see Harris, *Portable Writing Desks*, especially 22–23.

20. I include this reference to Jane Austen even though she precedes the Victorian age because her work made great contributions to it. See Carol Shields, *Jane Austen* (New York: Penguin, 2001), 45.

21. Briggs, p. 343.

22. Evans in *The Mulready Envelope* (217–221) is thorough in his discussion of temperance envelope designs but does not provide dates for them

23. An illustration of this pictorial envelope and further commentary about it appears both in Evans, *The Mulready Envelope*, 190, and Lowe, *The British Postage Stamp*, 94.

24. Debra N. Mancoff, *Love's Messenger: Tokens of Affection in the Victorian Age* (Chicago: Art Institute of Chicago, 1997), 46.

25. Evans provides commentary about and reproduces two examples from the series of "Ackermann's Comic Envelopes" in *The Mulready Envelope*, 176–181.

26. Valentine Cards collection, #268, Bath Central Library, Bath, UK.

27. The two collections I examined are the Valentine Cards collection, Special Collections, at the Bath Central Library and the Frank Staff Collection of the Bath Postal Museum, Bath, UK.

28. Item #253, Valentine Cards collection, Special Collections, Bath Central Library, Bath, UK.

29. Kate Greenaway, *Language of the Flowers* (New York: Avenel Books, n.d.), 36–37.

30. Greenaway, pp. 11, 36, 42.

31. Greenaway, pp. 10, 18, 15, 27.

32. Carroll, *The Annotated Alice*, 72.

33. Valentine 1993-08-29 forms part of the Frank Staff Collection, Bath Postal Museum, Bath, UK.

34. This quote comes from "Why is a raven like a writing desk?" accessed December 11, 2009. http://www.straightdope.com/columns/read/1173/why-is-a-raven-like-a-writing-desk.

35. The following website offers the Poe response and answers from famous people, such as Aldous Huxley: http://www.straightdope.com/columns/read/1173/why-is-a-raven-like-a-writing-desk. The website corrects the spelling of "nevar" to "never," following the lead of an editor who thought he caught a typo in Carroll's writing after the first printing; I have written the term as "nevar" here as Martin Gardner does in *The Annotated Alice*, 72. Clearly, Carroll wanted to spell the word "raven" backwards, and this "correction," as Gardner notes, "destroyed the ingenuity of his answer." Martin Gardner lists the answer about inky quills in his annotations to *The Annotated Alice*, 72. At the Fourth Annual Postal History Symposium in Bellefonte, Pennsylvania, Oct. 30–Nov. 1, 2009, one audience member suggested another possible answer: both ravens and desks hide valuable things.

BIBLIOGRAPHY

Adams, Cecil. "Why is a raven like a writing desk?" The Straight Dope, April 18, 1997. http://www.straightdope.com/columns/read/1173/why-is-a-raven-like-a-writing-desk. Accessed December 11, 2009.

Briggs, Asa. *Victorian Things*. 1988. Chicago: University of Chicago Press, 1989.

Carroll, Lewis. *The Annotated Alice: The Definitive Edition*. Ed. Martin Gardner. Illus. John Tenniel. New York: W. W. Norton and Co., 2000.

Cohen, Morton N. *Lewis Carroll: A Biography*. New York: Alfred A. Knopf, 1995.

Evans, E. B. *The Mulready Envelope and its Caricatures*. London: Stanley Gibbons, 1891.

Frank Staff Collection. Valentines. Bath Postal Museum, Bath, UK.

Fryer, Gavin, and Clive Akerman, eds. Fwd. Asa Briggs. *The Reform of the Post Office in the Victorian Era and its Impact on Economic and Social Activity: Documentary History 1837 to 1864 Based on Sir Rowland Hill's Journal and Ancillary Papers*. 2 vols. London: Royal Philatelic Society, 2000.

Golden, Catherine J. *Posting It: The Victorian Revolution in Letter Writing*. Gainesville, Fla.: University Press of Florida, 2009.

Greenaway, Kate. *Language of the Flowers*. New York: Avenel Books, n.d.

Hardy, Thomas. *Far From the Madding Crowd*. 1874. New York: Bantam, 1974.

Harris, David. *Victorian Writing Desks*. Buckinghamshire, UK: Shire, 2001.

Henkin, David. *The Postal Age: The Emergence of Modern Communications in Nineteenth-Century America*. Chicago: University of Chicago Press, 2006.

Lewins, William. *Her Majesty's Mails: A History of the Post Office and an Industrial Account of Its Present Condition*. 1864. 2nd ed. London: Sampson Low, Son, and Marston, 1865.

Lowe, Robson. *The British Postage Stamp of the Nineteenth Century*. London: National Postal Museum, 1968.

Mancoff, Debra N. *Love's Messenger: Tokens of Affection in the Victorian Age*. Chicago: Art Institute of Chicago, 1997.

Muir, Douglas. *Postal Reform and the Penny Black: A New Appreciation*. London: National Postal Museum, 1990.

Post Circular. Or Weekly Advocate for a Cheap, Swift, and Sure Postage. Ed. Henry Cole. Nos. 1–16. Wednesday, March, 14, 1838–Wednesday, November 20, 1839.

Shields, Carol. *Jane Austen*. New York: Penguin, 2001.

Thackeray, William Makepeace. *Vanity Fair: A Novel Without a Hero*. Ed. John Sutherland. Illus. W. M. Thackeray. Oxford: Oxford University Press, 1983.

Valentine Cards. Special Collections. Bath Central Library, Bath, England.

America's First Carrier Service: The U.S. City Despatch Post

Larry Lyons

The origin of organized carrier service using carrier adhesives is the basis of the 1842 U.S. postal reforms. The Greig's City Despatch Post local stamps were the first adhesive stamps printed in North America. The Post Office Department purchased this company for use as the first carrier service and adopted this first stamp. The postal reforms established in the United States by the U.S. City Despatch Post, America's first carrier service, can be summarized as follows:

1. The first use of a stamp for government purposes.
2. The established rate of three cents per stamp or $2.50 per hundred.
3. The first government handstamp. The creation of the "U.S." in an octagon to cancel stamps and prevent their reuse.
4. The first government datestamp to show the date and time of delivery.
5. The first adhesive design for use by the United States City Despatch Post, the *Scott Specialized Catalogue* listed 6LB3 stamp.
6. The creation of various color adhesives on unsurfaced paper colored through.
7. The first adhesive stamp printed on glazed surface colored paper for use by the government.
8. The first double impression errors.
9. The Postal Act of March 1845, effective July 1, 1845, putting the independent mail companies out of business for intercity mail.
10. The first use of adhesive stamps by the government for pre-payment of postage on intercity mail.
11. The first government overprinted stamp due to a change in the fee for carrier service.

This is a unique story about how the government started a carrier service in New York City with the issuance of carrier adhesives and handstamp devices and was forced to close down due to competition from the local posts. For once, free enterprise triumphed over the government. This was a first attempt at U.S. postal organization using carrier adhesives.

By an order of the postmaster general on August 1, 1842, a carrier service was established in New York known as the "United States City Despatch Post." In order to get started with carrier service, the Post Office Department felt it was best to purchase Grieg's City Despatch Post, a local post in New York City which had been operating successfully since February 1, 1842. The purchase also eliminated the competition from that particular local post. August 15, 1842, was the last day of the operation of Grieg's City Despatch Post, and on August 16, 1842, the service continued its operation but now was an official service of the post office with the name changed to "United States City Despatch Post." There was not time to print new stamps so the City Despatch Post adhesives created by Grieg (40L1) were now used as official carrier stamps (6LB1). These are two *Scott Specialized Catalogue* listings. One is a local stamp with an "L" prefix, and the other is a carrier stamp with an "LB" prefix. The 40L1 and 6LB1 are the same face picture stamps. The handstamps used were different and only used stamps can be differentiated. All unused stamps fall into the local stamp, 40L1, category. The stamps were sold individually at three cents each or $2.50 per hundred. This was the same rate Grieg had charged. The outer limit of operations of the U.S. City Despatch Post was Twenty-Second Street. The areas from Fourth Street to Twenty-Second

Street was known at that time as Uptown New York City. Central New York City was from Fourth Street south to Fulton Street and Downtown New York City was south of Fulton Street to the lower tip of Manhattan.

The Greig's City Despatch Local Post adhesive was to become America's first and most versatile stamp producing plate. It was now also the first plate used to make carrier stamps in the United States. The plate was made by Rawdon, Wright and Hatch. When Greig was operating as a local post he used a "FREE" handstamp in a fancy octagon (Figure 1). The "FREE" actually meant that the stamp was purchased and therefore the letter was prepaid. When Greig's became the U.S. City Despatch Post, the cancel used was a "U.S." in a fancy octagon shown in Figure 1. The U.S. City Despatch stamps were prepurchased and the "U.S." octagon cancel was to prevent their reuse. This was an innovative action by the carrier department based on the same action used by Greig cancelling his local post adhesives. The carrier service also had a circular datestamp which reads "U.S. City Despatch Post," with the "U.S." at the bottom. When Greig operated as a local post his datestamp read "City Despatch Post" with "N. Y." at the bottom. These handstamps can be seen in Figure 2.

Both the Greig's Local Post datestamp and the U.S. City Despatch Post handstamp were double lined circles with the middle reserved for a date and a clock time. Since this was the first government handstamp, the datestamp was an innovative action by the carrier department, as was the clock time, and it was based on the same action and design used by Greig when he ran his local post. Since Greig was running the U.S. City Despatch, he made good use of the handstamp design he developed earlier. Sometime in 1843 the U.S. City Despatch replaced its double lined circular datestamp with a single line datestamp which still included the clock time. See Figure 2.

FIGURE 1. The handstamps that identify covers used while Grieg operated his local post (left) and those of the U.S. City Despatch Post, the first government carrier service (right). From the 2010 Scott Specialized Catalogue.

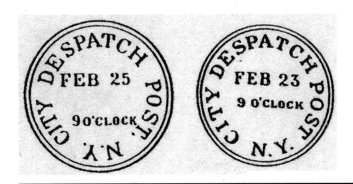

FIGURE 2. The datestamps that identify covers used while Greig operated his local post (left) and those of the U.S. City Despatch Post (right). From the American Stampless Cover Catalogue, Volume II, 1987.

FIGURE 3. The first new adhesive design for the U.S. City Despatch (6LB3) is shown at the left, and the Grieg's stamp (40L1) is shown at the right. From the collection of Larry Lyons.

THE SECOND U.S. CARRIER ADHESIVE

On September 1, 1842, the U.S. City Despatch Post came out with its first new adhesive design, which was black-on-light-blue unsurfaced paper (6LB3). See Figure 3. This was the first carrier adhesive printed by a United States post office. In Great Britain stamp production was in use since 1840. The use of prepaid adhesives was now proven as a great improvement over collect mail and manuscript notations. This was the beginnings of a postal reform equivalent to the invention of the wheel. The first new adhesive design reads "United States City Despatch Post" at the top, as opposed to the Greig's stamp which reads "City Despatch Post" at the top. The side ornaments were also changed but the general appearance with Washington in the middle and "THREE CENTS" at the bottom stayed the same. The original plates and printing size was not used. The new plate was also made by Rawdon, Wright and Hatch. The original Greig's local post stamps were printed in a forty-two stamp format of six-by-seven subjects, and the new U.S. City Despatch Post stamps were printed in sheets of one hundred subjects. Cal Hahn, a noted historian, plated the U.S. City Despatch Post stamps. He noted twenty-five positions on the left and twenty-five on the right which were repeated to make one hundred stamps. His plating analysis can be found in the *Lyons Identifier* in Volume III on pages 1055–1066.[1] Scott Trepel did pioneer work on the City Despatch Post adhesives; that plating analysis can be found in the study that he published.[2]

The United States City Despatch Post was initially very successful. By November 1842 they noted carrying 762 letters a day. They had 112 stations with collection boxes. Pick up was three times a day.[3] They employed eight letter carriers. The stamps were sold individually at three cents each or $2.50 per hundred.

THE UNSURFACED PAPER COLORED THROUGH ADHESIVES

The major stamp in this category is the black-on-light-blue adhesive (6LB3) which saw major usage. This adhesive was issued September 1, 1842, and is typically found on 1842 covers from September to the end of the year. According to Siegel Auction Galleries lot descriptions, the earliest recorded cover with the 6LB3 adhesive is September 2, 1842, the second day of its usage. There is a cover dated August 31, 1842, which is datestamped September 3, 1842, the third day of usage for this adhesive. Lot 201 in the Middendorf sale is a cover which is reported to be the earliest use of 6LB3. That cover is dated

September 1. There is a cover dated December 31, 1842, which is the latest usage in 1842. Sporadic late usages can be found as the purchased stamps were used. I note a January 31, 1843, cover, an April 2, 1844, cover and a February 14, 1846, cover, all with the early 6LB3 adhesives. The last three covers are not typical of when the majority of the 6LB3 adhesives were used.

Figure 4 shows an unsurfaced paper colored through adhesive which has been described as black-on-wheat. This stamp is cancelled with the U.S. in an octagon, the handstamp used by the U.S. City Despatch Post. This color is not listed in the *Scott Specialized Catalogue,* and it should be listed. The use of various colored papers was probably part of the experimentation process. These would have been color trials. Nothing went to waste, and all seem to have been used for postal duty.

There is also a black-on-rosy-buff (6LB2) adhesive listed in the *Scott Specialized Catalogue* in the unsurfaced paper colored through section. There is a note to the effect that "some authorities consider 6LB2 to be an essay." Only about eight to ten unused copies are recorded.

There is also an unsurfaced black-on-green adhesive (6LB4). There are only two recorded examples. Again there is a note in the *Scott Specialized Catalogue* to the effect that some authorities believe this color to be "a color changeling." It is a very valuable stamp with a *Scott*

Specialized Catalogue price of $11,500.00. No covers are recorded with this color adhesive. The Philatelic Foundation has certified the black-green unsurfaced paper adhesive (6LB4) as a genuine color and not a color changeling. The Philatelic Foundation is a not-for-profit foundation established in 1945 with a basis in education for philatelists. One function it performs is the certification of stamps and covers for genuineness. There is also a recorded apple-green adhesive which has been certified by the Philatelic Foundation and should be listed in the *Scott Specialized Catalogue.* Only one example of the apple-green color has been recorded. It has been suggested that the black-on-green adhesive was a trial color impression. This writer believes it was an issued color used for a very, short time. The one known example has been certified by the Philatelic Foundation as a genuinely used stamp.

THE GLAZED SURFACE PAPER ADHESIVES

The black-on-green glazed surface paper adhesive (6LB5d) printed in the fall of 1842 is the first glazed paper stamp issued by the government in the United States (Figure 5). Glazed paper adhesive labels were introduced more than four years earlier by the Eastern Express companies.

FIGURE 4. The U.S. City Despatch adhesive in wheat. This is an unsurfaced paper colored through adhesive which is not yet listed in the *Scott Specialized Catalogue.* From the collection of Larry Lyons.

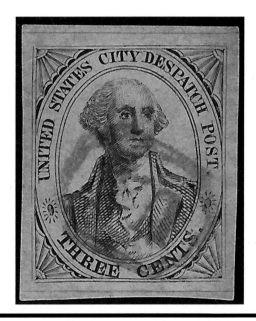

FIGURE 5. The 6LB5d adhesive is a black-on-green stamp on glazed surface colored paper. It is the first glazed paper stamp issued by the government in the United States. It was issued in the fall of 1842. From the collection of Larry Lyons.

The glazed paper adhesives were durable and took cancels well. Glazed paper was used by the carrier departments in Philadelphia and New York through 1852. This paper was more costly and was not used for the regular issue United States stamps which required large quantity printings. It was a logical step for the government carrier service to pursue the use of glazed paper for stamp use. According to research done by Bob Meyersburg, the earliest recorded date of the 6LB5d stamp, which is black-on-blue glazed, is November 26, 1842. The express companies were the pioneers in the use of glazed surface paper probably preceding the first government glazed paper adhesive by about three years. This color was in typical use for a full year to November 1843. There are four recorded examples of multiples of the black-on-green (6LB5d) adhesive with five stamps being used to pay the U.S. intercity postage to Philadelphia. There is also one cover with only four 6LB5d adhesives to Philadelphia because one adhesive is missing.

There are early examples of the black-on-green glazed adhesives, and there are late examples of black-on-green glazed adhesives. These colors have been lumped together under one generic color name. This author has extensively studied the colors of the adhesives, and they are not the same. The early examples are much greener and were probably printed in November 1842. These were in use until the black–on-light-blue glazed adhesives and the black-on-blue-green glazed adhesives were issued in January 1843. An example of the early black-on-green glazed paper adhesive can be seen in Figure 6. It is on a folded letter dated February 14, 1843, to 30 Wall Street. The early black-on-green glazed paper adhesives are very scarce. The later black-on-green glazed adhesives are basically variations in color shades of the black-on-blue-green adhesives issued and reissued from 1843 to 1846. The color variations resulted from the non-mixing of the large containers of colored glaze.

FIGURE 6. An early black-on-green glazed paper adhesive on a folded local letter dated February 14, 1843 to 30 Wall Street. The U.S. City Despatch Post datestamp is the double circle type. This is a true green glazed paper adhesive. Stamps issued later are not as green. From the collection of Larry Lyons.

Double impressions exist for the black-on-blue-green adhesives and are designated 6LB5a. Double impression examples of the black-on-blue adhesives are designated 6LB5c, and double impressions of the black-on-green adhesives are given the designation 6LB5e.

At the beginning of 1843 the U.S. City Despatch Post issued a black-on-blue-green adhesive on surface colored paper (6LB5). It is at this time that they also changed to a single circle datestamp. The double circle datestamp had been in use for less than a year. The recording of the time in the datestamp was evidently no longer important, and it would typically not be recorded in the new datestamp. It is quite likely that delivery was made at either nine AM or one PM, and it was deemed unimportant to note the time. Over the next four years through 1844, 1845 and into the fall of 1846 the black-on-blue-green adhesive would be the "workhorse" with various shades of reprinting.

The black-on-blue adhesive (6LB5b) does not appear until the fall of 1844 and is a very striking color. There are only two examples of covers with multiple black-on- blue adhesives (6LB5b). One cover has four adhesives and is addressed to Athens, New York, and the other has three adhesives and is addressed to Ridgefield, Connecticut. This black-on-blue color adhesive continued to be used until the U.S. Despatch Post closed in November 1846. The black-on-blue-green adhesive (6LB5) is also recorded on cover with the New York Provisional 9X1d.

Double impression errors on glazed surface paper adhesives occurred in three different colors, Black/blue green, black/blue, and black/green. A double transfer is a condition of a transfer on a plate that shows evidence of a duplication of all or a portion of the design. Occasionally it is necessary to remove the original transfer from a plate and enter the relief a second time. When the finished re-transfer shows indications of the original transfer, because of incomplete erasure, the result is known as a double transfer.

Last but not least there is a black-on- pink adhesive (6LB6). This stamp is on a cover dated April 7. The U.S. City Despatch circular datestamp on this cover is a double line circle which leads to the conclusion that the year date is about 1843. There is only one recorded example of the pink adhesive. It is shown in Figure 7.

FIGURE 7. A black-on-pink unglazed surface colored adhesive 6LB6, on a cover front dated April 7, (1843). This is the only recorded example. The datestamp is the double circle which was not in use after 1843. From the collection of Larry Lyons.

INTERCITY COVERS

The independent mail companies began handling intercity mail in 1839, started using adhesives in early 1844, and were put out of the intercity mail business by an Act of March 1845 which became effective July 1, 1845. This was a major postal reform intended to put an eventual end to private local posts as well. First the government would make it illegal for an independent mail company to carry mail intercity by declaring that all postal mail routes could only be traveled with mail by the government post office. The independent mail companies were therefore terminated by a government act. This was postal reform by decree. This reform did not apply on the west coast because there the government was not organized to deliver the mail and would not be organized in the west for twenty more years (until 1865). Express companies continued to operate because they were only allowed to carry packages and money and not letters by themselves.

There are eight recorded intercity covers with United States City Despatch Post adhesives. These covers mark the beginning of prepayment of intercity postage by adhesive stamps in the western hemisphere. This was pioneer activity in postal reform and set the stage for the first U.S. government regular issue stamps, which would come into use exactly two years later on July 1, 1847. The covers are recorded between the dates of May 25, 1843, and June 13, 1845. A listing of these eight recorded covers can be found in Table 1.

TABLE 1. The Eight Recorded Intercity Covers of the U.S. City Despatch Post

	Adhesives	Date	Destination	Note
1.	6LB5d (5)	May 25, 1843	To Philadelphia	Strip of 3 + pair
2.	6LB5d (5)	May 30, 1843	To Philadelphia	Two pairs + single
3.	6LB5d (5)	June 16, 1843	To Philadelphia	Strip of 4 + single
4.	6LB5d (5)	July 5, 1843	To Philadelphia	Strip of 5
5.	6LB5d (4)	August 23, 1843	To Philadelphia	4 singles + 1 missing
6.	6LB5d (5)	Nov. 1, 1843	To Pleasant Valley, N.Y.	5 singles
7.	6LB5b (4)	Oct. 18, ca. 1844	To Athens, N.Y.	Strip of 3 + single
8.	6LB5b (3)	June 13, ca. 1845	To Ridgefield, Conn.	3 singles

Five of the covers have five U.S. City Despatch adhesives, black-on-green (6LB5d). One cover has four black-on-green (6LB5d) adhesives with one missing. One cover has four black-on-blue adhesives (6LB5b) and one cover has three black-on-blue adhesives (6LB5b). The five covers with five adhesives are to Philadelphia. The rate was 12½ cents for the eighty-to-150 mile zone. At the wholesale rate of 2½ cents per stamp, the five adhesives would be correct for the 12½ cents U.S. postage rate. This fee was the intercity rate and included the carrier rate to the post office. The only cover with four carrier adhesives (other than the one to Philadelphia with one stamp missing) is to Athens, New York. The four carrier adhesives at the wholesale rate of 2½ cents per stamp accounted for the ten cent rate for the thirty-to-eighty mile zone. This writer believes the post office accepted the carrier stamps at the wholesale rate. The one cover with three carrier adhesives is to Ridgefield, Connecticut. The balance of the postage on this cover was presumably paid in cash. There is a manuscript notation "10" which has never been explained. This cover can be seen in the Middendorf sale catalogue.[4] The intercity carrier covers just described are among the most prized of all carrier covers.

THE FIRST GOVERNMENT OVERPRINTED STAMP

On July 1, 1845, the price of the U.S. City Despatch Post carrier service rose to four cents retail and 3½ cents wholesale. This was necessary because the post office "drop letter" fee was increased on the same day to two cents from one cent. Congress raised the drop letter fee out of fear that the new postage structure which established the five-cent and ten-cent postage rates would cause a severe decline in postal revenues. The five-cent and ten-cent rates laid the foundation for the first general issue adhesive stamps to be issued in this country in 1847 in the denominations of five cents and ten cents. Because the intercity rate was lowered, Congress hoped to offset some of the anticipated losses by raising the drop letter fee. A "drop letter" is a piece of mail that is brought to the post office for pickup by the addressee. Drop letters are not transmitted to another post office.

"The consequences of this legislation for the U.S. City Despatch Post were immediate and dire. Prior to July 1, 1845, a drop letter could be taken by the carrier to or from the post office for three cents, which included two cents for the carrier department and one cent for the post office (drop postage). Beginning July 1, an extra cent was required for the drop postage, making the total amount equal to four cents. Although other classes of mail were unaffected by the drop-rate increase (including carrier letters that by-passed the main post office), the U.S. City Despatch found itself at a severe disadvantage competing with local posts, who generally charged two cents for a city letter. In the post-July 1 period, not only did Boyd flourish, but many smaller local posts entered the scene, hoping to capture a share of the market for intra-city letter delivery."[5]

A new overprinted stamp (6LB7) came into use. The "THREE" in cents at the bottom of the stamp has a red line through it because the retail cost of the stamp was now four cents. The overprinted "2" was the cost of the "drop letter" rate. Covers without U.S. stamps that were dropped at the post office after this drop letter rate change have a large circular date stamp with a large "2" and "cts" at the bottom. The cover shown in Figure 8 has both the U.S. City Despatch Post handstamp and the New York City circular datestamp indicating the two-cents drop letter rate. It is the only recorded cover with both handstamps and the 6LB7 adhesive.

There are only three recorded covers with the red "2" surcharge on the U.S. City Despatch Post adhesive which is listed in the *2009 Scott Specialized Catalogue* as 6LB7 with a value for a cover shown in italic as $70,000.00. The

three recorded covers are dated January 9, 1846, February 14, 1846, and March 2, 1846. The stamp on the March 2, 1846, cover was originally affixed on the back of the cover and was torn in half upon the opening of the letter.

Previous research has indicated that the overprint was created in late 1845 or early 1846. The dates of the three recorded covers indicate early 1846. There was a fourth cover with an overprinted stamp dated October 29 (1845 or 1846) but the Philatelic Foundation determined the stamp did not originate on this cover and the adhesive was subsequently removed. The rarity of the overprinted U.S. City Despatch Post covers suggests that it was in use for a limited time.

There is also a decline in surviving 1846 U.S. City Despatch Post letters that reinforces the belief that the New York City carrier service was in trouble due to competition from the New York City local posts. If you ever wondered why certain New York City local posts first appear in the 1845-to-1849 time period, this is the reason. These included Dupuy & Schenck, Messenkopes, G. A. Mills, Bouton's Broadway Post Office, Gordon's, Hanford's, New York City Express Post, Union Post, Bouton's Manhattan Express, and Franklin City Despatch. Boyd's was already in existence, and it issued new adhesives in this time period which were used extensively and far in excess of Boyd's previously issued adhesives, which are much rarer.

FIGURE 8. The only recorded U.S. City Despatch Post cover with both the U.S. City Despatch handstamp and the New York City circular datestamp indicating the two-cent drop letter rate. The adhesive has the price struck out. This is the 6LB7 adhesive. There are three recorded covers with this adhesive. From the collection of Larry Lyons.

THE END OF THE U.S. CITY DESPATCH POST

The U.S. City Despatch Post had functioned well until mid-1845. The postmaster general discontinued the U.S. City Despatch Post on November 28, 1846. The government could not compete with the better service and lower prices offered by the local posts operating in New York City. The failure to expand collection and provide proper service could not be tolerated by the public. The government service itself was succeeded by a private post. This private post was "Mead's Post Office City Despatch." Abraham Mead had been a letter carrier for the U.S. City Despatch Post. An example of the Mead's adhesive and handstamp is shown in Figure 9.

After November 1846, outstanding U.S. City Despatch Post stamps were redeemable at the New York Post Office or remained valid for use locally on letters which were delivered by Mead's Private Local Post. Government carrier service in New York had been forced to stop its operations and would not appear again in New York City until February 1849. The U.S. mail adhesive, 6LB9, was issued at that time.

SUMMARY OF POSTAL REFORMS

The U.S. City Despatch Post originated from the purchase of Greig's City Despatch Post and used Greig's stamps with a different cancel. The U.S. City Despatch Post issued the second U.S. carrier adhesive (6LB3) in a slightly new design on unsurfaced colored paper on September 1, 1842. In 1843 the U.S. City Despatch Post began using glazed surface paper adhesives. This would be the first government use of a glazed paper adhesive. The Postal Act of March 1845, effective July 1, 1845, put the independent mail companies out of the intercity mail business. In early 1846 the U.S. City Despatch Post issued the first government overprinted stamp. This was necessitated by the increase in the post office "drop rate" from one cent to two cents. The U.S. City Despatch was unable to compete with the local posts due to the rise in the drop rate and the poor service it offered and was forced to stop its operations. The first attempt at the use of United States carrier adhesives was forced to end. It was put out of business by free enterprise.

FIGURE 9. Mead's Post Office City Despatch replaced the U.S. City Despatch Post when it was discontinued in late November 1846. The outstanding U.S. City Despatch stamps were valid for use through Mead's. The Mead's datestamp was similar to the U.S. City Despatch datestamp but with "P. O." at the bottom. The Mead's stamp has "TWO CENTS" at the bottom. Siegel Auction Galleries, Nov. 15–16, 2006, Lot 1227.

NOTES

1. *The Identifier for Carriers, Locals, Fakes, Forgeries and Bogus Posts of the United States*, Larry Lyons, 1998.

2. *The City Despatch Post 1842–1852 Issues: A Study of America's First and Most Versatile Stamp-Producing Plate*, Scott R. Trepel, Siegel Auction Galleries, Inc. 2003.

3. USA1, Robson Lowe, March 15, 1972, Lot 1011.

4. Richard C. Frajola, Inc. Sale No. 4. (Middendorf), May 1990, Lot 215.

5. Siegel Auctions Galleries, Golden sale, November 15–17, 1999, Lot 315.

BIBLIOGRAPHY

Lyons, Larry. *The Identifier for Carriers, Locals, Fakes, Forgeries & Bogus Posts of the United States: A Study of the Identification of the Local Stamp Adhesive from the Forgeries and Bogus Posts*. Westport, Ct.: Self published, 1998

Trepel, Scott R. *The City Despatch Post 1842–1852 Issues: A Study of America's First and Most Versatile Stamp-Producing Plate*. New York: Robert A. Siegel Auction Galleries, 2003.

stamps as the evidence of pre-payment of postage."[10] His grammatical tense was wrong, but his thought was right.

Did Congress, based on the 1847 experience, now agree that stamps were the answer—that they were all that was needed to eliminate the stampless system and thereby end the bane of unpaid mail? Well, that's the way they voted.

By 1850, in his "Report to the President," Postmaster General N.K. Hall recommended a further lowering of rates by two cents for pre-paid domestic letters.[11] This new rate was adopted effective July 1, 1851—three cents per half ounce for a pre-paid letter and five cents for a letter sent unpaid (both rates for letters traveling up to 3,000 miles).

This time there was much greater distribution of the stamps than had been the case in 1847, when only selected post offices received automatic distribution. The Act of 1851 (Section 3), required, "it shall be the duty of the Postmaster General to provide and furnish to all deputy postmasters, and to all other persons applying and paying therefore, suitable postage stamps of the denomination of three cents, and as such other denominations as he may think expedient, to facilitate the prepayment of postage provided for in this act"[12] all deputy postmasters— not just the four percent of postmasters who received the 1847 stamps!

Indeed, in terms of my hypothesis, it is noteworthy that in the first month of availability, 10.5 million stamps of the 1851 issue were distributed; this compares to 5.5 million stamps distributed for the full four years of the 1847 issue.[13] Clearly, by 1851 Congress and the Postal System had seen their way out of the dilemma of unpaid "collect" mail. Stamps would be the answer, and Congress wanted to be sure stamps were widely available.

The key factor for the public was, undoubtedly, the preferential rate for prepaid letter mail that was obviously designed to capitalize on the American core value of "thriftiness." Pre-payment was made a "bargain," and stamps were now readily available to facilitate that bargain. Would the two mesh? Would the plan work?

You bet it worked! It worked so well that by 1853, one reporter, who had conducted an extensive review of the New York Post Office, noted that: "the stamp system is now becoming generally used in the United States. Nearly four-fifths of the paid home letters which are posted at New York are paid by stamps." Furthermore, he said, "hardly three-fourths of the paid home letters which are received at New York are franked in this easy, simple process."[14] Think about that: after little more than one year of the preferential rate for pre-paid letters, stamps were becoming "generally used," with about 80% of paid domestic letters leaving New York, and almost 75% of paid letters coming into New York, being franked with adhesive postage stamps!

Prepayment had been established, and using stamps was obviously more desirable than cash from an administrative point of view. The public had also confirmed it—preferring stamps to cash as a pre-payment method.

It was all there, the stage was set. Congress now had the confidence that stamps could do the job. First they made pre-payment of domestic letter mail postage mandatory in 1855. Six months later, the final step was taken when stamps and stamped envelopes became the only acceptable means of pre-payment for domestic letter mail.

The loop was closed and the final piece of the Great Postal Reform Movement had been put in place. Postage rates were significantly lower (and would go lower still); service was better (there were 25,565 post offices in operation by mid-1856, compared to 14,183 in 1845);[15] communications were enhanced (there were an estimated 239,642 miles of postal routes in 1856, compared to 143,940 miles in 1845);[16] the use of the mails by ordinary citizens had grown exponentially; and, at last, "collect" letters (and the lost revenue and extra costs they engendered), had been eliminated.

Using the 1847 stamps to eliminate unpaid mail was probably the intention for many all along, but whether it was or not, the fact is that's exactly what stamps did. And that demonstration—that stamps had the ability to completely change the system—was, without question, the most important benefit of our first American issue.

NOTES

1. In 1845, for example, "net revenue, after deducting commissions of postmasters, contingent and incidental expenses, amounted to $2,942,217." This compared to expenditures of $4,320,732 (or a net deficit of $1,378,515) – *Report of the Postmaster General*, December 1, 1845, Doc. 2, pp. 850–851

2. Similarly, the privileges given to newspapers, in the form of preferential postal rates, were another very significant contributor to post office deficits. Indeed, in his 1845 *Report Of The Postmaster General (p.857)*, Cave Johnson noted that "It is confidently believed . . . that nine-tenths of the whole weight of the mails, and a greater inequality in bulk, is composed of printed matter, paying about one-ninth of the expense." Nonetheless, because of various political and philosophical reasons, Congress was unwilling to consider reforming those rates.

3. *Report of the Postmaster General*, December 1, 1845, Doc. 2, p. 857. (In his 1848 Report, Johnson increased the estimate to 2,000,000 letters annually.)

4. *Report of the Postmaster General, 1845*, p. 859.

5. *Report of the Postmaster General, 1845*, p. 859.

6. Senate *Resolutions*, 26th Congress, 1st Session, June 10, 1840

7. *Report of George Plitt, Special Agent of the Post Office Department*, February 3, 1841 (26th Congress, 2nd Session, Senate)

8. Tiffany, John K., *The History of Postage Stamps of the United States*, (C. H. Mekeel, 1887), p. 23

9. *Journal of the House of Representatives of the United States*, Volume 41, p. 405

10. *Report of the Postmaster General*, December 2, 1848, Doc. 1, p. 1253

11. *Report of the Postmaster General*, November 30, 1950, Doc. 1, p. 408

12. Chase, Carroll, *The 3¢ Stamp of the United States 1851–1857 Issue*, (Quarterman Publications, Inc., 1942), p. 3

13. Hulme II, W. Wilson, "July 1, 1851 Usages of the 1851 Issue," *The 1851 Issue of United States Stamps: a Sesquicentennial Perspective*, (U.S. Philatelic Classics Society, Inc., New Orleans, 2006), p. 107

14. "Metropolitan Post Offices-New York," *The Illustrated Magazine of Art*, (John Cassell), London, 1853, Vol. I, p. 268

15. *Report of the Postmaster General*, December 1, 1856, p. 764; *Report of the Postmaster General*, December 1, 1845, Doc. 2, p. 850

16. *Report of the Postmaster General, 1856*.

BIBLIOGRAPHY

Cassell, John. "Metropolitan Post Offices-New York." *The Illustrated Magazine of Art*, 1(1853): 268.

Chase, Carroll. *The 3¢ Stamp of the United States 1851–1857 Issue*. Lawrence, Mass.: Quarterman Publications, 1942.

Hulme, W. Wilson, II. "July 1 1851 Usages of the 1851 Issue." In *The 1851 Issue of United States Stamps: a Sesquicentennial Perspective*, ed. Hubert C. Skinner and Charles J. Peterson. New Orleans, La.: U.S. Philatelic Classics Society, 2006.

Tiffany, John K. *History of the Postage Stamps of the United States of America*. St Louis, Mo.: C. H. Mekeel, 1887.

U.S. Congress. House. *Journal of the House of Representatives of the United States*, 29th Congress, 1st Session. Volume 41. February 1846.

U.S. Congress. Senate. *Report of George Plitt, Special Agent of the Post Office Department, February 3, 1841*. 26th Congress, 2nd Session, 1841.

———. *Resolutions*. 26th Congress, 1st session, 10 June 1845.

U.S. Post Office Department. *Report of the Postmaster General, 1 December 1845*. Washington D. C.: Government Printing Office, 1845.

———. *Report of the Postmaster General, 2 December 1848*. Washington D. C.: Government Printing Office, 1848.

———. *Report of the Postmaster General, 2 December 1856*. Washington D. C.: Government Printing Office, 1856.

———. *Report of the Postmaster General, 30 November 1950*. Washington D. C.: Government Printing Office, 1950.

From the Pulpit to the Post: Anti-Clericalism and Communication in Orizaba, 1857–1867

Rachel A. Moore

In 1855, residents of Orizaba, a burgeoning town between Mexico's main Atlantic port of Veracruz and the national capital, saw the urban geography of their town change. In the first half of the nineteenth century, the town had been home to so many churches and religious orders that is had been called "one giant convent."[1] Indeed, one can see the many churches that dotted Orizaba's landscape in the nineteenth century in Juan Moritz Rugendas' depiction of the town. However, after the passage of laws that forced the Catholic Church in Mexico to sell off all property and allowed the government to seize church holdings,[2] new uses were found for the forcibly vacated religious buildings. In Orizaba, what had been the oratory of the religious order of San Felipe Neri was now occupied by the town's new post office.

The superimposing of a secular means of diffusing information over a religious one reflects the unique evolution of individuals' relationships with the postal service in Mexico. This paper will examine the ways in which the people of Orizaba and the larger state of Veracruz filled what one Orizaba newspaper called "the vacuum left by the exit of the religious communities"[3] with newspaper reading, letter writing and, as a result, increasing demands for a more comprehensive postal system. These demands included requests for more frequent and personalized postal delivery as well as more reliable and politically impartial postal employees. By the end of the nineteenth century, demands for an improved postal system drowned out any demands that might have been made for better treatment of the clergy on the part of the national government.

In their reaction to the expulsion of the religious community of San Felipe Neri, there seemed to be little sign of the renowned parochial nature of the residents of Orizaba. When the friars were abruptly forced to abandon the location, there was no outcry from the local population.[4] The litigation the event did generate involved what looks to be an intra-office squabble: for at least eight years after the passage of the Lerdo Law, the new postmaster of Orizaba lodged grievances with the government about the self-serving ways of his predecessor, who had requisitioned a house for his father-in-law. Nowhere in the documentation did anyone take issue with the expulsion of the religious themselves.

However in that same year, residents of Orizaba and the nearby town of Córdoba petitioned the imperial government of French interloper Maximilian for more comprehensive and reliable mail service. The following year they squabbled with one another over jurisdiction in censorship cases. Shortly after the execution of Maximilian, they continued to needle the federal government with complaints regarding the shabby appearance and vigilance of the police force. And through this all, no complaints surfaced in the same arenas regarding the treatment of the clergy or their Catholic followers.

In fact, Orizaba's intellectual community was quick to disavow the town's reputation as a mammoth monastery. In his *Essay on the history of Orizaba* (1867), Joaquín Arróniz refuted this reputation at length, writing,

> He who believes that modern Orizaba had monastic and clerical origins is mistaken. Although the preponderance of religious sentiment in the town supports this viewpoint, its religiosity is often overemphasized.
>
> The Spaniards who made Orizaba their principal residence were drawn to it neither by convent nor by cross. They were attracted by the opportunities this location offered merchants to conduct business with travelers. They also came in search of the healthy condition they had lost on the coast.
>
> The Church, the true center of all the populations of America and Europe, came later, once the light of the true faith was known, to further strengthen the vitality of our fledgling city. In this we differ from the foundation of the rest of our nation's cities since it can be said that they were born of the altar.[5]

Why this comparative complacency regarding anticlerical reform? I will argue here that the anticlerical reforms of the nineteenth century spurred on public debate regarding the obligations that the government assumed after depriving the public of church counsel. Correlations can be drawn between anticlerical initiatives and demands for improved distribution, regulation, and protection of private information circulating in the public sphere. That said, Mexicans in the nineteenth century acclimated to secular society at a pace that only *apparently* stood at odds with their "parochial reputation." Their demands conformed to a holistic concept of church and state in which the duties of governing society were shared between the two institutions.[6]

While residents of Orizaba demanded that the clergy retain their traditional duties through the first third of the 1800s, they rethought their appeals beginning in the mid-nineteenth century. Rather than seek to preserve the central public place of the clergy, *orizabeños* sought to foist some of the traditional duties of the clergy, namely the diffusion of information, on the government itself. What one 1870 *orizabeño* editorial called "the vacuum left by the exit of the religious communities"[7] needed to be filled. If the government wanted to assume the mantle of arbiter of public life, they reasoned, then the government would also assume the obligations that came therewith. These obligations included keeping the public informed and protected, both traditional purviews of the clergy in Mexico. The process of resolving themselves to these changes and responding with altered expectations of the clergy and the government alike represented a declaration of faith in the public sphere. The public sphere, and with it public service, became sacred arenas and occupations.[8] Here I will examine the chief government institution to which individuals turned for information and security in an increasingly anticlerical age: the postal service.

Several scholars have explained the growing "mass participation" in the postal system in the United States during this period as a result of improvements in print technology, literacy and transportation. The area under study in this essay experienced improvements in both print technology and literacy in the nineteenth century. Anticlericalism is an important additional factor that must be considered in studying the development of the postal system in any country in which the church played a central role in information diffusion. Many patronizing the postal system in the United States did so in hopes of maintaining contact with far-flung relations and friends. By contrast, those patronizing the postal system in Mexico often experienced less mobility and craved news of the wider world in the form of newspapers and, to a lesser degree, personal letters. Before the liberal reforms of the mid-nineteenth century, many individuals turned to the Church as a source of information and answers. The closing of churches deprived them of this uniquely sanctioned information.

Orizaba and Córdoba are particularly interesting cities to study because residents simultaneously bore the consequences and enjoyed the fruits of nineteenth-century modernization. The anticlerical initiatives and demands for improved government services manifested in these towns fit squarely into two larger processes at work globally in the nineteenth century – secularization and centralization. In Mexico, the Bourbon dynasty spearheaded both processes in the late eighteenth century with reforms that minimized the influence of the clergy and the autonomy of the colonial government. Secularizing and centralizing initiatives persisted after Mexican independence. They experienced renewed popular approval after several stormy years under the passage of a federal constitution in 1824.

The allegedly parochial *orizabeños* reacted to early anticlerical reforms in the expected manner. In 1827, nineteen of the thirty-five friars working at the Propaganda Fide College in Orizaba were forced to return to Spain when the Mexican government expelled all Spaniards from the country. According to Francisco Morales, "the city's inhabitants threatened to guard the convent to prevent the government from expelling the Spanish friars."[9] It would not be until 1834 that *orizabeños* followed through on that threat.

In 1834, the state government ordered that all religious houses with fewer than twenty-four residents be closed. "This," wrote local chronicler José María Naredo, "amounted to abolishing them all since none of them had this many residents."[10] The anxieties of local residents mounted as they awaited the promulgation of the decree. The arrival of five empty carriages heightened suspicions that the religious community of Orizaba would soon be forced from their residences and the town. When authorities finally moved to expel the religious, they did so in the middle of the night. However, residents noticed this activity as well. According to Naredo, one resident left her house at two in the morning alerting the town that "They are taking the priest! They are taking the priest!" Naredo wrote that,

> News spread like a bolt of electricity. Townspeople came out of their houses armed and ready to act and soon the bells of the Church were ringing, sounding the alarm. At dawn the group of armed people had grown and the church bells continued sounding until noon. Upon hearing the news, many combatants left their ranches and came into town, forming a large squad with those already there. . . . At midday the uproar was horrible and everything was in disarray, so much so that some people stepped forward to impose some order. These individuals, along with Fathers Llano and Mendoza, engineered a truce with the armed forces and they put down their arms. The whole thing had come to a close by six that night, and the ringing of the church bells, as well as the fireworks, announced the triumph of the townspeople.[11]

Even in a moment of victimization the clerical community of Orizaba demonstrated the strong sway they continued to hold over popular action to this point. After diffusing the situation with government authorities, the priests implored the irate population to return to their homes. "The obedient townspeople withdrew, forming groups and singing hymns to the Lord," wrote Naredo.

However, as the nineteenth century progressed there were an increasing number of instances in which public sentiment overrode public deference to representatives of the church. In 1834, the priests of Orizaba had successfully prevented residents of the town from retaliating against government authorities for attempting to drive the clergy from their homes. Just four years later their entreaties were not as effective. The devaluation of currency by the Mexican government in 1837 incensed *orizabeños*. When they threatened to march on the textile factory at Cocolapam, located on the outskirts of Orizaba, priests attempted to dissuade them. Naredo wrote that, "The people listened to the arguments of the priests and seemed to calm down; and when it seemed like each and every one of them would return to their homes, a voice started to chant 'To Cocolapam! To Cocolapam!'" When French workers at the factory fired warning shots at the menacing group, the demonstration escalated into open violence. Two Frenchmen were injured and the factory suffered an estimated 1,200 pesos worth of damage. Naredo described the event as a gross aberration for the people of Orizaba. "The moderation and docility of the people here is proverbial," he wrote.[12] However, in light of their subsequent demands of the government, this would not seem to be the case.

With the clerical community under attack, *orizabeños* turned to other means of gathering information. *Orizabeños* conceived of themselves as active participants in the burgeoning print culture and legal system of nineteenth-century Mexico. They were avid newspaper readers and frequent correspondents. Documents make reference to no less than six newspapers published or circulated within the city itself.[13] Much of the population was keenly aware of the way in which information circulated. In addition, they had strongly held opinions regarding the quality and integrity of information to which they were entitled. In the aftermath of local and national anticlerical initiatives, residents of Orizaba became increasingly vocal in their demands for a more reliable and secure postal service. These demands grew as much from the unique intellectual environment of Orizaba as they did from the larger dialogues occurring in Mexico at the time regarding the transparency of government.

While Orizaba did not boast the same concentration of educational institutions as neighboring town of Xalapa, the tobacco barons responsible for many of the improvements to the town made certain that residents had access to secondary education. The *Colegio Preparatorio de Orizaba* opened thanks to their sponsorship in 1825.[14] For their primary education, *orizabeños* had several options of varying scholarly rigor. The two most respected primary schools in the center of town educated their students in "reading, writing, Christian doctrine, math, drawing, manners, and morals." In addition, several schools for girls offered classes in "reading, writing, counting, cooking, keeping house, and many other manual skills appropriate for the fairer sex."[15]

Residents of the town of Orizaba itself were as engaged as circumstances permitted with the larger literary community of Mexico. Especially after the rapid growth of the periodical press in Mexico during the nineteenth century,[16] orizabeños relied to a great degree on the postal system for contact with the larger intellectual community of the nation. They often found themselves frustrated with an understaffed and underfunded post office.

The postal regulations instituted by the Bourbons in 1794 remained the foundation of Mexico's postal code until 1883.[17] The Bourbon administrators created two principal postal administrations with this set of laws: that of Veracruz and that of Mexico. In 1821, Mexico's newly independent government eliminated the first eleven provisions of the Bourbon regulations but left the larger organization of the postal system intact. Orizaba numbered among one of four principal post offices operating under the main post office in Veracruz. Campeche and Mérida also had principal post offices as did Xalapa, Orizaba's mercantile rival to the north. However, where Campeche, Xalapa, and Mérida had three or even four full-time postal employees, Orizaba had only two. The budget of the Orizaba post office was less than half that of the Xalapa post office, despite their similar size and location.[18] This disparity grew in large part from Xalapa's prominent commercial role during the late colonial period as the site of Mexico's only trade fair. In addition, Xalapa served as the major travel hub for those in transit from Veracruz to Mexico City.

While regular mail service was reinstituted in Mexico in May 1823, postal patrons continued to face delays and unreliable service throughout the first half of the nineteenth century. In 1838, mail arrived in Orizaba biweekly on Tuesdays and Thursdays. However, the town lacked direct mail communication with Veracruz. Those letters bound for the port, according to Segura, "had to pass through Nopalucan and Xalapa and, for this reason, are much delayed." By 1854, sufficient progress had been made on the route between Orizaba and Veracruz that weekly mail service existed.[19] Five years later, residents of Orizaba could both send and receive mail three days a week.[20] The ability to both dispatch and receive correspondence on Sundays—the only day on which this was

possible—alluded to the anticlerical bent of the national government at the time.

However, in the years of political instability ushered in by the beginning of the French intervention in 1862, the postal system suffered near financial ruin. According to postal employee Manuel Aburto from late April to November 1862, "the revenue of the post office was insufficient to cover our salaries and other costs, forcing us to leave nearly all employees unpaid."[21] When the post office failed to return sufficient revenue, the responsibility of covering expenses often fell to the postmasters themselves. In 1863, postal employees working in Orizaba appealed to the government for financial assistance in at least two separate instances. In October, the postmaster requested that the expenses of correos extraordinarios be transferred from the post office of origin to the central post office in Mexico City.[22] A month later, the same official petitioned the government for assistance in paying rent owed from April to November 1862. "At that point in time," wrote the official, "this office had no income at all."[23] The post office was in such financial straits that French officials reduced their staff to just two: the postmaster and a postal inspector.[24]

However, the indigence of postal workers in Orizaba does not necessarily indicate that individuals were not using the post office during this period. Rather than posting mail, orizabeños were eagerly anticipating it. After the installation of Maximilian of Austria as emperor of Mexico in 1864, the demands for postal service by both the new government and civilians increased markedly. Maximilian wanted to stay in closer contact with provincial outposts, and civilians sought to apprise each other of developments through letters and the growing number of newspapers in Mexico. As a result, the frequency of mail service between Mexico City, Orizaba, and Veracruz increased to six times a week.[25] However, postal employees continued to be poorly paid and poorly monitored. In 1864, the postmaster of Córdoba wrote to officials in Mexico City complaining that, "Being that mail is now being sent and received daily, both from above as well as from below, the duties of this office have quadrupled and I am stretched to my limit in dispatching with them. This makes it imperative that I have someone to help me."[26] He wrote again the next year appealing to authorities for more pay since "within a short while" mail service from Córdoba was set to include Coscomatepec, Huatusco, Xalapa, and the tierra caliente.[27] Authorities relented at this point and granted the overworked civil servant a raise in salary to 400 pesos.